The Awakened Self

The
Awakened Self

Sharon Joy Ng, Ph. D.

For more information contact:

Wu Chi Creations

1010 Foxchase Drive Suite 315
San Jose, California 95123
wuchicreations@sbcglobal.net
www.wuchicreations.com

Book cover design by Kameron L. Montgomery

Photo credits:
     Kameron L. Montgomery, p. 170 image creation
     Sue Graue Photography, p. 212
     Haily Gwynn Shaw, p. 270, artwork
     William Nathan Hale and Sharon Joy Ng, all other photos used

To Your

Awakening

Contents

EXERCISES

Preface

The *Awakened Self* is a collection of topics that together, provide important tools for your journey towards awakening to your highest potential. Awakening needs to occur because our inherent human nature is such that much of our behaviors, thoughts, feelings and beliefs have been programmed into our subconscious early in life. We have been conditioned and reinforced to conform in many ways to the standards set for us by our families, cultures and society. As you will learn in this book, so much of our behavior is unconscious as if we were in a "waking sleep." Yet, there comes a time when it is healthy for us to begin questioning why and how we have grown into the person that we have become. Are we done, or is there still room for us to grow, evolve and change towards a Self that is centered and aware of automatic behaviors that arise, giving us the chance to choose different behavioral, emotional, and thinking responses?

With this growing awareness, we slowly come to realize that the life we are living may in fact, not be our own. With trepidation, we search to unravel and uncover the nature of these conditioned aspects of ourselves and wonder what we will discover. We fear that if we let go of the known, that there will be nothing to hang on to. How will we stay grounded in the world as we search for new meaning to our lives? Will we get lost? What internal demons will we confront as we traverse this unknown territory into our own psyche?

As is true with any new undertakings, there is anxiety, yet, simultaneously excitement permeates the discovery process. Anxiety can turn into fuel to drive us towards our Awakening, expending this extra energy to free ourselves from conditioned living. The extra energy of the psyche can move us forward in a constructive way if we focus and harness that energy towards growth and awakening. We are the sculptor, standing ready before a large slab of granite, and with tools in hand we chip away at the stone to see "who" is underneath all the environmental molding. Many of us have not had the chance to even hear that voice from within because life did not accommodate this discovery process. It was more important "to be nice," "to be smart," and "to be a good boy/girl." Did we grow up being encouraged to explore and discover our unique individuality or were we told how we were expected to be, to behave, to think, or to feel?

There are both topics to read and exercises to complete. The exercises are located at the back of the book. The topics are ordered to lead you through a logical sequence to build your knowledge base that will equip you with important tools to living the *Awakened* life. The exercises will facilitate the journey while also teaching you tools that will help you throughout your life to stay awakened. After Topic Four would be a good time to complete Exercises 1-4. These three exercises will help you discover how you may be creating obstacles to awakening. The remaining exercises indicate that there are particular topics to read before attempting the exercise.

The website to accompany this book is found at http://www.wuchicreations.com. There you will find a wealth of information to continue your journey to the Awakened Self with articles, links, exercises, videos and more. Join me and together we can continue to live an Awakened life!

Bon Voyage!

Dr. Sharon Joy Ng
January 2015

Introduction

The twenty-first century has brought with it an awakening on many levels. People are waking up to the fact that much of what we took for granted is simply not workable. The consciousness of the planet is evolving towards a different way to live in the world. This psychological awakening to a new worldview calls each of us to become stewards of the Earth and we feel compelled, more than ever, to find sustainable solutions. We sense a shift in consciousness on many levels—from a growing political awareness and the importance of our participation in shaping our government to an increased concern regarding our environment and the impact that human activity and consumption have had upon the earth's limited resources. We seek alternative solutions for harnessing renewable resources of energy and to restore our environment, or at the least, to halt the damage that we have done.

Growing concern over the effects of global warming is warranted. It has been predicted that with rising temperatures, we will see corresponding changes, such as rising sea levels, the extinction of certain species and the emergence of more virulent strains of viruses, bacteria, and diseases. In the last few years alone, Ebola, SARS, West Nile Virus and the Swine Flu have challenged our medical communities and with more virulent drug-resistant strains of malaria, tuberculosis, and bacterial pneumonias, we are facing emerging health issues that will call for different approaches to prevention and treatment. We also face increased flooding, drought, and other natural disasters as the Earth continues to warm. The economic downturn of the American economy, the global financial recession, and the continued fighting across the globe are all cause for concern during this time in human history.

These concerns and more are forcing us to examine the interrelationships that exist between and among Earth's inhabitants and its natural resources. People are becoming more concerned about finding solutions to living that will not destroy our planet or further compromise the world we leave to our children, grandchildren and future descendants. Humans are challenged on many fronts to live in harmony with the earth and move beyond the "divide and conquer" mentality that has taken us to this point. Former vice president, Al Gore, explained the consequences of not changing our habits in his film, *An Inconvenient Truth* where he succinctly outlines the consequences of continuing our current trek that is destroying the world as we have known it. Unfortunately, those born today will never know the beauty of clear running streams and lakes, drinking tap water that is not filled with chemicals and pollutants, nor see the untouched beauty of the earth as we continue to mine, dig, and destroy our natural habitat. What will it take to change the course we are embarked upon? Can each individual contribute something of value to this process? Worldwide, the power of our individual voice is being realized and we are beginning to find and use that voice to bring about global change. Tradition is being questioned and many now realize that new technology may not provide the answers as we move into the future, but that we also need a new perspective on the world as well. We realize that a new perspective must begin with us, as individual people, and therefore we are called to the path of greater self awareness. Each person can help to shape the future world that we will create because *changes in consciousness result in changes to the choices that we make.*

Many of us struggle in our search for happiness and fulfillment, not knowing what it is that stands in our way. We live our lives driven by our beliefs of how the world works, never knowing if these beliefs and our efforts will bring us what we seek. We swallow whole much of what we are fed, resulting in a belief system that reflects what we have ingested: "Work hard, and you will be rewarded." "Be loyal to your employer and you will have lifetime security." "Sacrifice yourself to those that you love and that love will be returned." "Men have no emotions!" "Women are too emotional!" You get the picture. These beliefs are called *memes* (as opposed to genes) that we inherit unconsciously, incorporating these beliefs without scrutiny. How many people actually stop and question how they developed their belief system? Maybe we would live differently if we were more aware of how we got to this point in our lives. Greater awareness of the mechanisms that drive our feelings and behaviors leads us to make different choices. As our awareness grows, we open our eyes to the fact that much of our current belief system may be riddled with fear, prejudice, anger and other negative emotional states, fueling our choices that may not be quite so wise or informed.

"What are my beliefs? From whom did I learn these beliefs? Do these beliefs fit who I am? In fact, who am I?" That last question, "Who am I?" is perplexing because it leads to more questions: "How did I become the person that I am? Who can I become? What factors have helped to shape my perceptions, expectations, hopes, fears, dreams, thoughts, curiosities, and goals? What role have my parents played in who I am? How do my peers influence me? Do I fit in?" We look to others for our answers and feel dissatisfied. Eventually, we are faced with a choice between living the status quo or to evolve. Living the status quo requires little effort or consciousness. We just keep doing what we have

3

been doing, seeing the world in the same way that we've grown accustomed to perceiving it.

Human beings are not required to be conscious. In many ways, we are similar to other lower forms of life on earth. We are instinctual creatures, learning behaviors through a stimulus/response process, being conditioned and reinforced just like B.F. Skinner's rats in the lab. Although we have the capacity for creativity and thought, how much of our behavior actually lies outside of our conscious everyday awareness? We drive our cars, brush our teeth and can even do much of our day-to-day routines without thinking because once the neural pathways have been established in the brain and strengthened through repetition, we don't have to "think" about how to do those things anymore. We have learned the behavior. Now the memory for how to "do it" is reassigned to a different part of the brain—the *cerebellum*, also referred to as our "little brain."

Habit and routine are stored in the cerebellum, allowing us to act without thinking. This is great for routines in our lives such as walking, running, riding a bike, driving a car, cooking, playing sports or musical instruments that we've learned, or even working at our jobs. The question is, does habit serve us well when we are dissatisfied with our lives and ready to change our reactions and habits? In other words, our emotions become "habits" as well which are wired into our brains in a similar manner to how learned behavior is reassigned. We learn that certain things make us mad, sad, frustrated, scared, anxious, happy, or excited. We even anticipate (through our thoughts) that we might be entering into a situation that is similar to a past trauma, so that we are "prepared" to fight, freeze or flee before the situation has even unfolded. Therefore, our behaviors and emotions can both be seen as "habits."

Part of the process towards greater self awareness is to understand how these habits were formed so that we can break the bonds and create new behaviors that are more functional. When we understand the origins of our beliefs, perceptions, attitudes, expectations, desires, fears and traumas, self-awareness grows. This knowledge about the self gives us the insight and motivation to change. Change requires consciousness. To stay conscious requires work, but it leads us towards the discovery of our unique individuality and potential. When we can discover the assumptions that we hold about the world, we begin to open up to the world in a way that can lead to greater happiness because we have removed the blinders. We see life with what Buddhists refer to as a "beginner's mind." Like a child, we see the world with openness and wonder, fresh and new, not colored by our expectations and fears. In this way we can begin to truly live our lives as the "Lived Life."

The "self" and How It Develops

The *self* may not be aware of the possibility that we can awaken our consciousness to a greater *Self*. We can call this *self* our *ego* because it is the result of having incorporated the do's and don'ts that we were taught as we were growing up. As you will learn in later chapters, what we hear, learn and experience are simply downloaded for the first 5-6 years of life. There is no process of scrutiny because our brainwaves are basically in a hypnogogic state, similar to a hypnotic state. This fact implies that if we are to lose some of those old habits and reactions, we will first need to recognize when they emerge or are activated. Without recognizing the reactions and behaviors that stem from our habitual *self*, I doubt that we have much chance of evolving into our *Self*. The reason I believe this is because as biological creatures, we are similar to the rats, monkeys and pigeons used in experimental psychology to learn more about human behavior. We know that humans are wired in similar ways to other creatures, learning much basic behavior through *reinforcement* and *conditioning*. If you have taken a basic psychology course, you will remember that *reinforcement* is the application of a reward for a behavior that strengthens that behavior, making it more likely to be repeated again in a similar situation. You bring flowers to your partner to make up after a fight, it works to bring you back together, so the next time you are in a similar tight situation, you reach for the flowers to appease hurt feelings in your partner. *Conditioning* occurs on a more automatic level. We hear a song, we are in a romantic setting with a desired partner, and subsequently, we feel these same emotions whenever we hear that song again. Classical conditioning like Pavlov's dog, salivating to the sound of the bell.

As humans, we tend to believe that we are much more complex than dogs, cats, and pigeons! We believe that "thought" or thinking is the greatest tool that humans possess and we give much weight to our cognitions. In fact, it is safe to say that we have pushed emotions to the back burner, believing that our emotions are the source of all our problems. But how often has thinking been the culprit that has gotten us into trouble, a funk, or a tight spot? Thinking is a capacity that we have, but what happens when we use erroneous or outdated information to base our thoughts and decisions upon? Where does that lead us? We do this almost everyday as we go about our lives? We hear something and immediately have a set opinion about what is happening. We make up stories that fit our world—stories that are based upon our expectations and earlier experiences. It may be that our ability to stop the thinking process and rest in the awareness of just simply "be-ing" that is our greatest hope to become more aware and awaken to our potential. Our capacity for reflection allows us to stand back and observe ourselves in action, whether that action is thinking or doing.

What is Self Awareness?

Self awareness is an interesting journey because the *self* actually covers up the authentic *Self*, but the Self needs help in order to emerge. Developing greater *self* awareness implies that there is a "self" to discover. Is the *self* the same as the *Self* (small versus capital S)? If you describe your *self* to another person, how do you describe your *self*? Most of us start out by telling others our name, our age, our birth order, our ethnicity, our profession, where we live, who we are partnered with, how many children we have, where we grew up, etc. We might even tell others that we are fun, happy, creative, patient and caring. But do these words really inform others about who we really are at the core? Don't these words tell more about where we came from, what we do, what we care about, and who is in our lives? Even if these terms arise from our conscious beliefs about ourselves, do they include what we know about our inner nature—core values, beliefs and desires? We need to ask ourselves if our lives reflect an *examined life* or are we just acting out and regurgitating things that we learned without questioning their value to us as individuals? Where and from whom did we learn these things? How did they become *our* truths? Do they still have value for us? Have we ever taken the time to consciously examine their origin or meaning?

As we begin to contemplate the nature of *self* and *Self*, a definition of each might be helpful. The *self* can be described as the *ego's* description of who we are and can be referred to as the *conditioned self*—the *self* that has been conditioned to fit in and hide those things that we fear may make us unacceptable to others, so we conceal this knowledge—from others and oftentimes from ourselves as well. Thinking has been seen as superior over our emotions and in many ways we have discouraged emotion based living. We are told to "get a grip!" The *ego*, or *conditioned self* lives life putting great value on the thinking process because we have been told this by society. This is the *ego's* problem because it makes decisions in ways that often exclude deeper, heartfelt feelings, pushing them aside in favor of logic. Logic is a left-brained activity and uses *external criteria* to form conclusions. Why would this cause us problems? When we think, we use a ranking system that tells us one thing is better than another, but this ranking system will probably not reflect our deepest felt heartstrings. It is a ranking system developed by society that is patriarchal and hierarchical and not necessarily reflecting what is held deeply within one's heart. So the *ego* has the tendency to use thinking exclusively. We learn, however, that our truth lies within our hearts and not necessarily our thoughts so without checking in with our deepest heartfelt beliefs and desires, we end up cutting off vital aspects of who we are.

To make this clearer, let's look at an example. Think of one of your "buttons." You know what I mean. It's one of those sensitivities that you might hold, or it might be a "readiness to react" in certain situations. If you grew up being put-down by your parent or parents, you will likely be sensitive to any criticism from others. Just the anticipation of being criticized can set you off and push your button, resulting in whatever usual reaction you have to criticism—your heart beats faster, your breathing gets shallow, you feel angry, or you close yourself off to others, feeling inferior, etc. So, simultaneously, we *react* on a physical level and an emotional level. This happens because the neural nets that formed when you reacted to criticism as a child are now firmly established in your brain and need nothing more than even the simple anticipation of being criticized to set the reaction pattern rolling. Before you know it, your heart is beating faster, you are being overcome with the emotion, and then you lash out—even when you had vowed to change your anger patterns! So the desire of the heartfelt *Self* to not *react* gets overridden by the habitual reactions of the *self*.

So the *self* really needs to be noticed if we want to become more *Self* aware. As we learn to understand the *self*, we have the opportunity to evolve and free the *Self*. We have to move out of unconsciously reacting to these same situations and teach ourselves to recognize when we are caught up in a *reaction pattern*. Once we have taken that step backwards and have become the observer of our behaviors and feelings instead of seeing ourselves as the *actor*, we start the loosening process of the brain's neural nets that fire in those situations. We see that things unfold around us, but that we don't have to necessarily *react* to them because we have made assumptions about what is happening.

We have the opportunity to choose a different perspective by learning to see the situation with *non-attachment*, which is to let go of our expectations and fears about why something is happening or not. Much of human suffering comes from what Buddhist refer to as *samsara*, created through our minds—we enter situations expecting certain outcomes and when they don't materialize, we become angry, frustrated, sad, or anxious. Or we have been hurt, so we are primed to be hurt again by others because we expect it. These reactions can be called addictions as you will learn in a later chapter. We are addicted to our emotional reactions. If we can release these fears, expectations and desires and step back from our reactions to situations, we take a step towards the path of awareness and awakening. We loosen the reactionary patterns of behavior and learn to just *be*.

Slowly, we learn to rest in the *here and now*—being present so that we can really take in what is unfolding around us. To be in the *here and now* implies that we are not applying any definitions, stories, or storylines to what is happening in the moment, but that we keep our awareness open and unfettered by past memories, fears, or situations. By calming the neural nets to our former ways of reacting to the world, we open ourselves up to the possibility of leaving our addictions behind and living life more functionally, happily and creatively. This allows the *Self* to emerge—the highest potential of the individual in which the illusions and blinders have been removed. This represents living an *Awakened* life—not always needing to have it our way, applying our expectations, fears, and desires that create our own suffering. We allow to unfold, that which is about to unfold.

The *Self* is more than the *self*. The *Self* is the *Awakened Self*. It is that *Self* that emerges once we have recaptured and integrated what was denied or neglected in the process of growing up. It is the *Self* that is stripped of the protective masks, bravely stepping out into the world with knowledge and compassion for oneself and others, seeking to evolve itself to a greater sense of oneness and centeredness in the world. It is the *Self* that is energetically connected to others and the universe, understanding that interconnection exists in all aspects of life. This *Self* empowers us to live authentically, being fulfilled, and joyful because we have worked through the impediments to conscious living. We vibrate at the level of unity or cosmic consciousness, a place where the boundaries we have erected in our lives no longer rule how we see or experience the world.

Summary

I propose that we are never *done* with our development and evolution. We are continually in the process of *becoming*, giving us the opportunity to discover and evolve our uniqueness. By forging psychological tools that help us awaken this complex *Self*, we become active co-creators of our destiny. We take an active part in shaping who we are and who we can become. We call forth our strength to face our past with renewed vision and to turn our hearts and minds towards a path of greater awareness in the future of possibilities. By honing psychological tools to help us in this process, we can face the future with strength and confidence that we can and will strive towards living a more *Awakened* life. We do not travel with blinders on, but prepare ourselves with knowledge, insight and wisdom so that we move forward with understanding and hope.

The Awakened Self takes you on a journey to explore where you have been so that you can navigate and chart a new course for yourself. This quest takes you back in time to explore what has shaped your personality, providing tools that lead you to a clearer sense of where you have been, how you got there, and simultaneously providing you with the knowledge necessary to set the pace for actualizing your real *Self*, and developing lifelong tools that will help you to stay your course on the *Awakened Self* path. You will reclaim what has been left behind, discard what is not worth keeping, and actualize new choices that lead to greater happiness and a more fulfilled life.

Topic One

My Guiding Myth

Often, we find our reality does not fit our preconceived notions about the world around us. We adjust and distort our perceptions to fit the pictures we hold in our heads (Glasser, 1985). These pictures contain the behaviors and solutions to some past goal and, quite often, we continue to use them even though they may no longer work. These "pictures in our heads" (e.g., beliefs, ideas, behaviors, responses, manipulations) were created through our early experiences and provided workable solutions for the time, but unless we update these "photos" we will continue to draw upon them, even though they may well be outdated. We attempt to distort the reality around us so that we can assimilate the new experience. We cannot tolerate cognitive dissonance; thus we rationalize, displace, project or utilize any of the other Freudian defenses when accommodation would be more functional. If we find that we prefer to create change, then a formula for implementing change is useful.

It is not so much *what* happens to us that affects us so deeply. Much more poignant is our perception and thus, *how we live*. Our perceptions invariably dictate our reactions or responses. If we see ourselves as victors, then we will be triumphant; if we see ourselves as victims, then we will be overcome. Basically, we can abdicate the victim role. We can become the masters of our destiny through our willingness to shape the course of our lives, choosing which direction we will take and then taking responsibility to make it happen. If our choices fall short of our expectations we can swallow our pride, pick ourselves up, brush ourselves off and try another solution. This differs from sitting, pointing the finger at others, and blaming them for the things that go wrong in our lives.

The mode of our travel may seem inappropriate for the times in which we find ourselves as well. Slowly, we may come to realize that we have been pressured into conformity, not taking the time to evaluate the structure of our prevailing belief system until we are in crises. So much of our myth was already "written" for us as we were growing up and we simply began to live it out in an unconscious manner. We were subtly being shaped into little female and male tin soldiers probably not questioning how well the design fit us individually. There comes a time when we realize the pattern of our lives may not be of our own design. It slaps us in the face and we say, "Enough!" and so, we must reckon with ourselves. Painful as it may be, we embark upon the dialectical process of evaluating, dissecting, and sorting out the values and beliefs we have grown to believe in. In our youth we are "like the sun rising over the horizon and climbing towards the meridian." We are focused upon establishing our financial independence, finding a mate and a niche in life. If we felt subtly uncomfortable because we had to "put aside" other parts of ourselves, we found it necessary to do so. Beliefs, desires, or experiences that are contrary to our personal belief system—our prevailing myth at that time—were probably suppressed or repressed so as not to disrupt the process.

When we come to this juncture in our journey it is neither wise nor necessary for us to discard all that we have collected. It would benefit us to keep that what we value and treasure has worked for us. What we will discard are the worn-out aspects of our personality and belief systems that are no longer functional. By combining the old with the new, we rewrite our myth and create a new workable roadmap that will work for us in the present. Thus, we can integrate the thesis of our present state with the antithesis of the emerging myth and transform the two into a synthesis— a gestalt.

Discovery and Revision

"I can only answer the question of 'What am I to do?' if I can answer the prior question, *What story or stories do I find myself a part of?*" These stories are metaphors for how to live. In our media-oriented society, we are continually bombarded with various answers to these questions. We are shown how to live, whom to marry, how to act in our relationships, what to do for a career, and much more, simply from watching television or movies. Add the influence of magazines, comic books, newspapers, Hollywood and the Internet and we have all shapes and sizes to choose from for our models. These forms may have different faces, but the message is fairly distinct regarding societal ideals about success, happiness, relationships, fulfillment, femininity and masculinity.

In this chapter we are exploring the idea that there are stories about people and life that guide our perceptions, choices, behaviors, thoughts, feelings, and attitudes. All around us are stories being told from which we fashion our own path in life, thinking that if we emulate the model, we too will get what they have achieved in life. We are conscious of some of our stories and some of them lie in our subconscious and unconscious. The stories that we live by from our subconscious would be those habits that we have formed. The unconscious houses those stories that we have yet to unearth. They influence us but we are not aware of why we feel the way we do, or do what we do. This is where awakening to what is unconscious can significantly change your life.

Let's examine a few things that together constitute the story or myth by which we live. In the late 1980's, Warren Farrell, author of *Why Men Are The Way They Are, The Myth of Male Power,* and *Women Can't Hear What Men Don't Say* examined magazines and found that men's magazines centered around beautiful, sexual and sensual women. *Playboy* and *Penthouse* were the best selling men's magazines according to 1985 figures. Farrell believed that these magazines metaphorically represented the male Primary Fantasy where a man can have unlimited access to beautiful women with no fear of rejection. The equivalent Primary Fantasy for women was represented by *Better Homes and Garden* and *Family Circle*— being a wife, having children and a husband, and financial security with all the trappings of material success. If what America reads represents what is important to them, we need only look at what sells. Although these examples are dated, they are instructive.

In 1986, 40% of all paperback sales were romance novels. Six of the top 11 magazines were traditional women's magazines. In fact, *Better Homes and Garden* outsold *Playboy* and *Penthouse* sales combined. None of the top 11 magazines were men's magazines, nor were they of the working women type. Interestingly, Farrell looked at the second ranking magazines for each sex to discover the means by which each sex achieves the primary fantasy. For women, it was *Cosmopolitan, Glamour, Seventeen* and *Teen*— beauty and men. Over 90% of the ads in those magazines focused upon glamour, beauty and fashion. The articles in these same magazines were divided between glamour and men.

For men, the focus of the most read magazines was an emphasis on heroism or performance. Second ranking men's magazines were *American Legion* (war hero), *Sports Illustrated* (sports hero), *Boy's Life* (childhood preparation to perform) and *Forbes* (business hero). Of course, there are other societal mediums through which we are led to believe that traditional values of feminine and masculine behaviors will help us achieve a more fulfilling life. Television commercials, billboards, the Internet and movies convey messages that *we can have it all* if we can just conform to the images that they flash before us. When we fall short of these idealistic images, we feel somewhat inadequate and incompetent.

Let's look at today's top selling men's magazines. They are, in rank order, *Esquire, Playboy, Sport's Illustrated, GQ (formerly Gentlemen's Quarterly),* and *FHM (For Him Magazine).* The only theme to have dropped out for males is the war hero, but the emphasis on beautiful, sexy women remains as well as the sports hero. For women, not much has changed it seems. Today's top selling women's magazines, in rank order, are *Good Housekeeping, Ladies Home Journal, Better Homes & Gardens, Redbook and Family Circle.* Looks the same as the 1980's list.

The movies of our times also continue to depict themes that reveal the prevailing mythology of our society in regards to gender behavior. Another older movie, *Hook,* featured the late Robin Williams as Peter Pan who had grown up into an adult. His quest was to save his own children from the clutches of Captain Hook. To do this he had to *re-member* (i.e., to join together) the child he once was. He had forgotten that part of his life, but when he goes back to *Neverland* with Tinkerbell, he slowly remembers his "lost self." Through the help of the "Lost Boys" Peter Pan joins the forgotten aspects of his personality with his adult self. This contemporary myth for males illustrates a shedding of more traditional male values, which enabled Peter to enjoy life once again. This particular myth is a rendition of the current movement for us to find "the child within." If we are to save ourselves from the hooks of traditional gendered behaviors, then we must reclaim the joyful child that once existed within each of us.

How many of the current movies are similar to the 1990's movie, "Pretty Woman," starring Julia Roberts? According to this movie, we are led to believe that by being a high-class call girl, we can be "flashdanced" to happiness (Farrell, 1986). "Flashdance" was another movie that basically portrayed a woman as rising to the top through her relationship to a rich and powerful man. This perpetuates the societal myth that a woman can be magically transformed if she finds the *right* man. She does not have to get a college degree, find a job, "pay her dues," or set up a retirement plan. These movies perpetuate the notion of women as objects and that happiness is attained through the life of a man. Females get the message in a subtle manner that beauty is indeed skin deep and is prerequisite to having it all. Although there are more movies today that portray strong female role models (e.g., *The Hunger Games, X-Men*), too many movies still instill myths that perpetuate the status quo where gender roles are concerned. When we become aware of this type of influence, our awareness leads us to make different choices that do not follow these stereotypes.

These stories serve to fashion male behaviors in relation to females and vice versa. If a male continually sees ads that assert that love is best expressed in the form of a $10,000 diamond ring, then, "Hey! What's a guy to do?" Flowers on Valentines Day (Don't forget the chocolates!), presents for every conceivable holiday, and a man's worth is based upon his ability to provide. He must not only be a provider, but he should be able to protect as well. And what will a woman think if he cannot do this?

Fifteen minutes of viewing the Francis Ford Coppola film, *Apocalypse Now* is enough to make males reevaluate societal definitions of a real man. This film depicts the horrors of the Vietnam War and the viewer is forced to imagine the psychological effects upon the veterans who were engaged in this type of warfare. It is a poignant example of the effects of patriarchal expectations of male warrior behaviors and the resulting inevitable feelings of betrayal experienced by many of the young men who served and trusted the decisions of the all knowing "father." Today we have numerous movies that continue to portray the hero and heroine as warriors, perpetuating the myth that a "real" man or woman must be at war. I wonder how the men, women and veterans of our current wars, including the Iraq and Afghanistan wars, feel about trusting the government to do what is right?

These are but a few examples of the societal myths for women and men today—they are not personal. They do not fit everyone. Some are good and some are not. We have to be discerning when we fashion our definition of what it means to be a "real woman" and a "real man." We need to take into account our individuality and not force ourselves into the Procrustean bed. By trusting our inner wisdom, we can explore, define and redefine our beliefs and mythologies regarding femininity and masculinity—our *Self*—so that we actualize the authentic self and all the potential that is within. With this, integration of the personality will bring the fullness of experience that individuation promises.

Myths, Fairy Tales and Folklore

What can we learn from stories? Myths, fairy tales and folklore have throughout time addressed the issues of life. These stories have illuminated the all too human situations in which we find ourselves—love, hate, war, birth, death, maturity, femininity, masculinity, and separation to name just a few. As the great mythologist, Joseph Campbell (1983) described, the function of myth is to provide a blueprint which delineates the road we will travel, with markers to indicate the inherent joys, sorrows, obstacles,

19

and consequences of our actions. Myths enable human beings to code and organize their lives so that they can see their destination and the path they will travel (Feinstein, D., Krippner, S. & Granger, D., 1988).

These stories reveal our human strengths and weaknesses. By studying mythical characters and their personalities, we gain insight into the spectrum of human related ways of being in the world. These stories give us some indication of what we can expect of life, of our predisposed human ways of reacting to situations, and of our possible and probable solutions to the dilemmas in which we find ourselves. By examining the lessons inherent in myths, we are better prepared to venture forth upon our own personal journey through consciousness of the challenges we may face and the psychological pitfalls, which may impede our growth.

Myths are a fundamental expression of our experience (Fordham, 1963). In his autobiography, Jung (1961/1963) wrote, "Everything in the unconscious seeks outward manifestation, and the personality too desires to evolve out of its unconscious conditions and to experience itself as a whole. What we are to our inward vision...can only be expressed by way of myth" (p. 3). Jung was implying that forces in the unconscious that we have tucked away, ignored or have not yet acknowledged continue to influence us. These neglected aspects of our personality continue to seek acknowledgement and expression, however, clamoring for attention and impacting our behavior, thoughts, and perceptions. Even though we may not be able to explain why we are overcome with certain moods or thoughts in particular situations, we "know" on an intuitive level that something does not feel right. It is not so much that these unconscious aspects of our personality want to "take over" but that they need to be acknowledged, accepted and integrated into consciousness.

Can myths be taken as truths? Can we rely on the lessons inherent in these stories to guide our behaviors and choices? Will they illuminate the road before us that we must travel like so many sojourners? The psychologist, William James asserted that our beliefs are sustained by our ability to obtain proof that there is truth in those convictions, yet, before we could discover that proof, one of the necessary conditions for a *particular class of truths* was belief itself (Cited in Daniels, 1988). In other words, until our *faith* makes it so, something cannot be true for us. Truth requires that we accept and believe in the premises of that *truth* without solid proof of its existence. We must then act upon the faith of that belief, trusting that it will lead us to where it purports to take us.

Mythic structures are based upon make-believe which is the ability to play with and react to symbols or words "as if" they were what they represented, a concept that is similar to Adler's idea of *fictional finalism* (Daniels, 1988). This is the case with mythologies. If we live "as if" our myth is true, then the message of the myth may become a truth for us in the consequence of our guided actions—similar to a self-fulfilling prophecy. We are thus pulled toward the future, so to speak. The future is not yet at hand, yet we act "as if" this future self or goal is, in fact, a reality. Living creatively empowers us to live fully and in an inspired manner. In times past, the word "myth" implied a falsehood, something we could not depend upon to be true; but, today, the word "myth" has taken on a quality wherein the understanding of life and the quests we embark upon can be better understood by looking to these stories for meaning. Myths speak to our human condition at a metaphorical level.

Why is it that myths and fairy tales do not die out as we continue to develop as a technological society? The mythical settings speak to a time long gone and yet the stories continue to reveal pertinent and timely issues. Perhaps it is because dilemmas addressed in these stories are timeless in nature and common to all humanity. Myths refer to experiences of the collective race, as Jung would assert. We continue to confront the same situations, predicaments, paradoxes and sentiments that our ancestors experienced. Only the setting is different. The human condition is not bound by the strictures of time for the tasks are existential. None of us are immune from the common situations life will present to us. We must all face our developmental tasks and with some guidance from mythical sources, the process or passage will be easier.

Our Personal Mythology

The current societal myth appears to be the quest for the golden fleece of power and many of us are led blindly to strive for that prize regardless of the ramifications we may experience because of this (Ng, 1989). What is power? Power can be said to have various qualities, such as material power, military power or the power of persuasion. Regardless of its form, power speaks. The paths to power in our society are part of the mythological structure of gender related behaviors. We learn from an early age that the contemporary image of woman or man is the ideal for which we must strive. If we want to fit in and excel, we must adhere to these images and emulate those behaviors. We then feel that we will be successful. We will gain acceptance and power in the larger grouping of society. This is success to some.

We stretch or stifle ourselves to fit the societal prescription for success, yet so many times we must deny our inner self in the name of conformity. We come to believe that certain personal qualities will assure success, so we go about the task of adding here, subtracting there to accommodate our perception of the path we must follow. We think that if we follow the same path of someone that we admire, we too will have an admirable life.

In our hands we hold a map that was formed in the developmental process. This map consists of the paths we have learned that will lead to success, happiness, femininity, masculinity, etc. We plod along, referring to our old map for guidance but invariably at some point in our lives, we notice that there are holes in it and that it is faded at important junctures. The folds in the map have become worn and unreadable. So what we are left with is a worn-out, outdated "map" which includes our preconceived notions about life. If we are honest with ourselves, we realize that we must create our own path rather than blindly follow preset standards and old role models.

The irony of this situation is that most of us do not have solid role models to follow regarding the path to wholeness (Moore, R. & Gillette, D., 1990). Traditional models of belief no longer fit our contemporary world. Change occurs rapidly and we are at a loss regarding the transitions of life. We have come to a point where the guiding myths or rituals necessary for transition to more mature ways of being are absent. We grope in the dark for the light switch, but cannot see. What we each need is a mythology that is more personal, individual and current—one that will guide us on our unique journey. Ironically, we are already living by some form of personal mythology but we may simply be unaware of the content of those myths. We are, nevertheless, guided by certain principles, beliefs, values, expectations, desires and standards that in turn form the pattern of our lives.

This personal mythology consists of the guiding myths that we have construed in the process of our development—a belief system that directs us in our thoughts and actions. It is a constellation of ideas, images and emotions with a central theme that serves as an inner model for us. It becomes the template that "we create to fit over the realities of which the world is composed" (Feinstein, 1979). In this way we learn to interpret the world according to our myths, which give color and meaning to our experiences.

Cognitive Structures as Templates for Belief

Perhaps digression will illuminate the developmental process of our personal mythology. Feinstein (1979) proposed several concepts of cognitive structures that reveal the scientific basis of personal mythologies as a model for psychology. It gives credence to the idea that similar to myths, a personal mythology is more than a falsehood. By examining cognitive structures, we can use this paradigm to help us understand how we developed the current form of our belief system—our personal mythology:

Self-Statements

Self-statements are the cognitive structures that provide the "internal dialogue governing understanding and behavior." These cognitive structures are a basis for our *self-statements* and help us to interpret our experiences. We evaluate stimuli and sensory experience through these *self-instructions*, which create our perceptions and beliefs about life. They guide our behavior and are the components of our personal mythology. They are the self-messages we tell ourselves regarding life.

This would be an opportune time to begin noting when your thoughts, feelings or behavior stem from a self-statement. This would refer to resultant feelings that arise from the self-statement or the resulting behavior acted out. We then need to re-examine the self-statement that we are using to see if it really does apply in the situation that we find ourselves.

Coding System

Our coding system consists of structures that provide a means of verbal and pictorial coding. They are a parallel system that results in "verbal material and mental imagery." Our preference of the coding system we use tends to result in either a predominant verbal or pictorial expression of our personal myth. Emerging from this aspect are either the "pictures we hold in our heads" or the self-statements we utter. Do you code primarily in pictures or words? What are the forms of those statements or pictures? More importantly, when events happen, what are the pictures that arise or self-statements that you say to yourself that have an impact on how you process what is going on in situations?

Unconscious Templates

Cognitive structures act as "templates that mediate perception, thoughts, and behavior" that may be out of our conscious awareness. This means that through use and repetition, ways of thinking and being can become habitual and do not require our conscious attention. Personal myths often operate at this level so that we can direct our energies to more demanding tasks at hand in the moment. At other times, we use defense mechanisms because if we became aware of our unconsciousness, it might cause us too much anxiety. We just keep doing what we've been doing, even when it doesn't work. Although this prevents us from developing more workable ways of seeing and thinking about the world, it also keeps our anxiety at bay. Until we become conscious of these unconscious templates, it is difficult to recognize that a personal myth is in operation. We are thus unconsciously guided by a belief system that may be unworkable, but familiar.

Neuronal Connections

There appears to be genetic and experiential determinants to our cognitive structures. Neuroscientists now know that "neurons that fire together, wire together." This implies that when we have experiences that are repeated often enough, that they will become second nature to us. This involves not only the ways in which we see the world, but it also involves emotional states that we experience habitually that also wire together. When these emotional states are repeated again and again, we develop a chemical craving for these same hormones and neurostates.

25

We form new neuronal connections that influence our behavior as we have matured with new nerve fibers forming as we encounter new experiences. At the same time, connective patterns among neurons are altered. Many forms of social organization have been attributed to our biological nature and Feinstein (1998) suggested that personal myths may originate from the genetic structure of the brain as well as in the accumulation of ongoing experiences. He feels that "personal myths are biologically coded organizing models for behavior that exert their influence on consciousness and behavior from the bottom up.

Developmental Processes

Feinstein suggests that our personal myths become activated at the appropriate time in our development. What will be activated in our personal myth is part of the developmental process. For example, we do not begin to think and act like a teenager until we have come of age at puberty. At that time, we find ourselves breaking away from established childhood behaviors and attitudes, attempting to form our own identity and rebelling against the established ways in which we have lived as a child. In other words, it is not until we come of age as a teenager that this myth or belief system is activated. These activated belief systems are unconscious and may work for a while, but eventually, like many of our naive illusions, we are compelled to find a more individualized, workable path. When it is appropriate to do so we will recognize the time to reassess and revamp our personal myth.

Identification of Our Prevailing Myth

The myth that currently guides our attitudes and behavior is called our *prevailing myth*. It is the most recent version of the developing myth that has emerged from the integration of our experiences. As Feinstein (1998) described, the basic postulates, or beliefs, in one's personal theory of reality are generalizations derived from emotionally significant experiences in childhood. These events and our reaction to them exert a strong influence in the development of our later beliefs. As we grow in awareness, we open our eyes and understand that the past does color our present. If we are to uncover the *Self*, we need to see how the *self* was formed and identify the beliefs that stemmed from those past experiences and our reactions to those events.

Human beings are often resistant to change. Stability and consistency help us to feel safe and comfortable. The problem resides in the fact that change is inevitable. Life presents us with challenges, and we must meet those hurdles with the knowledge and skills necessary for this accomplishment. New information that runs counter to our current myth is either subject to defense mechanisms or is assimilated or accommodated into our current schema—our prevailing myth. If we try to *assimilate* this new information in our attempt to prevent a disruption to our current mythic structure, we end up distorting events so that it fits our beliefs. *Accommodation*, however, requires that we get out of our comfort zone and update our previous beliefs so that we can adapt more successfully to the present circumstance. In the process, our old myths are refined or eventually are completely replaced by newly formed ones, but most often the renewed mythology will be a blend of the old and new.

The Dialectical Process and the Emergence of a Counter Myth

A *dialectic* is the practice of "discussion and reasoning by dialogue as a method of intellectual investigation; the Socratic techniques of exposing false beliefs and eliciting truth; the Platonic investigation of the eternal ideas" (Webster's, 1973). This is a rudimentary element of uncovering our personal mythology in that we begin the process to discuss and question the assumptions by which we live. Mythical thought flows "from an awareness of contradictions towards their resolution, attempting to mediate opposites and resolve them" (Feinstein, et al, 1988).

In other words, when our outer experiences do not match our inner perceptions, conflict and its resulting anxiety ensue. We feel torn, not knowing which way to turn, but we do realize that some change is necessary. We just have to discover the direction of that change. Quite often, anxiety leads to using *defense mechanisms* rather than changing because this allows us to protect our current operating myth and maintain the status quo. Defense mechanisms lead to another kind of psychic threat, however—we repress the emotional energy created from this battle and it festers within the unconsciousness, which can lead to an unexpected outburst on our part. By understanding how the psyche works, we are armed with the knowledge of how to identify and create the positive changes that we seek. The upcoming topic on Jung's Theory will help explain this concept.

We hold onto our old beliefs but desperately need a new answer. The greater our anxiety, the more rigid our posture becomes so that we can maintain our old ways of being and believing. What happens in the psyche is that our *libido* (fuel for the psyche) gets polarized, creating an imbalance. This is like forming two opposing teams, each side fighting for its belief system to win. Our *libido,* or psychic energy, becomes imbalanced that eventually leads to a "snap" in our minds. The more highly charged material from the unconscious flows into the conscious mind and attempts to burst through, and we lose our cool.

We may find ourselves acting out, saying and doing things to the extreme. What we try to repress can pop up unexpectedly and in a more extreme expression. For example, when we don't allow ourselves to do or think of something that we actually really want to do, there is a danger of building up resentment. We may not allow ourselves to act on our thoughts because if we did, it goes against our current values or beliefs and makes us uncomfortable. In fact, we often won't even allow ourselves to think such thoughts! The desire to do or say the act is still within us, however, and each side of the conflict has psychic energy attached to it. It is not lost simply because we push it down. It's like a bubble in the unconscious that naturally moves up (and into consciousness), but when we push it down again, it just gains more power. Eventually the psychic pressure builds and we burst! What comes out is an extreme form of your former feelings, however.

As an example, there are many people that I've met who tell me that they have trouble telling others, "No" although that is their true feeling. They want to say no, but because they see themselves as kind, caring, and helpful, saying "no" doesn't match their self-image. When we tell others "yes" when we mean, "no" the psychic energy becomes more charged and creates an imbalance in the psyche unless we are conscious of our ambivalence. Being aware of our conflict, we can say "yes" this time, but can also promise ourselves to engage in some much needed self-care. That keeps the libido more balanced. If we miss this last step, we are likely to just berate ourselves for being "so selfish" so we say yes, and build up more imbalance in our psyche. When we have told others "yes" too often when we really wanted to say "no," eventually we will snap. Instead of a simple "No," we yell out, "Hell no!! All you ever do is use me!" You then decide to not help anyone anymore. Does this sound familiar?

This emerging material can be considered the "counter myth" or antithesis to our prevailing myth. Feinstein, et al (1988) stated that counter myths often arise to support aspects of our personality that are undeveloped because of our current mythic structure. The counter myth thus pushes "toward further expression" but will be an extreme form and must undergo the same scrutiny applied to the prevailing mythos.

Symbolism can become a tool for uncovering the opposing forces we are facing at this time and dreams are a rich source symbolism that reveal the nature of our unconscious. The gift that dreams provide is a peek into our unconscious to discover what we may not be aware of. Dreams have three characteristic functions: reinforcing the old myth, advancing the counter myth, and promoting a synthesis between the two. Dreams can become an avenue to reconciling the conflict. Through dreamwork we can listen to the messages emerging from the unconscious that symbolize the compensatory nature of dreams (See the topics on *Understanding Dreams* and *Dreamwork Exercise*). The themes in our dreams would be the opposite of how we see the situation consciously; thus, missing pieces of our puzzle are discovered through dream work.

Many of the people in our dreams represent other forms of our *Self*. An older male or female may be the archetypes of the *Wise Old Man* or *Wise Old Woman* speaking to us. These archetypes represent the *wiser* self that is within all of us. This inner guide leads us to answers that are healing. By tapping into our own inner wisdom we can become the mediator between the old and emerging myth. Acknowledging the emerging myth, we can reevaluate our existing myth and synthesize the two to form a new myth that incorporates the positive, workable aspects of each subsystem of belief. We glean the best from both worlds and create new pathways for us to follow.

The Process of Discovery and Revision

Feinstein and Krippner (1988) described their five-stage model that delineates the path we will traverse when our old mythologies no longer work. One constant in life is change, and so with awareness of our need to update our mythology to accommodate our changing needs, we can implement the following model when necessary.

Stage 1

This necessary first step is the recognition and identification of the conflict that is arising between our old and emerging myth. The old or prevailing mythic structure needs to be identified along with the submerged counter myth. Some of the signs that precede this stage are "difficulties making decisions, unfamiliar fears and anxieties, puzzling dreams, self-contradictions, nagging confusion, ambivalence, and even physical symptoms" (Feinstein, et al, 1988). This is the time when we experience all the ambivalence, conflict and confusion that comes when we are wanting to grow and evolve out of our old habits, but have not quite identified the elements of the old myth that are causing us problems.

Stage 2

At this stage, the prevailing myth is examined noting its history and consequences. This stage is when we distinguish the nature of any illusions we hold, leading us to ask how this illusion serves us. Identifying the counter myth is also required during this stage because we will need to recognize how this emerging myth is probably just as extreme as the current prevailing myth. It is our task to determine and recognize that the elements of the emerging myth are just as one-sided as the current mythology guiding our behaviors. Through conscious exploration of the two myths, neither of which is entirely satisfactory, a more workable resolution can be reached that incorporates constructive elements of both myths.

It is useful at this stage to engage in some exercises that help you get in touch with the stories that you may have inherited from your family. Try to put yourself into the shoes of your grandparents and ask what she or he would say to you. What belief would they pass on? Then do the same with your parents. These statements will likely reveal

31

elements of your mythology and at the same time help you identify their origins.

Stage 3

In stage three, the integration of the old myth and the counter myth begins. Resolution to the conflict identified in the first two stages is focused upon. In this process, a transcendence of the old and the new is achieved. This is a time when you need to ferret out what is workable and what is not in both the old and emerging mythologies. There will be a refinement of the extremes of both myths, when you can consciously create and commit to a new path.

Stage 4

The choice is now ripe for a renewed mythology wherein the new mythic integration is examined. At this point we would need to articulate and refine the new myth sufficiently, enabling us to consciously and maturely enter into a commitment to the newly synthesized myth. To accomplish this stage, it is helpful to make lists of how you are going to incorporate the newly synthesized mythology into action. Identify specific things that you can do to demonstrate your commitment to this new way of living.

Stage 5

In this last stage, a weaving of the renewed mythology into our daily life has begun. This requires focused attention and commitment to be our own monitor so that we can achieve the harmony we have mythically fashioned. With conscious awareness, we guard ourselves from acting out and believing in our old ways of "being" and we become the champions of our newly formed belief system. This is when living the new mythology happens.

After exploring the thesis and antithesis of our present mythology, however, our job is not done. Carl Rogers wrote, "To be what one is, is to enter fully into being a process" (Cited in Ginsberg, 1984). Life is not static. We need to continually assess and re-assess the stories we are living out. We must take what we have learned and develop a plan or guidance system so that we can have a clear path to follow—then we must act.

Summary

Our personal mythology was formed as we developed. We probably never questioned whether some of these values and ethics felt right for us, but simply took them on as if they were a part of us. Their influence was felt in countless ways—what we valued in a mate (or thought we did); what we believed was feminine or masculine; our career goals; our biases, opinions, and morals. Most of us traveled along our marked path with these preset notions of how we should construe the world and never paused to challenge our assumptions. When we reach a point of crisis, however, we find it to be an opportune moment that sets us towards reevaluating our goals and beliefs with our external life. As described by New York based Jungian analyst, Sylvia Perera (1990), we can descend to the Dark Goddess and "sit, wait and rot" to discover the internal solutions to our dilemma. Through this introspective process, we generally sense the incongruity that exists between our gut feelings and what we have been doing. We take first one side and then the other. We examine the paradoxes and polarities of life. By daring to involve the dialectical process, we can assess the tasks that remain before us. Introspection often requires that we wait for the answers to bubble up from the unconscious, however; thus, as we sit and wait, we allow that which is putrid to our soul to rot.

Topic Two

Psychology In Perspective

As we search to identify the nature of our *self*, it is helpful to have a framework that guides our exploration. In this topic we will examine the historical roots of the discipline of psychology in order to build some of those tools that we will need along our journey to awaken to our greater *Self*. Rather than traveling through each psychological perspective as if they are separate and disconnected, we will use the analogy of a cut diamond to illustrate the interconnectedness of the various viewpoints.

Like a diamond, human behavior is multifaceted—a complex combination and interaction of processes occurring simultaneously. In this analogy, humans can be seen as unique diamonds, each with its own characteristic color and clarity. The psychological perspectives can be likened to the separate facets that are created in the cutting of a diamond. Each person is like the diamond, and the facets are the various perspectives from which we can scrutinize individual behavior. The facets provide a more detailed picture in the language of that perspective's focus, but remember that each facet is *reductionistic* and requires us to remember that *the whole is more than the sum of its parts*. We only see part of the picture when we peer through each facet, providing us with a valuable peek into our human nature. Each lens helps us more fully understand the mechanisms that govern our behavior, but it is the *sum,* or totality of all this information gained through the various perspectives that brings us closer to understanding the meaning of the phrase, "To be human." We must, therefore, remember that after we have examined behavior from a particular facet or psychological perspective, we need to draw back from this *reductionistic,* microscopic analysis to see the person as a whole.

To understand the nature of behavior we embrace a pragmatic approach that essentially strips the individual and experience into smaller, more manageable pieces. The scientific approach is *reductionistic* by nature because we take a larger object or complex creature such as a human being and try to identify and understand the smaller units that make up the bigger picture. This is helpful because we learn about the nature of the component parts that make up an individual on some level; however, an important step of the process is to be certain that we piece the person together again to see how the various "parts" interact within the whole organism or human being. We reduce the individual into component parts, much as we take a car apart to understand the different mechanisms that, when combined, create a moving vehicle that allows us to go from point A to point B. But we know that the transmission is not the same as the vehicle. It is only a vital part of the total machine. The facets serve to magnify and illuminate the parts, but to be a human is to be more than the sum of our parts. Each perspective provides an invaluable lens through which we can more fully understand the patterns and processes that result in human behavior and experience, but they are not the same as the person.

So, we will begin our journey by taking a brief tour of the history of psychology and an examination of how each force and facet has influenced what is studied in the discipline. You will be introduced to the driving forces that have shaped psychology and the ways in which behavior has been categorized, understood and explained. This historical adventure will illuminate how the discipline has grown, changed, and evolved thus revealing the current metamorphosis that is happening in the discipline.

As we apply the *Diamond Perspective* to our examination of psychology, we break down the component parts that make up the individual, walk around that person as if she or he is a Diamond and peer through each facet to determine what that "lens" reveals about the behavior(s) we are examining. As in all pursuits where we must disassemble something to see what makes it "tick," we have to put it back together to form a working whole again. Thus the saying, "The whole is more than the sum of its parts," informs us that we cannot know a human being by simply disassembling him or her. Like a symphony, where each instrument provides an important part to the complete sound experienced, human beings are a combination of different facets that together, produce a unique individual. Like the instruments in an orchestra, each instrument adds a vital piece to the whole sound. We study the separate pieces in order to discover the components that make up the total sound of a symphony. It's often hard to imagine or hear the separate parts that each instrument plays in a song, because the combined sound of all instruments playing their separate parts produces a more complex sound that is hard to imagine from the separate instrumental parts. Human beings, too, are like an orchestra. We are more than the sum of our parts.

Psychology is Born in the Lab

Before we begin our journey into the various perspectives within psychology, it is useful to know a bit of psychology's foundations. Psychology emerged from the combination of two existing disciplines of *philosophy* and *biology/physiology*. Philosophers had formerly entertained the questions about human existence that have plagued our species, but was accused of being confined to the armchair—there was no proof to their claims. Philosophers could just sit around and speculate about the meaning of life and the reasons for human existence without conducting any research to prove or disprove their claims.

On the other side of the discipline of Psychology, the fields of Biology and Physiology had always used a strict scientific approach to gain a better understanding of the human body and its processes. This adherence to the scientific method allowed for what we believe are objective and observable conclusions in biological research. Combining the disciplines of philosophy with biology/physiology to form the discipline of psychology was an attempt to wed the basic questions that philosophers held about human existence with the methods of science. Questions about human nature could now be put to the test by using the tools of science: observation, experimentation, case studies, correlations, surveys, theory, hypothesis formation, random selection, and representative sampling to name a few.

Psychology may have some built-in limitations because of this unique combination of these two different disciplines. Because much of human behavior is not observable (e.g., consciousness, thought processes and their interaction with our emotions), there are certain human experiences that are difficult to measure. The hallmark of the scientific method is to measure whatever phenomenon is under consideration, yet the tools to measure these states may not yet be in existence. This poses a problem when psychologists are interested in studying aspects of human nature but lack the necessary technical equipment to ascertain the data. Simultaneously, even when the equipment and technology are in accord with our endeavors to scrutinize a phenomenon scientifically, it takes time to develop appropriate methods of measurement in research. For example, in research being conducted to determine the efficacy of acupuncture to help people suffering from various problems, both physical and mental, new procedures had to be developed since acupuncture theory is based upon the concept that the body has energy meridians. These energy meridians carry what Chinese medicine refers to as *chi,* but these meridians are not physical structures that we can see like blood vessels. There have been 12 major meridians identified, however, with hundreds of acupuncture points that lie along those meridians. So how would scientists design a study to "measure" the efficacy of acupuncture treatments? Is it sufficient to simply compare two groups, the experimental group receiving treatment using bona fide acupuncture points and in the control condition, to insert needles in other areas of the body that are not mapped as points along one of the known energy meridians of the body?

Continued debate rages regarding the methodology applied to studying the subtle energies of the body (e.g., chi, consciousness). This illustrates the split within the discipline of psychology between the hard-core materialists and the more esoteric questions of humanistic and transpersonal psychologists. The use of the scientific method to philosophical questions of being human is a worthy endeavor and has helped us find answers and develop effective treatments to many human problems. It has, however, simultaneously prevented research into interesting and esoteric areas because we are posed with the problems of how to measure the phenomena that we are exploring.

The nature of consciousness is another one of these problematic arenas to study because research is constrained by technology. If we don't have the instruments to measure what we are exploring or if those instruments simply tell us that a phenomenon is occurring, we risk the danger of assuming that *correlation implies causation.* We mistakenly see the action going on in the brain as evidence that the brain *caused* the resultant or accompanying experience and forget that the brain may simply be recording what we as sentient creatures can generate.

For example, much hesitation, bad press, and skepticism have colored research conducted to better understand some realms of human experience that are difficult to measure (i.e., psi phenomena). We need to consider that it may not be that these phenomena do not exist, but that we cannot detect it properly because we lack the necessary technology or equipment to detect what we are investigating. If the methods we employ do not lend themselves easily to measuring the phenomenon under question, should we simply refuse to research these phenomena, claiming that they do not exist because technology and science have not discovered the means to do so?

I am reminded of how our understanding of the cosmos has grown over time. What we knew about the cosmos in the 1900's pales in comparison to what we know today! As we continue our trek into the 21st century, we need only to look back 100 years and compare our body of knowledge in astronomy, physics and cosmology to what we currently know in the 21st century. How could we imagine that the Hubble telescope, the Cassini mission or any of the more recent probes launched into the universe would reveal what we now know? How many of you are still debating whether Pluto is a planet or not? Cited as a fact not long ago as being the ninth planet in our solar system, we are now reduced to only eight planets, but there are some new contenders for the title of the ninth planet in our known solar system. Additionally, medicine makes claims based upon current knowledge, but as new information is discovered, those assumptions have to be revamped or discarded entirely.

Is psychology an exact science, or is it possible that we must wait for more sophisticated technological advancement and understanding before we can reach a more complete understanding of what makes us tick? We may also have to devise new perspectives of how to research the unknown territories of the human experience. Near-sightedness arises when we become obsessed with the methodology rather than the question. Given these restrictions, should psychology venture into research in areas where we cannot apply the scientific method easily? Can we live with the knowledge that our understanding may be incomplete? This has been the nature of the science of psychology as it has evolved over the past 135+ years.

A Brief History of Psychology

In 1879, in Leipzig, Germany, *Wilhelm Wundt* established the first psychological laboratory wherein he systematically observed and recorded phenomena about human experience. Considered to be the "father of psychology," Wundt used the methods of science to explain human behavior where he investigated the structure of human consciousness. Thus, born in the lab, psychology began its quest to answer the questions of human experience by using the scientific method. This method is not without its problems, however, as we have noted earlier.

We can reduce human experience to the questions that we ask, and in that pursuit we have been able to put behavior under the microscope. At the same time, we realize that explaining our humanity is not a simplistic endeavor. These narrow interpretations of human experience that arise from our research findings have given credibility to the discipline of psychology and have attracted interest from those corporations in our society that profit from research results. For example, although there are many facets through which we can understand and treat behavior, research seems to focus primarily on the biological approach without equal attention and funding being channeled towards research that could make people more self-reliant and healthier. We are focused primarily on treatment rather than healing or

41

prevention when we stick to only one facet of the Diamond Perspective. We need only to look at the pharmaceutical industry to see the connections. Much research is funded by drug companies in their pursuit for better living through chemistry. By looking at what gets funded and the resultant drugs that are developed, we find that studies that do not enhance further drug development generally don't get funded.

Society becomes myopic when we only advance one way of looking at behavior. All facets of the Diamond Perspective provide valuable information. It seems that much of psychology has forgotten to draw back from the microscope, developing a sort of tunnel vision in our quest to establish psychology as a "hard" science. We know that there some aspects of being human that are difficult to investigate empirically, but we need to continue on if we are to compile a complete body of knowledge about psychology.

For example, can we truly understand the concept of "love" in the lab? Conversely, can we understand what it means to be human if we do not at least pursue the question, "What is love?" Another realm of human experience that is difficult to find hard and fast answers to deals with our search for meaning in life. Is there only one answer to this question that could be applied to all humans or is the answer as individual as the people who seek an answer? Is it possible to discover our unique gifts and potential? When we do uncover these truths about ourselves, what are we to do with that knowledge? Is the answer within us or must we search outside ourselves for our potential? What will foster that growth and what conditions will serve to thwart it?

What can psychology teach us about the human experience that has, up to this point in history, defied scientific investigation? There are areas of human behavior that psychology has had difficulty incorporating into its research repertoire. Should psychology simply ignore those human related phenomena because we have not been able to prove how those processes work [e.g., extrasensory perception (ESP), premonitions, mental telepathy, clairvoyance, energy healing, out-of-body experiences, or astral projection] or should we continue even though we have limited insight into how to investigate these phenomena? Does psychology have a responsibility to help humans find answers to our ignorance about the realm of our psyche or soul?

Another consideration is the old nature/nurture debate. Although many argue that the debate is over, it appears to be alive and well in the discipline of psychology. We find it difficult to unravel the effects of our physical self with the environment we are in, whether that environment is the womb or the workplace. Can and should behavior be dichotomized into either black or white or is there a large grey area to consider? Is the mind connected to the body or is it separate? In other words, do our thoughts affect our physical body and vice versa? Although this debate has settled into an uneasy alliance among psychologists, it serves to illustrate the point that to be human is to be complex.

It is doubtful that psychology will ever become a "hard" science, such as biology. There are many questions regarding the nature of how human observation affects the situation or object being observed. Subject/Object. Quantum physics is showing us that the subject and object are always "entangled" and that one does not exist separately without some relationship to the other. In other words, we are faced with the age-old dilemma: "If a tree falls in the woods and there is no one around to hear it, does it make a noise?"

We need to question research design when we pursue phenomenon that has not been amenable to traditional inquiry. The healing effects of imagery, acupuncture, meditation, and the like are examples of non-traditional areas to be investigated scientifically using revised research designs that consider the basic nature of the phenomena being investigated. This is being done in regards to research into the contemplative practices such as different forms of meditation (e.g., mediation, mindfulness, compassion meditation) and the effects on brain function and structure.

It therefore becomes apparent that many of the questions for which we seek answers may not be quantified or measured in any exact method. We must be satisfied that the pursuit of knowledge is sufficient for our inquisitiveness in some areas of understanding human behavior. Also, we must remember that those behaviors that we can reduce to more simplistic explanations are only part of the picture and therefore, only partial explanations for the experience of being human.

As we begin our adventure, the ideas that form the foundation of psychology are essential tools to take with you on your journey. These tools will help you to stay open and receptive to the many ways in which behavior can be interpreted. Just remember that psychology is an analytical discipline that forces you to critically examine what you are studying. This endeavor can create a nearsighted viewpoint and we have to remember to pull back and try to see the whole picture.

Forces and Facets of the Diamond

Using the Diamond Perspective, we will each find a favorite perspective or lens that helps us to better understand the world and people. That is natural and normal. As psychologists, you will better serve others if you will remember to use all the tools available in your quest for understanding such a complicated creature as a human being. To use tools from different perspectives in psychology is to be *eclectic*. The Diamond Perspective is useful because it:

- Helps us see each person as a multifaceted & complex being
- The facets represent the major psychological models or perspectives and are the tools of a psychologist
- Allows for a holistic approach to assessment and understanding behavior
- Breaking down behavior into different facets facilitates a critical analysis of the problem.
- It is an *eclectic* approach. In other words it allows us to borrow from many different schools of thought so that we can better understand the complexity of human behavior.

At the core of our sense of self are the personal sets of characteristics that we each perceive to be peculiar to ourselves. As will be described in the Diamond Perspective, Behaviorism and Psychodynamic thought shaped the early years of the discipline. Behaviorists believed we were animals that could be taught anything through conditioning and reinforcement. Psychodynamic theories grew from the work of Sigmund Freud who saw human behavior as the result of the mediation of our instinctual drives, which were primarily sexual or aggressive, with the demands to conform by society. From this viewpoint, human beings are the same. If it looks like a duck and acts like a duck, then it must be a duck. Individuality and potential are not a concern from these theoretical viewpoints. As the discipline developed, changes came about that broadened the ways in which we came to investigate and therefore, understand behavior.

Mental illness, its descriptions, definitions and therapeutic interventions have always reflected the *zeitgeist* of the psychological cultural context in which these problems were defined. Behaviorism, or the first force in psychology, focused on observable behavior and limited its investigations to that realm. It helped psychologists answer questions about how we learn through conditioning and reinforcement.

This focus on observable behavior and its quantification fit neatly into scientific methodological schemes and gave the discipline of psychology more credibility in the scientific community. This narrow focus limited the realm in which psychological research could occur, however. Additionally, because animal models formed much of the knowledge gained in behaviorism, generalization to human behavior was often criticized and looked upon with skepticism. Humans are considered to be much more complex organisms than the animals being used in these behavioral studies. It represented a reduction of the total human experience into its component parts, but did provide explanations for simple human learning.

Behaviorism: The First Force
(Key associative term: Learning)

Behaviorism essentially sees behavior as being the result of learning. This learning is the total accumulation of the different sets of conditioning and reinforcements that we have acquired in the developmental process. According to radical behaviorists, personality is not an existing condition ready to unfold. Instead, on the simplest level we learn to do what we do just like other animals learn. We do something and if what follows is what we were hoping or expecting, then we are likely to repeat that behavior again in the future. Behaviorists also describe how our emotions and physiological reactions emerge from the combination or association of an event with the emotion experienced. If we were teased a lot as a child, as an adult we tend to still react to teasing with the same network of emotions and thoughts. Essentially, Behaviorism can be characterized by the following:

> • Behavior is explained as stemming from the notion that we are born "tabula rasa" or like a "blank slate." If we are born as a blank slate, then our personalities are simply the result of the experiences, reinforcements, and conditioning we have received within our lifetimes. The unconscious is not a consideration from this perspective.

• It understands behavior only from the perspective that all behavior is learned. This is the nurture side of behavior that shapes what we do and what we react to in life.

• Behavior is learned through *operant conditioning* according to B.F. Skinner. In operant conditioning, behavior is seen as the result of having received *reinforcement*, or reward, for any given behavior whether it was intentional or not. In the future, when we desire a similar reinforcement, we are more likely to act in the same way as before. We are motivated by our expectations. If we get what we want by doing or saying something, then we are likely to repeat the behaviors when we want the same type of reward or result. When a child throws a tantrum and gets the attention she wants, she's likely to throw another tantrum when you are ignoring her.

• We also learn through *classical conditioning* according to Ivan Pavlov. We associate certain stimuli with a particular reaction within our emotional or physiological self—we react. In other words, if the very first time I give a speech in class and I am ridiculed, I will continue to have the same feelings of anxiety and shame in future situations where I might have to be in front of people to speak. Again, my behavior, which is reflexive in this case, is conditioned.

We are human animals...human, but animals nevertheless. Behaviorism conducted much of their research using rats, pigeons, monkeys, cats, dogs and other animals to determine how learning occurred. The information gained from this comparative research was then generalized to the human population. There is a similarity of human response and conditioning to what happens in animals, in general. It was a good starting point for psychological research in the early days of the discipline. It did, however, severely limited the range of human related behaviors and complexities that psychology could address but the types of behaviors that were studied were those that were easily amenable to the current scientific design at the time.

Albert Bandura established another form of modified behaviorism. He believed that we still learned behaviors even though we might not be rewarded right after we performed an action. Through *Social Modeling* or

Observational Learning we learn many, many ways of being in the world. We observe our parents as children and learn from what they model for us. We watch our peers and emulate what they do or say. This is the basis for concern of parents who restrict their children's exposure to violence on television or movies.

Psychodynamic or Psychoanalytic Perspectives: The Second Force
(Key associative term: Unconscious)

The second force driving psychological research is the Psychodynamic perspective, which focused more upon the instinctual nature of human behavior and the processes that governed psychological functioning. This force is primarily concerned with the unconscious and it's impact upon behavior. Psychodynamic thought, as proposed by such early psychoanalysts as Sigmund Freud (Hall, 1954), explained behavior as the result of the clash between inner drives and cultural expectations.

Carl Jung, a follower of Freud, also believed that we were instinctual creatures, but he believed that we were driven more by our inherited human tendencies, predispositions and preferences of our ancestors that he called the archetypes. He called this our *psychoid* inheritance, which stems from the influences within the collective unconscious (Hall, 1973). Jung's theory will guide much of our exploration into our understanding of the *The Awakened Self.* His theory will be covered in more detail in a later chapter.

Alfred Adler (1957) and Karen Horney (1966) were also both contemporaries of Freud and Jung. Adler advocated that the ego was the crucial factor in determining personality and that the internal sense of fragility—being a vulnerable, mortal human being—set the stage for our strivings in the world. He did believe that humans were goal-oriented creatures who live teleologically—with an aim towards the future. According to Adler, if you really wanted to understand a person, you should examine his or her goals. These goals indicate the personality type and *fictional finalism* that drives the individual.

Fictional finalism is a concept that he described wherein we live by our beliefs even though our beliefs may not be verified as a truth. For example, I may believe that if I am a kind and nurturing person, then my life will be filled with love, happiness, and friendship. I cannot verify that this belief will result in what I believe to be true, but because I hold it in my mind as a "truth," it guides my choices and behaviors. I live "as if" my belief is true, thus it can be called a "fictional finalism." This was a creative concept that allowed for individual growth, adaptation and change since the ego was in charge from this theoretical viewpoint. If we find that our beliefs are not getting us what we want in the world, we can examine those beliefs, or fictions, revise them, update them or discard them so that we can live by a more realistic belief system that works for us. Adler referred to this as *the creative power of the self.*

Karen Horney believed that we are all seeking safety in an insane world where love is difficult to find. Through our childhood environment, we learn to relate to others by adapting our behaviors to bring ourselves a sense of safety. This safety is in relationship to the physical environment as well as our interrelationships with others. We will do what it takes to feel safe. In the healthy personality we learn to relate to others depending on the circumstances and we adapt our behaviors accordingly. We would know when to *Move Towards People* because we can trust them in those circumstances, or we *Move Away From People* because we sense that we are not safe and would be wise to leave the situation. Additionally, we may find that we need to stand up for ourselves and assert our rights, boundaries, and beliefs. She called this *Moving Against People*. All three of these trends are adaptive if used in the right circumstances.

In neurotic development, we get stuck in one primary mode of relating to people that is habitual but not necessarily adaptive as adults. As children, we learned how to relate to others in ways that would make us feel safe, regardless of the dysfunction of our behaviors. As adults we continue to adhere to limited ways of relating to others based upon what Horney called neurotic needs (e.g., an exaggerated need for affection and approval, a dominant partner, for power or to exploit others; an exaggerated need for social recognition or prestige, admiration, ambition or personal achievement, self-sufficiency, independence, or perfection; or an exaggerated need to restrict one's life).

These psychodynamic approaches were early pathways to understanding the nature of the psyche and provided theories to explain personality development. If we see the psyche as a dynamic system where much of the action takes place below the level of consciousness, then we are better equipped to understand how we have become the person that we seem to be. Psychodynamic thought helped us understand the workings of the unconscious and how this affects our perception and behavior. These forces provided different paths to understanding about human behavior and were limited in their nature, but it was a beginning for the discipline of psychology.

The psychodynamic viewpoint teaches us that our motivation for behavior is outside of our awareness. Our perception is colored by experience, and often we say, do and feel in particular ways because of our past. Our sensitivities and "buttons" are formed in the process of development and serve the function of shaping our reactions and perceptions in the future. We end up reacting to situations instead of responding to them.

Psychodynamic theories are considered drive theories because all behavior is driven from internal needs according to these theories. As in Freud's theory, he believed that the driving forces of behavior were the life and death instincts and that they manifest as sex and aggression. These instincts govern all behaviors, but the social environment conflicts with these needs causing us to push down our impulses, or modify them into more socially acceptable forms.

Bubbles in the Unconscious

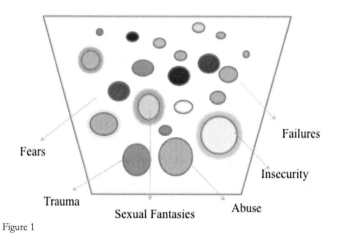

Fears

Failures

Insecurity

Trauma

Sexual Fantasies

Abuse

Figure 1

Psychodynamic thought also teaches us that we will push into the unconscious anything that is threatening or distasteful to us about our basic nature, our thoughts, or our traumatic experiences (see Figure 1). This material may sink into the unconscious, but it continues to exert its influence on what we say, think or do until we become *conscious* and override it's influence. What is forgotten by the mind is not gone and will rob us of psychic energy in the process. Freud's theory is a good example of this perspective.

These first two forces in psychology, Behaviorism and Psychodynamic thought, thus set the stage for how we would come to understand and explain human behavior in the early days of psychology. We were either simply animals that learn as other animals learn through conditioning, reinforcement and observation (behaviorism), or we were animals with particular human instincts, that when thwarted, could lead to mental illness (psychodynamic theories). These two early driving forces in psychology, behaviorism and psychodynamic thought, provided valuable but limited insight into human behavior. What was missing from psychology soon emerged in the Humanistic Movement.

The Humanistic Perspective: The Third Force
(Key associative terms: Potential, Individuality, Uniqueness)

Humanistic thought emerged in the midst of the changing psychological landscape of the 1960's. This was a time of great social and political change. This was mirrored in the discipline of psychology where there was growing dissatisfaction with the limitations of psychological thinking. Since behaviorism focused upon human behavior as it was reflected in animal studies, and psychodynamic thought gave us an apparent pathological viewpoint about humans, leaders of the humanistic movement turned their eyes more towards the future unfolding of the individual. It asked questions about human potential and the necessary conditions for its flowering. With the emergence of the Humanistic Movement, psychologists were now able to go into a different realm of inquiry. They studied a different set of questions about human potential and its actualization.

Humanistic psychology didn't discard the knowledge gained by the earlier psychological perspectives, but used this information to help reveal the nature of how we can achieve our best. What were the conditions and mechanisms involved that fostered or hindered the full blossoming of an individual? A think tank emerged in California at Esalen in Big Sur where many of the founding thinkers of the Third Force gathered to contemplate the nature of human potential: Abraham Maslow, Fritz Perls, Stanislav Grof, Michael Murphy, Charles Tart, and Rollo May joined in the movement and devised other strategies for exploring the humanistic realm. Over the years, Esalen has been the west coast site for study in Humanistic and Transpersonal psychology, somatic education, and holistic medicine.

What was significant about Third Force psychology was the conceptual reintegration of the bodymind split. Before the work of the pioneers of this movement, the body and mind were essentially seen as separate: the body did not affect the mind, or vice versa. Third Force practitioners worked on bringing the physical body back in tune with consciousness, or the mind. Body-based therapies were emphasized to help people "get back into their bodies." Massage, acupressure, acupuncture, yoga, meditation, chi kung and other martial arts, Rolfing, Lomi therapy, Feldenkraus method, and gestalt therapy all helped a person to understand how emotions get locked into the body. It became conventional wisdom in this group that the body must be worked with in some manner if the depth of pathological behavior was to be positively resolved. The body and mind were seen as interrelated facets of experience. One affected the other. Knowing the interaction of the bodymind connection paved the path to greater understanding of how thought, attitude, and belief affect an individual's mental and physical health. The humanistic movement expanded the realm of inquiry for psychology allowing for a more positive approach to understanding human desire, and the intrinsic mechanisms for evolving the self.

Humanistic psychologists believed that as therapists, we could not pretend to be the expert of another person's experiences. At best, we could "walk a mile" in his or her shoes and convey this understanding We learn to empathize and express this understanding through paraphrasing what we believe the person is trying to convey. We help by actively listening and helping the person to discover his or her own answers. Through the study of *phenomenology*, or the study of the direct experience as it is consciously experienced in an individual, humanistic psychologists could assist others to find their own answers. Pre-formed theories could not be used to explain the causes of a person's experience. The explanations had to be direct and related to the person having the experience.

In other words, it is an approach where we must take care to not base our understanding upon unexplained preconceptions and presuppositions. We have to "walk a mile" in another person's shoes to know what it is like to be that person and to understand what it must be like to be in that person's mindset. This allowed humanistic psychologists to guide the questioning and focus of therapy that was truly *client-centered*. Client-centered therapy, a term coined by Carl Rogers worked in therapy with *clients*, not *patients*. He felt that the term, patient, implied a hierarchical relationship, which he found erroneous since a therapist could only facilitate the discovery of answers for another person. We must be able to relate and empathize with the struggles that person is going through, withholding any judgment and seeking only to understand so that we can assist that person in their self-discovery process.

There are no blanket prescriptions providing relief from anxiety, or *angst* from this perspective. Instead, a private and personal search is required of each person who seeks to actualize the authentic self and one's inner potential. With the humanistic perspective, human "will" was now linked with choice and responsibility. Choices confronting a person are happening now, in the present situation and decisions need to be made from today's "reality." Regardless of past influences, each person has the responsibility to make wise choices and discover meaning within the current context of living. Learning and childhood experiences hold less power over an individual from this perspective.

This perspective thus puts the responsibility for existence squarely in the person's lap who is having the experience. Happiness is our responsibility to create. By exercising human will towards meaningful goals and making choices that reflect our sense that the future is up to us, we can move towards living our truest potential. Regardless of past influences that have either served to limit or harm us, we are no longer in the past but are here in the present. We have choices to make that will either allow us to unfold and blossom or remain wrapped up in a cocoon of protective behaviors and perspectives. It is in the "HERE AND NOW" that we each are called to discover our unrealized potential and individuality. It is a positive viewpoint of the best in humans. Abraham Maslow, the father of the Third Force, stated, "What a man (woman) can be, he (she) must be." Like an acorn, we have a unique potential to reach the heights of being a great oak tree if the conditions are right for our growth. Even if the conditions are compromised, we will still feel the pull towards self-actualization. This is similar to a plant that is in a dark room where there is only one window...we will stretch to grow towards that light source. It is an inner need to become.

Existentialism
(Key Associative Phrase: Finding Meaning in Life)

Existentialism is not a force in psychology, but a facet of the Diamond Perspective. Existentialism is probably best known as a philosophical viewpoint. Because psychology emerged from philosophy and biology it is not surprising that much of psychological inquiry focuses upon the very same questions that philosophers posed. After all, philosophy proposes to address the dilemmas we face within our lifetimes and the questions of existence that arise in the process of living. Humanistic thought grew out of this philosophical approach to understanding the problems that humans face. Life, by itself, results in questions with which we each struggle. Once we become conscious of our basic mortality we struggle with this knowledge and are faced to create a meaningful life knowing that it will be over before we know it.

The basic premise of existentialism is that psychological problems stem from our search for meaning in life—What is the meaning of life? What is the meaning of death? Why must we suffer? Why was I born? Who am I? We seek ways to live a meaningful life and in that pursuit we are challenged to find an answer that is personally meaningful. We search for meaning in what we do or don't do; we look for meaningful love; we desire to work in a meaningful career; we hope to leave some mark in the world that is meaningful. When we fail to provide ourselves with individual, meaningful answers, we become lost in the *angst,* which is a German term for fear or anxiety.

Being human is not easy. We are born with a veil of unconsciousness and as consciousness emerges, we realize that we are mortal. We know at some point in our lives that it will end in death. According to existentialism, this is the paradox of life. At some point in our lives, we are faced with questions about finding meaning and purpose in life knowing that we won't be here forever. We search for meaning in what often feels like a meaningless life. As a person plunges into what is called an "existential crisis"—or crisis of existence, the questions begin to emerge. Existentially, the problem of existence is our perpetual struggle for meaning in the face of our inevitable demise. This dilemma confronts us with the questions of life: "Why was I born? What is the meaning of life? Is there meaning to life? What is my purpose? Where am I going? Who will go with me? What makes me happy? What is love? Can I love? What must I to do to live life fully?" In the face of our mortality can we create a meaningful existence that carries us through, not simply to the point of death, but through the death process as well? How would we be able to prepare for such as event? These are the questions for which we seek answers and in the search for meaning we struggle with the anxiety aroused by our inquiry.

We are thus called to the task of creating a life that has meaning and purpose at a deep level, yet we are not sure of how to do that. We plod along, often driven as if something were chasing us, hoping not to get caught. At other times, we chase whatever it is that has eluded us hoping that if we catch up with "it," our problems will be solved. Do we run towards or away from whatever it is? Do we run forward to embrace life, or do we flee from living because of our fear of death? This is the paradox of life.

Being human makes us vulnerable because we have consciousness, calling us to live consciously and, from an eastern viewpoint, to die consciously. Existential psychology thus does not use different therapeutic techniques to help people adjust, but is instead considered as an "approach" to working with people in therapy. From an existential viewpoint, being human implies that we are born with *will*. Our will drives us towards our *choices* if we exercise this freedom. If we assert our will, we have the opportunity to explore and examine the many choices before us. It allows us to see the wisdom in taking our time to discover all our options. Then it will be up to us to make those choices that lead us towards a more personally fulfilled life.

Consequently, if we embrace our freedom to make our own choices then we also see that we must take *responsibility* for our choices as well. We have to stop blaming others for our lives. Our choices are not limited to those things that are external to us, but also include the internal choices we make regarding our perceptions in life and about life. Do I choose to focus on those things that make me happy and excited about life or do I choose to focus on the things that bring me down and make me unhappy? What happens to my brain when I continually experience the same negative states? Can I change this mindscape? How do I do it? We are each faced with questions that lead us to the discovery of how to live a life filled with personal meaning. This step towards a more evolved consciousness forces us to begin a journey to uncover the many contributors to our sense of reality. We embark upon the Hero's Journey, as a man, and the Heroine's Journey, as a woman.

Transpersonal: The Fourth Force
(Key Associative Phrase: Evolution of Consciousness)

The Humanistic Movement expanded psychology's repertoire but there was still something missing from our search for understanding human behavior. Although a bridge was formed that linked the earlier two forces with the Third Force, issues that related to the soul were still not being addressed. The existence of a soul and the needs of a soul were seen as the province of theology or philosophy, yet the humanistic psychologists pursued the questions of spirit and soul in our quest for understanding human behavior. They believed that if the spirit or soul were not included in our considerations of psychological research, then we were missing a big part of the puzzle. If the humanistic movement moved us towards a more positive view of human nature, then the transpersonal promised to bring the core of the human spirit in line with the meaning of the word, psychology.

The term, psychology can be broken down into "psyche" and "-ology." "Ology" refers to "the study of." *Psyche* is literally translated from Greek to mean "soul." Thus the name of the discipline tells that psychology's founders believed in the importance of the soul when trying to understand human beings. If we examine the term, *psychotherapist*, for example, we find that the term, *therapist* can be translated into "an attendant or servant." *Psychotherapist* would therefore be translated into an "attendant of the soul."

This tells us that if we want to help others then we must therefore "care for the soul of the other person." If what we are doing in therapy is strictly biological or does not include *tending to the soul needs of the individual*, then we are missing the point. The emerging fourth force in psychology seeks to bring the soul and spirit back into the discipline of psychology.

In the pursuit for objectivity (if this is possible), psychology appears to have lost its soul. From the world of quantum mechanics, we know that observation of an object changes the nature of whatever is being observed. Yet we continue to pursue research as if we can be truly objective and that the act of observation or measurement has no affect on the process. If we are to advance in our knowledge we will need to update our assumptions. The placebo effect is a very good example of this phenomenon. Belief alone can produce drastic changes in our physical bodies.

The word *transpersonal* refers to those aspects of human experience that are *beyond* the personal and that connect us to the world and others in it. We move beyond the realm of our personal lives and explore our connection to others and the universe. This includes seeing our commonality with other humans but also taps into what are called the *subtle energies* of being human. They are subtle because they are often difficult to detect and are generally not something we can observe with our senses. Science is attempting to discover ways to measure these subtle energies that accompany different states of consciousness. A transpersonal approach to understanding the self is to evolve beyond our conditioning and learning, enabling us to go deeper into the roots of the self and evolve our capacity for consciousness. With greater consciousness, our perspective changes as we begin to see our interconnectedness with others and the universe, but we also develop greater skill by developing our own abilities to detect these subtle energies—ESP, lucid dreaming, clairvoyance, out-of-body experiences (OBE) and precognition to name a few. Great interest is also being taken to understand the nature of the *near death experiences* (NDE) that some have reported. We learn how to connect to our deeper powers of co-creation and begin to consciously take part in the reality we are forming.

Trans can refer to *that which is beyond*, or it can also refer to *across*. Cortright (1997) explained that

> Transpersonal approaches move across the personal realm and take in…(and)…explore all aspects of the self and the unconscious that traditional psychology has discovered while also placing…personal psychology in a larger framework…. (T)he self is very much the focus in transpersonal psychotherapy. But by moving across traditional personal psychology to the larger spiritual context, the individual self moves out of its existential vacuum into a wider dimension to which the world's spiritual teachings point (Cortright, 1997, p. 10).

The transpersonal is defined as "that which is beyond the personal or individual." This pursuit into studying the nature of human consciousness takes us into many interesting and controversial realms. In the past, more importance has been given to the observable and the methods of science rather than the questions that we have about human behavior. Psychology without a soul can thus be defined as simply measurement or quantification of behavior without a true understanding of the basic nature of the being. Although much valuable information has been achieved through the scientific method, we mustn't become so wedded to the means that we forget the goal. Is it possible to understand what it means to be human if we do not also consider the very core of what makes humans unique?

The primary focus of transpersonal psychology is its concern with the evolution of human consciousness and the development of our human ability to discover, develop and evolve our consciousness. Evolving consciousness allows us to use more than our five senses but the difficulty of verifying how these subtle energies are perceived has limited research into states of consciousness.

Science is verifying our interconnectedness through many avenues (Radin, 2006). We are learning about the commonality of our DNA regardless of our racial heritage. We are also discovering how the elements that make up the known universe are the same as that which is within our own cells. We are made of cosmic dust. From particle physics we know that when a particle is split into two parts, even though those two parts may be long distances apart, there is an instant communication between the two when changes are made to one of the pair. We are challenged to explain how this happens, but the fact that it happens is what is intriguing. Could our ability to scientifically explain this phenomenon in quantum physics provide us with an explanation for extrasensory perception (ESP)? We shall see.

To evolve human consciousness is an exciting proposition. We can achieve this within our single lifetime and do not have to submit the evolution of consciousness to the Darwinian model of chance mutations and time. What does it mean for us to *evolve our consciousness*? Becoming aware is the first step to evolving one's consciousness—awareness of the present moment, awareness of our conditioned reactions, awareness of our perceptual attitudes, and awareness of how we filter our experiences. This awareness allows us to remove the blocks that hinder our growth, and to actively engage our minds to the task of creating a better reality for ourselves. If there is one thing within our control, it is our perspective on how we see the world. Our attitude can make us miserable or make us hopeful.

The tools to evolve consciousness are within the grasp of every individual and do not have to be bought through prescription drugs. It is the ultimate self-empowerment! What if we could all learn self-healing tools that would help us overcome depression, anger, pain, trauma, frustration, and anxiety? Transpersonal research is helping clinicians to develop effective non-prescription approaches to helping people gain relief from psychological suffering. Currently, therapy for psychological disorders is mediated through the use of prescription drugs. The medical model is dominating the psychological approaches to understanding and treating mental illness and disease. As more prescription medicines are being developed and used to treat every imaginable malady that humans experience, it is time for us to step back and examine the wisdom and effectiveness of limiting our approaches to this paradigm (Lipton, 2005). While the medical model has provided us with the biological knowledge necessary to understand the mechanisms of behavior, using the biological model as the primary approach to treatment neglects important information we know about the interrelatedness of the human organic system. What we do to our bodies affects our mind. What we think about affects our bodies. This interconnected system must be treated as a whole, or holistically, if healing is to occur. We need to use holistic and integrated approaches to fully address the complex nature of being human.

The western scientific model, which focuses on measurement and observation, has been the primary force in shaping what psychology investigates. We progress, inch by inch, as we discover new technologies to help explain what is happening. With the advent of more sophisticated technology in the 1970's, the MRI and PET scans allowed us to peer into the structure of the brain and the physiology of consciousness states, yet, many questions remain regarding the more subtle energies of consciousness. For example, how do we measure what is happening when a person is able to use subtle forms of consciousness (e.g., ESP or remote viewing) to help government intelligence efforts? I recently read an account about Paul Smith, who worked for a CIA funded research project called Center Lane as a remote viewer. In essence he was a psychic spy. So, even though we cannot explain why some people can "see" what is happening somewhere in the world even while they are at a different location, even the government has employed people who can work with these subtle energies to help them in their investigations (Smith, 2005).

In spite of the limitations of our ability to measure and explain consciousness states, the transpersonal paradigm is providing the foundation for understanding this aspect of our humanity. Transpersonal research is often criticized for not adhering to strict scientific methodology. This is inaccurate, however, because psi researchers realize the intense scrutiny that their type of research will undergo. If you conduct a literature review of the methods used in psi research you will find that these researchers are even more scrupulous with their methodology. You can investigate the early work of Professor Emeritus Charles Tart from the University of California, Davis who conducted the early ground breaking studies in extrasensory perception (ESP). His research was nontraditional, but his methodology was impeccable. Tart understood the skepticism to this type of research, so he applied even more stringent standards to his ESP studies while he was a tenured professor at UCD.

The transpersonal encourages practitioners and researchers to examine what is difficult to measure—human consciousness and its energy system—but that are important to our understanding of being human. By acknowledging the limitations of our technological abilities to study human consciousness, the transpersonal paradigm has forged ahead to expand the ways in which we treat human mental illness and is helping us to find ways to prevent problems. These approaches are more humane and less invasive than surgeries or drug treatments. Current studies are underway throughout major universities in the United States. Through investigations using hallucinogens (e.g., LSD, MDMA, psilocybin) and non-drug means, (e.g., *Holotropic Breathwork©*), psychologists and psychiatrists are finding ways to help people who are suffering from anxiety, depression or post-traumatic stress disorder. The studies being conducted at prestigious universities such as Duke University, the University of Arizona, and the Salk Institute in California, appear to be helping those suffering providing long-lasting relief from psychological suffering in a significant number of subjects who have participated in the studies. Some topics of psychological research from this perspective that are being investigated are:

- Using psychedelic drugs in the treatment of PTSD, OCD, anxiety disorders, pain
- Utilizing treatment methods that tap into the energy (chi) channels of the body to address all facets of psychological and physical *dis-ease.*
- Exploring the powers of consciousness and human capability to heal and treat disease
- Researching the holographic nature of consciousness and the implications that these findings hold for creating mental health and happiness
- Willingness to research human experiences of psi phenomena, extrasensory perception (ESP), telepathy, out-of-body experiences (OBE), near-death experiences (NDE), remote viewing, premonition, psychokinesis, lucid dreaming

There is great interest in NDEs. A near-death experience is the term used to describe when a person has clinically died (i.e., the heart has stopped and brainwaves are no longer detected by conventional means), but has been resuscitated or spontaneously returns to the realm of the living. According to Marrone (1997), in NDEs

> Loss of control of the body and the mind is often experienced, as though the mind is taken to a special place while the body is left behind. Movement of the mind occurs through darkness or into a dark space and then travels through a tunnel or underpass filled with a bright light—a heavenly place filled with love and awe. Some people are allowed to enter the light, and some are not. The mind then emerges into the bright light where it is allowed to converse with people or a supreme being…In the midst of this light, escorts, in the form of angels or beings of light, accompany the mind in this phase of the near-death experience (pp. 92-93).

In our death-denying society, it is vital that we learn more about what happens at death so that we can help those who are diagnosed with terminal illnesses. Hospice work is important soul work and rewarding for those who find meaning in helping others transition into the next phase called death.

Research into NDEs is providing comforting anecdotal evidence that consciousness does survive bodily death. These near-death-experiences have been reported throughout the world and through case studies we are learning that about 30% who have died and returned report having an NDE. Since 1998, the Esalen Center for Theory and Research in Big Sur, California has convened a conference each year where researchers report on further evidence that supports reincarnation and the survival of bodily death. It is listed as Survival Research.

To realize our connection inspires us to learn more about this interrelatedness of all things. Transpersonal psychology is embarked upon an exploration that will provide us with more insight and knowledge into this essentially unexplored aspect of our humanity. This journey expands the realms of experience that will be investigated through scientific means and is beginning to provide essential information about the limits or capacities of human consciousness. We also gain a sense of community rather than alienation when we understand this connection. Transpersonal consciousness may be our collective ability to effect worldwide change.

Cognitive Approach
(Key Associative Terms: Thinking or Thought Processes)

The cognitive perspective is not a force in psychology, but a facet of the Diamond Perspective that presents a viable perspective from which we can understand behavior. In a sense, it is a sub-branch of the transpersonal because it deals with consciousness. In cognitive psychology, however, the discipline has restricted itself more towards the investigation of the mechanisms of consciousness and thinking. It focuses more on the structure and function of thinking and thus explores such subjects as memory, reasoning, thinking, language, and intelligence.

A cognitive approach to therapy would focus upon the thinking patterns one is having that may be contributing to the problems one is experiencing. Thoughts are examined to uncover any irrational thoughts or beliefs one may be having about a situation, or catastrophic thinking that may lead to negative emotions. Sometimes when we fail at one thing, we may globalize our situation and feel that we are failures at everything. This type of thinking could prevent us from looking at the situation more objectively to see what we could have done differently. It can prevent alternative solutions from being tested and therefore stop us from achieving a desired goal.

The cognitive approach causes us to listen to our self talk. It helps us to see how we may be embedded in negative thinking, feeding our worries and fears in a feedback loop. We think what we think, we feel what we feel because of these thoughts, and then we simply feel more of the feeling. This doesn't sound too bad when I think of positive

66

thoughts and uplifting experiences, but when I focus on my fears and worries, it can send me into a downward spiral. Negative thoughts can create negative feelings and a gloomy outlook on life. These negative thoughts do not exist in a vacuum, either, but affect our physiology and immune system. By changing our thinking into more positive directions, we can create happier thoughts and experiences. The cognitive approach guides us to become more aware of how our thinking can produce the reality we are experiencing. How we see a situation evokes certain emotional reactions that may not be necessarily linked to the present. We could very well be applying old pictures in our heads to new situations, thereby distorting the experience. By examining our thinking we are able to make changes to our perceptions of situations.

Cognitive psychology does not dive into the formation of these negative patterns of thinking, however, but focuses on thought rather than the origins of that way of thinking. If we delve deeper into the roots of consciousness we then enter into the psychodynamic realm and even broader realm of transpersonal thought and consciousness studies. The cognitive approach studies the more complex aspects of learning in humans and therefore differs from behaviorism.

Biological/Medical Approach or Neuroscience
(Key Terms-Organic, of the body, Physiology, Genetics)

Whenever we read about the roots of behavior as stemming from the biological processes or from the structure of our brain or genes, we are learning about the world of neuroscience. This perspective focuses upon the material aspects of our being a human organism and is another facet in the Diamond Perspective. The biological approach seeks to find answers to behavioral deviations through examining abnormalities in the structure or function of the various systems of the nervous system. It looks at the structure of the brain, the hormones and the neurotransmitters that mediate the way our nervous system behaves. Treatment for behavior through the biological perspective uses some form of biological intervention—drugs, hormones, or psychosurgery.

Much of what we know about the brain has been acquired only recently. Before the 1970's, we were hard pressed to find out what was going on inside the living brain. Research was done on cadavers or by comparing behavior before and after head injuries. Some manipulation of the living brain could occur during open brain surgery, but brain surgery could not serve as an investigative method. It was only through chance when a person needed brain surgery that researchers were able to manipulate the brain to discover its secrets. Wilder Penfield, for example, proposed that memory is stored in the temporal lobes of the brain because when he stimulated that portion of the brain during open brain surgery, he could evoke memories in the patient. His ideas were wrong, however, because it is now believed that memories are not stored in brain cells, but are distributed in a wave interference pattern. This supports earlier research on the brain by Karl Lashley who after teaching mice to run a maze, would destroy portions of the brain without erasing the memory for how to run the maze. One disconcerting time period in neuroscience was attributed to Dr. Walter Freeman, known as the *Lobotomist*. Between 1936 and the late 1950's, it is estimated that 40-50,000 Americans had undergone the procedure. These lobotomies were performed in a crude attempt to address mental illness. I refer you to the film called *The Lobotomist*.

The medical model is important to our growing understanding of human behavior, but care needs to be taken to assure that pharmaceutical companies are not gaining an unfair advantage in determining the direction of research in mental health. Too often drug lobbyist carry greater influence in what gets studied than what is needed by humanity. Much research in psychology is funded by pharmaceutical companies. Researchers seeking funding must appeal to those companies, but many studies are rejected, not because these studies are not worthy of investigation, but because of the lack of interest on the part of the drug company. If the proposed studies are not geared toward future pharmaceutical development, they won't be award funding. These researchers must then rely on private donations or use their own funds to conduct their studies. This is creating a false sense that neuroscience has all the answers to our psychological problems. As more and more drugs are developed, consumers will have to empower themselves to seek additional or different approaches to their problems. Drugs without therapy does not work well since it is not complete. The biological approach can only provide part of the answers to our questions.

Evolutionary Perspective
(Key Phrase: Behaviors as Adaptations, Survival of the Fittest)

Evolutionary psychologists seek to understand the persistence of various human behaviors from the viewpoint that these behaviors had adaptive value in the survival of the human race. Based upon Darwin's ideas on natural selection, human behavior is believed to consist of those adaptive characteristics and preferences that were passed down through the generations. From this facet of the Diamond Perspective, we are all constrained by our biological inheritance. We have variations of the same genes as our ancestors that shape our preferences and behaviors. Males and females have survived because the behaviors that were selected for increased the likelihood that they would procreate and have their genes survive. The preferences and behaviors that attract each of the genders are within us all and continue to exert their influence on our choices.

The evolutionary perspective sees behaviors as adaptations to the early environment and societies in which humans emerged. Certain characteristics increased the likelihood of survival, finding a mate and passing on our genes. These behaviors persist even today, making it difficult to determine whether it is biology, culture, or society that makes men act like men and women act like women.

Family, Culture and Societal Factors

When we consider the influences of our family, cultures and society, I liken these aspects of the diamond to what is considered the *color* of the diamond. Similar to diamonds that come in different colors, we each grow up being influenced by our particular family, the different cultural factors that we are exposed to, and the societal era in which we live. Although these are not necessarily fields of thought in psychology, it is well known that nurture exerts a powerful influence on our body, mind and psyche.

Family influences have perhaps the greatest impact upon the development of our self. The presence or absence of a family shapes the world that we come to view as the normal way of being. It isn't until we step out into the greater world and gain exposure to other ways of living and being in the world that we begin to see that perhaps there were things about our own family that may have skewed the way we see ourselves or the world.

Communication patterns are established in our family of origin. We learn ways of interacting through observing our parents and through the rewards or punishment that we receive for our actions. We can consider our family to have a long lasting influence on our personality since personality is formed early in our development. According to Freud and other psychodynamic theorists, our basic personality is formed by the age of 5 or 6. We learn about our selves, love, friendship, and commitment through our family interactions. Those influences that are supportive and positive have a profound affect on our sense of safety and security as do the opposite environments of ridicule and negativity. We take with us what we have learned and unless we consciously examine the makeup of this childhood environment, we may carry into our own families the same thinking patterns, ways of relating to our spouses and children, or dysfunction.

Cultural factors to consider on our journey to self discovery are those particular cultural pockets to which we were more intimately exposed that differ from others around us in our immediate neighborhoods or city. These cultural pockets may be all around us, but unless our families are immersed and live within these cultural environments, we will not gain the same perspective that someone within that culture has developed.

Some of the cultural landscapes to consider are demographics such as ethnicity and race; economic status of our childhood family; the region of the world in which we were reared; the historical era of our lifetime and the significant events that shaped history; religious influences; sexual preference; being reared in a military environment; and our peer groups. All of these factors, and more, will have an impact on how our personalities have been shaped and how we see ourselves.

What we believe in, who we feel are insiders or outsiders, or what we believe is *normal* is shaped by the microenvironment of our cultural surroundings. Without consideration of these factors we will miss important contributions to understanding the self that we are seeking to discover. Although we may all be human and thus similar in our organic composition, our mind and psyche are developed and shaped by other forces that come from these *cultures*.

Societal factors are what I consider to be the mass media influences of our particular era. The television, music, books, commercials, magazines, historical events (9-11 for example), radio, billboards, movies, newspapers, and technological advances such as cell phones and the internet have all created societal influences that have shaped who we are and who we will become. These societal influences have all differed depending on when we were born, but there is no doubt that these mediums of influence have had a profound impact upon how we see the world and ourselves.

Can you imagine growing up in a world that did not have cell phones or the internet for example? Many of you probably remember when these devices were only seen in science fiction movies. What of the images that we are exposed to daily in commercials and television programs? Don't they have a sculpting effect upon how we see ourselves and what we deem to be normal? How many of us judge ourselves according to these external standards? How would we be different if the mass media in all its forms crashed tomorrow?

Gender

Last, but not least, is the shaping influence of our gender. We are discovering the vast differences between females and males in their physiology and biological makeup. These basic biological differences have a strong influence in the capacities of both genders and warrant strong consideration when comparing women and men. Aside from the biological forces that shape what we call feminine and masculine behavior, there is also the influence of our expectations and attitudes towards each gender that will affect one's sense of self. Both females and males are expected to fit within the behavioral norms of their respective gender, even when they do not fit us as individuals. We treat each gender differently and thus the psychological makeup of males and females differs in self-esteem, self-efficacy or ego strength.

Our gender determines the attitudes that others will have towards us because we live in a patriarchal society where historically, males have held a dominant place in all areas of power. Throughout the world, parents prefer males over females. Maleness is preferable to femaleness. Even when females began to gain more equality in the workforce, they found that they needed to act more like males if they were going to be taken seriously. It is important to remember that in our society, it was not until 1920 that women won the right to vote. When trying to understand a person's personality, the atmosphere that has surrounded our ideas about gender must not be forgotten. We may be in the 21st century, but old attitudes die hard and there is still much gender discrimination today that affects both females and males.

Even when we consider that males have had more political rights than females have had, we also need to remember that power belonged primarily to Caucasian males who have held the most prominent positions of power in our society for much of our history as a union. The Civil Rights Movement ended racial discrimination and restored the right to vote for African-Americans in 1964, but does that imply equal treatment for all? Psychological understanding must consider the long history of prejudice, discrimination and violence against minorities, whether they belonged to a different racial class or sex and how this has shaped the collective minds of the members of those groups.

Most conversations about gender will focus on Women's Rights, but a compensatory consideration is to examine how the same biases that have placed women in a subservient and secondary position in society has also had a damaging affect on the male psyche. Societal expectations for males are more stringent, thus when a male does not meet those expectations, the consequences can be quite cruel. The men's movement has concerned itself with an examination of the damage done to the male psyche under patriarchy.

We expect males to be dominant, competent, the breadwinner, unemotional, strong, competitive, and to always be in control. These expectations limit the range of human emotions and talents that can be expressed, similar to how expectations of typical feminine behavior have limited females from pursuing and excelling at atypical female endeavors. The Men's Movement is working towards changing societal perceptions of males as being unemotional and encouraging males to reach within, discover and express their needs and emotions and to pursue what has meaning to them internally. They are reaching out to fathers and potential fathers to curb the stereotypes from being imposed on their growing male children. One of the key elements to the wounded male psyche is an examination of how these gender role expectations have affected a man's ability to love and be loving. Confronting the pain of a childhood with an absent or a demanding father seems to be one of the primary roads to healing.

Much has already been written about women's struggle for equality, so I won't repeat it here in too much detail, but the Women's Rights movement has been a historical struggle long before the 1960's. Women continue to fight the good fight and have made great strides to equalize the disparity between the genders in many areas of life, but work remains to be done to change our perceptions, expectations and attitudes towards either gender.

Lastly, in psychology, much of the research in psychology before the 1990's was conducted using mostly white, male subjects. This has had broad implications for the generalizations that have been made to other ethnic male populations and to the female population. Research focusing on differences between these groups has only just begun. In the 1990's a research initiative was passed that funded research to focus on problems that particularly affect females. Some research is now being conducted to analyze any differences that may exist between the males of different ethnic groups as well. This information will help psychologists to more successfully address problems that face each gender, whether those problems are physical or psychological. Given the recent findings of clear gender differences in health and brain function, research must continue to differentiate between the two sexes.

Topic Three

How Consciousness Works

Being human is an interesting journey. We are intelligent creatures who are only just beginning to tap into the hidden potential of the mind. Researchers and scientists are beginning to see that reality is not necessarily *out there* waiting to be discovered but that reality is a part of our own creation. We focus on particular aspects of the world around us and as a result, that reality forms. Think about a time when you perceived a situation to be a certain way. You saw what you thought was the truth of what happened. Upon further examination you realized that your perspective was skewed by the emotions you were attaching to the situation—your fears, doubts, memories—and so you *saw* what you believed was the truth of that reality. After you realized that it was your *reaction* that fueled the situation, you realized that you were mistaken. How many times has that happened to all of us? We are co-creators of our own realities.

The late Candace Pert (2005), co-discover of the opiate receptor site, believed that dysfunctional behavioral patterns are repeated over and over again because each time we experience an emotional state and it is repeated, those neural pathways, or *neural networks*, are strengthened in the brain. These networks stand at readiness for the next similar situation that will fire off the same neural pathways so that we experience that emotional state again. Like a drug addict, we get caught up in the emotional reactions and act out from the feelings that are evoked. This also serves as a negative reinforcer because if we indulge ourselves in the emotional state again, we feel relief for a short time, but that relief is short-lived. The only way to change this craving is to recognize that it is happening in a repetition-compulsion cycle and that our perception and behavior is being influenced in a manner similar to what happens to a drug addict who needs a fix with the drug of choice. In this case, however, the drug is our own chemical cocktail that is released when the neural nets fire and release the combination of neurotransmitters, hormones and excitation. Candace Pert explained this process in the groundbreaking film, *What The Bleep Do We Know!?!?!?!*

Consciousness can take on a higher level of awareness so that we transcend our preprogramming and make positive changes in our lives through choices that allow us to experience a different reality. We become co-creators of our lives. What this implies is that if we are unhappy with the way we see things, we can change our perspective. This requires for us to stop feeding into our emotional reactions, however, so that the neural networks that keep the emotional addiction going can be broken (Dispenza, 2005; Pert, 2005). Like any physiological process, our emotions produce a flood of chemicals in the brain and body, similar to the when a drug user gets high from a drug fix. As the effects of the *chemical cocktail* wears off, the craving for another fix comes on. The drug user in this case would seek out more of the drug of choice while "emotional addicts" seek out a repetition of the situations that result in getting another chemical flooding from our emotional "state of choice" (e.g., anger, sadness, victimization, impatience, etc.).

To break this cycle of emotional addiction is really a simple process. Joe Dispenza (2005) described that we must stop, take a breath and step back from ourselves. We have to stop *being* the emotion and simply observe the emotion arising. We can say to ourselves, "Wow! I am really angry!" or "Wow! That really pushed a button in me!" Emotions are a physiological process and not necessarily *who* we are. I can ride the emotion out and rather than fueling the emotion by giving it more energy, I can defuse it, thus breaking the neural nets that have formed in my brain that mimic addiction. I now have the opportunity to make another choice in my perception and behavior. Why do I want to continue to feel upset? Why not let it go and focus my awareness on what I want rather than stewing over something I probably cannot change anyway? By allowing the emotions to settle down, I can then rationally devise a plan of action to open up communication. Once I have stepped back and allowed my conscious awareness to change my "reaction," I can avoid the emotional turmoil and the resulting havoc that reactionary responses usually create. To actively and consciously recognize and choose which elements are impacting our perception, we can then embark upon a conscious path to greater awareness. But, first, we have to know how consciousness works and understand the limitlessness of the capabilities of our consciousness.

We are much more powerful than we have been led to believe. Each person is conscious to a different degree, which means that some people seem to have a greater awareness of themselves, others and the dynamics of their experiences. Knowing the inner forces that govern our behaviors allows us to choose *not* to act on them, but to form new choices of behavior and perception. I liken this process to the difference between *reacting* to a situation versus *responding* to what is happening. In the first scenario we are simply repeating the cycle of our emotions without conscious intervention. It's like a reflex. In the second case, when we respond, we are using the power of our consciousness to intervene in the emotional reflex and move towards greater awareness.

The key to healing is to grow and expand the limited ways in which we use consciousness. It means we have to understand how these limitations have been ingrained in us by our society, families, cultures, and through our experiences so that we can begin to hear our inner truth. This doesn't imply that our parents have deliberately instilled in us a limited way of being in the world, but that much of humanity is unaware of the unlimited potential of the mind. It is so powerful that it can either free us or keep us locked in a prison that is bleak and demoralizing.

Once we change old patterns of reaction for new ways of being in the world, these changes become more ingrained through repetition and we are on the healing path. We must stop reacting to our emotional baggage, step back and imagine different choices we can make—ones that feel better. If we are constrained by our biology to be addictive creatures, then why not choose what you will be addicted to? How about being addicted to happiness, love, peace, compassion, joy, spirit or soul? With each pause we take when our emotions clamor for attention, we move a step closer towards healing from behaviors that characterize dysfunction. We can see how our perceptions in situations do create our behaviors and actions. As Joe Dispenza stated in the film, *What the Bleep Do We Know!?!?!?* each morning before we arise, consciously spend the time to actively create in your mind what you want to experience that day. We let go of the emotional hunger to recreate the pain and suffering in our lives and throw off our victim mentality.

Is Truth or Reality Fixed?

Our concept of reality and the knowledge we apply to ascertain these truths are subject to what we know as a species. The truths discovered in one era must withstand revision in our attempts to better understand the world around us (Welwood, 2000). The great thinkers of our time—Galileo, Kepler, Copernicus, Schroedinger, Newton, Einstein, Bohm and Bohr—have all contributed to the changing conceptions of "truth" and reality. Each of these scientists contributed new knowledge to the human pool of truths that had to be revised when the discoveries of each were finally accepted.

Transpersonal psychology is attempting to explain the notion of *reality*. Reality is determined by a set of perceptual beliefs or lenses applied to interpret that reality. According to the physicist Werner Heisenberg's *uncertainty principle*, the simple act of observation will change the nature of what is being observed. At the same time, when one reality is perceived, all possible realities in the same situation are not. We only see what we focus upon. Yet, in accord with Heisenberg's ideas, one can never be certain of more than one aspect of an event at any given point in time (In Talbot, 1991; Zukav, 1979). When the elements of a situation coalesce into a pattern, that particular reality becomes true to the perceiver. By focusing on only one interpretation of a situation, all other possible interpretations are ignored. He also wrote, "What is observed is dependent upon the *measuring device* or unit of measurement being utilized" (in Talbot, 1991). Heisenberg believed that all things in the universe are potentials waiting to be observed and it is not until we focus our attention that reality comes to the forefront. The chooser determines the nature of the chosen in this instance.

This is similar to the "truths" that have been gained through research. Every truth must, in fact, be viewed as a tentative truth, a *good enough* explanation for now. It is the best explanation that can be given considering the limitations of human knowledge at that point in historical time. We apply these "truths" to applicable situations and until more

81

information steers us in a different direction, we continue to make our choices based on those assumptions. We rely upon these "truths" in lieu of greater understanding that may be forthcoming as we advance technologically. With new technologies and progressive vision we grow in our understanding of how the universe works.

For example, we knew very little about the human brain until we were able to invent devices that would allow for measuring what we formerly could not (e.g., magnetic resonance imaging [MRI], positron emission tomography [PET], or laser technology). As mentioned before, the MRI and PET scans were not invented until the 1970's therefore our knowledge about the inner workings of the brain were limited to the technologies that were developed before that time. Thus, the "truths" and "facts" that guided our research and interpretations, once again, had to be revised. As has been true for any generation of thinkers, we ascribe meaning to experience through the lens of the time. We explain history according to the perspective from which the situation is being viewed.

Thinking can be seen as a system that is self-perpetuating. Once we see things in a particular way, it becomes a *known* value in our world. Each time we apply this perceptual lens, it brings order to the chaos of life. When we meet another similar situation in the future, in most cases we will again apply these *known* factors about life without conscious appraisal of the new situation. I think that this borders on the edge of reaction rather than responding, but, this method usually results in a reduction of psychological tension because we don't have to start from square one again. We don't realize, however, that we may be applying erroneous concepts to understanding our world. Sound familiar?

We attach meaning to situations based upon our definitions and expectations that we apply to the experience, even if those definitions are wrong. Old paradigms are applied to new situations because they have worked in the past. Like a habit, we do the same repetitive things again and again in our lives. These thoughts, or words and their definitions continue to be applied to all situations that use similar concepts because they bring order out of the chaos of living in a modern world. Our thoughts create physiological changes in the brain and we become conditioned to react to the world in the same way over and over again until we intervene consciously (Bohm, 1994).

Chaos generates anxiety because humans don't do well with the unknown. We like order and predictability. When we are anxious, we call upon strategies to reduce the tension and get things under control again. Many of these strategies are reactions, or a knee-jerk reflex. Unless we become aware of how reality is formed, we are likely to continue the automatic, habitual programming we have learned so well. We are like Pavlov's dogs and Skinner's pigeons. We learn a connection between two things either through classical conditioning or through reinforcement, repeating the same behaviors and feelings, because we have learned these connections and we do not need our consciousness to do so. If we want to change, however, we will need to come to conscious awareness of these patterns.

Certain circumstances evoke particular emotional reactions and physiological responses that become hardwired into our brains. We hear the bell and then salivate like Pavlov's dogs. We also learn that if we behave in a particular fashion, it prevents chaos from breaking out or anxiety from getting out of hand. In this repetitive cycle we unwittingly strengthen the likelihood of our acting out the same reaction patterns again because we have repeatedly been conditioned and reinforced. We learn these behaviors.

Using old outdated experiences to live today's life is to live *from the past* using preprogrammed behaviors. In his book,

Control Theory, Glasser (1984) refers to this process as living from *old pictures* that we store in memory. These old pictures prepare us for action should similar circumstances arise. Problems arise when we *react*, rather than *respond*. Growing up in a dysfunctional environment will predispose us to resorting to the "old pictures" or old tapes in our attempts to control our world but we need to develop new strategies and update the old pictures for new perceptions that allow us to truly see the current circumstances. Behavior change requires reflection to understand the nature of our reactionary mechanisms. This reflection is done with the help of language and its usage.

What's That?

Little children reach a point when it seems that their favorite phrase is, "What's that?" So we tell them *what it is*. What we tell them can be our truth or the truth that our parents told us or the truth that society wants us to believe. It can even be something we make up. The result is the same. That child applies the definition learned to everything and anything that resembles it without regard to the accuracy of the information. If when they see a bird for the first time and ask, "What's that?" and we tell them, "It's a bird," then the next time they see something similar flying, such as a butterfly, then they will point to the butterfly and call it a bird. If we are there, we can correct them, but if not, they carry on their misconception to all flying objects until they learn how to better differentiate and identify the things in the world.

Words make up the primary form of communication between two beings and are a symbolic system used to represent experience (Bruner, 1990; Fromm, 1951; Fordham, 1966; Glaser, 1984). At best words approximate our meanings and help us describe the *reality* that we are experiencing; however, words cannot convey the totality of an experience (Wilber, 1979b). Experience is a total picture of what happens on all levels—it is phenomenological. It's impossible for any of us to convey that in words. But it's generally the best form of communication that we have. Together, they form a narrative of what we saw or felt, but even then, we are limited because words cannot describe our feelings. The names and labels we use help us categorize and define the world.

This is something to consider when we examine how consciousness is formed by the reality applied by the person doing the thinking. I can tell you that the sunset in Monterey is so unbelievable that you must see it, but that does not describe the totality of the experiences I've had while viewing those sunsets. Words are like a map. They are useful to describe experience but they cannot convey the experience itself. On a map, there are markings to help me locate places of interest, and the map helps me to find those places. However, those map markings cannot do justice to the experience I will have once I am there. I have to be there and experience the place to really *know* it. Our consciousness is a subjective state and consists of all aspects occurring in a particular moment. To translate that consciousness into a form others can understand we have to use language. It has allowed humans a symbolic way to exchange information and experience.

Like all reductionistic pursuits, we know that the parts are only part of the picture. When we put all the parts together we realize that *the whole is greater than the sum of its parts.* For example, listen to a symphony in its fullness with all instruments playing their respective parts. Now break down the parts to the different sections of instruments—the woodwinds, brass, percussion, strings or voices. By themselves, the different sections sound one way. Put them all together and you have a masterpiece of creativity that surpasses the individual instruments and players themselves. When we apply this concept to human behavior we realize that although we may understand the mechanics of how human beings work, it is not the same as the experience of being human.

The nature of consciousness and our use of language create the schemas or cognitive structures that help us organize our world. This categorization creates our initial sense of separateness at the same time. We use words and descriptions to describe ourselves. There are those things that we *are* and those things that we believe we *are not*. Those things that are not a part of me are outside or apart from me—they are *not me* (Wilber, 1979b).

We erect artificial boundaries and create a sense of separation from others. We form boundaries and separation from things that are not us, while all around us things remain interconnected. We forget that the naming of *me* and *not me* categories was simply a way to describe things. We create separation where there really is none and then go about defending our artificial boundaries from invasion by others.

In other words we identify with those things that are familiar and that fit into our definitions, but find it difficult to think outside of the box. We struggle to imagine that perhaps what we are experiencing can be seen from a different perspective. We think that what we interpret is what is really *out there*. Ken Wilber, author of *No Boundary* wrote, "The Mind appears as a subject and an object. The creation of two worlds from one is like when you place an object in front of a mirror—you get "two" objects where there is in fact but one…we reflect upon the world and get "two" images, a seer and a seen, but actually the Mind is one." Thus reality may not be so much "out there" as it is "in here." Perception and the definitions we apply to that perception become our reality.

Because there are so many definitions and gradations to meaning that we can apply to any thing or situation, communication that involves language can be problematic. We think we understand the meaning of what another person has just said and we react or respond to that reality. It could be that we have misinterpreted what has just been said, however, and this teaches us to become better listeners. We need to examine the assumptions we have applied to what we just heard—the content of the sentence(s) and the meaning of the words used by the other person. We must meet the other person in the middle where we can agree upon the definitions we are each applying to the words used enabling us to effect clear communication.

The point here is that much of what we have learned about the world may actually be false or erroneous. When we are told that we are "worthless," this concept may become a truth for us but, in fact, it is simply a label someone applied to describe us. It has no basis in reality. It is not who we are. So by examining our assumptions we begin to see how the assumptions may have given us erroneous information about the world outside (and inside) of us.

These aspects of consciousness formation make it difficult for us to see that we may be our own worst enemy at times. The good news is that we can revise and update our notions of reality. Updating implies that we begin to use words based upon *our own meaning* to those words. We take our expanded awareness and begin to experience each new encounter as if we see the world through the eyes of a baby. We strive for what Ken Wilber calls *No Boundary* thinking.

Behavior and meaning cannot be understood without understanding how the mind determines reality. A person explains reality through the assumptions or implicit "truths" held about the world and those in it. These "truths" may be incomplete or outdated, however; thus feelings, thoughts and behaviors based upon these personal truths reflect those biases. Reality is the result of assigning meaning and value to internal processes. Transpersonal approaches propose that reality is a more complicated process than simply discovering what is "out there" or external to ourselves.

Evolving Consciousness

Julian Jaynes (1990) examined the evolution of the human mind in his book, *The Origins of Consciousness in the Breakdown of the Bicameral Mind*. He described the bicameral mind in which humans appeared to not be aware of themselves as individuals, but that they were part of a collective state of consciousness. These people were guided by visions and voices from above. Each individual still acted individually, but there didn't seem to be any indications or references to the words "I" or "me"—a sense of self. As the bicameral mind gave way to our present right/left brain, conscious/unconscious arrangement, humans attained greater consciousness, especially of the self. According to Jaynes, humanity had not yet developed the self-reflecting ego that characterized modern consciousness prior to the second millennium B.C. (Feinstein, 1990b, p. 170). The dawning of the Mythical Epoch, roughly 10,000 B.C., was when language sophistication reached its full influence.

> With language, the verbal mind could differentiate itself more definitively from the physical body. People began to understand that the word is not the object for which it stands. Language was the major psychological vehicle for...consciousness. (Without it)...humankind...was... incapable of projecting into the future or of organizing itself in large membership communities...Because language embodies mental goals and futures, the new self could delay and channel its bodily desires (Feinstein, 1990b, p. 168-169).

Language and mythmaking have replaced genetic mutation as the primary mechanisms by which awareness and innovation are carried forward (Feinstein, 1990b, p. 165).

As consciousness evolved, so did the ability to reflect, to step out of the myth and consider the way the myth structures experience...Stepping out of a particular myth is neither easy nor instinctive. The capacity to do so marks the birth of psychological freedom...mak(ing) it conceivable that a people can speed the process by which they free themselves from the inadequacies of their mythic inheritance, a particularly critical matter in a rapidly changing world...The mind becomes capable of turning back upon itself and reflecting on what it perceives (Feinstein, 1990b, p. 171).

Ironically, greater self-awareness meant less awareness of the collective or our link to the universe. Visions and voices of guidance ceased and each person was left to find his or her own answers. Jaynes (1990) referred to this as an advancement in the evolution of the human mind, but at the same time separated consciousness from access to other sources of information that were common in the bicameral mind (e.g., auditory and visual hallucinations). Having visions and being led from "voices above" were considered blessings from a universal spiritual source. They were not signs of pathology as they are now perceived.

Modern, traditional psychology has seen hallucinations as symptomatic of a psychosis and therefore something to be rid of through medication. In the bicameral mind, however, these same voices and hallucinations were seen as a form of divine guidance from a higher source that collectively led societies towards a common purpose (Jaynes, 1990). But the mind evolved and with the advent of our sense of individuality, it seems that humans stopped having these hallucinations as a regular route to divine guidance.

When we are ill, our body regresses to earlier states. Our mind can regress to the earlier bicameral mind where we hear voices again or see things that are not there. Psychologists understand that the precursor to the onset of psychological illness is usually associated with undue stress in a person's life. Stress makes us vulnerable and breaks down our immunity. It wrecks havoc on our psyche. Modern medicine now treats hallucinations as a sign of pathology and therefore in need of medical treatment, such as shock therapy, drugs or a lobotomy. Yet, how many of us experience hallucinations when we are ill? What of our dream world? Every night when we dream, we hallucinate or are psychotic because we hear voices and see things that are not really there. We see and interact with people who are dead and some of us even fly unaided by mechanical contraptions! Some people even undergo a form of somnambulism and have sex in their sleep without knowing it (called sexsomnia)! Does this imply that we are all in need of psychological treatment to rid us of these "psychotic" symptoms?

Transpersonal psychology treats psychotic symptoms differently than does traditional western medicine. If the psychosis is due to disease, such as schizophrenia, then treatment with a neuroleptic is prudent. But there are other forms of psychoses that emerge from great inner turmoil and psychological distress. Transpersonal psychologists handle these forms of psychotic symptoms differently. Instead of masking the symptoms with medication, the symptoms are viewed as a means to tap into deeper layers of the psyche beyond the biographical contents. Stan Grof's work with LSD and the healing potential of non-ordinary states of consciousness have provided strong evidence for this different approach to psychoses. He and his late wife, Christina, developed the *Holotropic Breathwork*© technique, which is a non-drug route to non-ordinary states of consciousness that mimic the effects of psychedelics. By seeing the psychoses as a cry for help and using the contents of the psychoses to better understand the psychological trauma that is attempting to work itself through, transpersonal psychologists are able to help psychotic patients to emerge with a renewed sense of self. Grof wrote,

From the viewpoint of observations from deep experiential therapy, determined striving for external goals and the pursuit of success in the world are of little value in overcoming the feelings of inadequacy and low self-esteem, no matter what the actual outcome of these endeavors turns out to be. The feelings of inferiority cannot be resolved by mobilizing one's forces to overcompensate for them, but by confronting them experientially and surrendering to them. They are then consumed in the process of ego death and rebirth, and a new self-image emerges from the awareness of one's cosmic identity. True courage lies in the willingness to undergo this awesome process of self-confrontation, not in a heroic pursuit of external goals. Unless the individual succeeds in finding his or her true identity within, any attempts to give meaning to life by manipulating the outside world and external achievement will be a futile and ultimately self-defeating quixotic crusade (Grof, 1985, p. 165).

Because of work in the transpersonal domain, a new category was added to the 1994 Diagnostic and Statistical Manual of Mental Disorders, 4th revision (DSM-IV). It is called Religious or Spiritual Problems and its inclusion in the DSM indicates an advancement over earlier approaches to working with people who experience psychotic symptoms.

While the acceptance of this new category was based on a proposal documenting the extensive literature on the frequent occurrence of religious and spiritual issues in clinical practice, the impetus for the proposal came from transpersonal clinicians whose initial focus was on spiritual emergencies—forms of distress associated with spiritual practices and experiences. The proposal grew out of the work of the Spiritual Emergence Network...to increase the competence of mental health professionals in sensitivity to such spiritual issues (Lukoff et al, 1998).

Consciousness evolution may well represent the evolution of the human spirit (Wilber, 2000). This evolution can become a collective endeavor if each person takes personal responsibility for one's consciousness progression. Whitfield (1987) stated that, "If man is really to evolve, then he must develop depth, and power over his own depths" (p. 125).

When we mistake our cognitive schemas for reality, especially when those schemas bring us pain, we are creating what Buddhists call *samsara*, or "delusive appearance." We think that our perception is the truth but our need to be right often creates our sorrow. Even when I don't want to feel bad, I can make myself feel bad by simply *seeing* the situation around me as an oppressive one rather than a challenging one. *Samsara* creates human suffering because we expect or cling to what we want rather than seeing what *is* (Yeshe, 1987). Welwood (2002) described this as clinging to the stories in our head. We often perceive that the stories or myths we believe in are reality when in fact they are nothing more than guiding principles of how to live. In a transpersonal setting, these stories, or mythologies are identified, updated, and revised.

Awakening

To awaken consciousness implies that normal consciousness is similar to being in a trance state, or *waking sleep* (Tart, 1986). *Waking sleep* is induced by our unconscious use of predefined notions about life because we have used these descriptions and definitions learned during the developmental process regardless of their applicability to us as individuals. As mentioned earlier, the labels we use and the preconceived ways of understanding the world limit consciousness to known forms of taking in experience. They are the storylines we use to establish and maintain predictability but which can keep us stuck. This prevents our growth and access to our creativity and resources that allow us to deepen our experiences. To awaken, we need to become aware of the many forces that shaped our perceptual world, or *personal mythology*. This concept was introduced in an earlier topic and will be further explored when we explore the topic of *Jung's Theory*, which is foundational to understanding personal mythologies (Feinstein, 1990a).

Awakening is a process outlined by Welwood (2002) that helps us discover how the perceptions that we use to explain reality may be preventing us from tapping into the possibilities of a more creative formless state of awareness. *No form awareness* lets us take in the world without having preset notions about what is occurring. We discover the soul cages or prisons of conditioned self/other concepts that we have learned.

The first step to awakening is *identification*. These early identifications form our reality about who we are and how the world works, but we awaken to how we learned this information as well.

The second step entails *conceptual reflection*. In conceptual reflection, or the active participation of increasing consciousness through therapy, we come to understand how we label the world and our experiences and the guiding principles that we have lived by have coalesced to form the reality we experience and create. Perhaps for the first time, we process and relive the pain of any trauma, neglect, or abuse we suffered, feeling the experience in its fullness.

The third step is called *phenomenological reflection* and marks an awakening of consciousness. We need to take this step that is beyond simple conceptualization or the ability to talk about what happened. *Phenomenological reflection* requires that we feel the fullness of whatever the memory or emotion holds and then proceed to complete any unfinished business that we may have with that memory.

The fourth step, *mindfulness* requires that we become aware of the labels we have been using to explain our memories and experiences. We learn to stop labeling our experiences as good or bad. What happens in our lives is simply observed and taken in without numbing ourselves nor trying to find an explanation for it.

Mindfulness, or open-monitoring meditation, is a state of consciousness wherein we are present, in the moment. We are tuned into the moment without applying the labels habitually established to understand reality. In Scientific American, authors Matthieu Ricard, Antoine Lutz, and Richard J. Davidson (Nov. 2014),

> Mindfulness…requires the meditator to take note of every sight or sound and track internal bodily sensations and inner self-talk…stay(ing) aware of what is happening without becoming overly preoccupied with any single perception or thought, returning to this detached focus each time the mind strays. As awareness of what is happening in one's surroundings grows, normal daily irritants…become less disruptive, and a sense of psychological well-being develops(p. 42.)

As these skills become honed, *unconditional presence* leads to self-liberation. This last step is the ability to rest in being fully present with each experience. Nothing is good or bad, but simply *is*.

Welwood (2002) wrote, "Meaning, purpose, support, direction, stability, coherence—none of these are givens on which we can securely rely. Since our mind creates them, we can just as easily see through them, or suddenly find ourselves unable to depend on them" (p. 149). Existential angst occurs at *the moment of world collapse,* when the known structures, forms, expectations and beliefs that one holds, collapse and what is left is a void or emptiness in its place. This tends to create anxiety that existentialists refer to as a *loss of being*. We dread the sense of empty space because our mind wants to fill the silence. This type of chatter in the brain is what has been called *monkey mind* (Chia et al., 1993). The constant *roof brain chatter* must be stilled in order for us to hear our inner self.

When we release our former ways of filling experience, a space is created that makes room for growth and expansion of consciousness. When our known boundaries of conditioned consciousness collapse, anxiety arises, but also allows for the wisdom inherent in problems to emerge. When emotions are allowed to emerge and to be experienced, the implicit felt meaning or the enfolded reality can emerge.

Body and Soul

Traditional techniques of psychotherapy are first used to help the client to begin the process. When these methods are combined with spiritual meditative traditions to awaken consciousness, we learn how to be more present in everyday experience.

Meditative techniques and psychotherapy both represent polar ends of therapy for awakening from our *waking sleep*. This includes other therapeutic techniques such as chi kung, biofeedback, yoga, aikido, energy techniques, acupuncture or other methods of manipulating bodily tissue or skeletal alignment (e.g., chiropractic work, Rolfing or massage). These methods of working with the energy of the body and the resulting effects on the mind "fit into the body-mind relationship….(A)ny process that organizes and patterns the nervous system and the body, whether by mantra, yoga, etc. is likely to affect the consciousness of man" (Lee, Ornstein, Galin, Deikman, & Tart, 1976, p. 10).

The emphasis towards meditative tools for awakening consciousness is not a negation of traditional psychotherapy but represents a joining of hands. "Each of the differing schools of psychotherapy—East and West—are primarily addressing different levels of the spectrum" (Wilber, 1979b, p. 119). Firman et al (1997) wrote,

> The psychoanalyst and depth psychologist expect us to be able to observe and report upon our inner flow of experience; the cognitive-behaviorist teaches us to study our behavior and uncover the cognitive and affective underpinnings of our actions; the existentialist-humanist invites us to experience the here-and-now of our personal existence, take responsibility for this, and make choices regarding this; and, the transpersonal therapist understands the human being as capable of moving among a stunning variety of states and levels of consciousness (p. 68).

Cognitive-behavioral approaches help explain the surface mind. Psychotherapy delves a bit deeper to help us unravel the dynamics of the psyche in action. Humanistic therapies go a step further to assist in the reconnection of the mind and the body.

Meditation is used in the transpersonal setting to expand awareness and introduces a person to

> develop the sustained attention necessary...to stop being 'hijacked' by...thoughts. When...(one)...enters an emotion in this naked way, it cannot persist for long because it does not actually have any independent, solid existence of its own, apart from (one's) concepts or reactions (Welwood, 2002, p. 190).

In meditation, we access a direct opening to our feelings without needing to find out the meaning of the feelings. Going within and deepening our meditative states allow us to have a greater sense of awareness and freedom, even when we get caught up in emotional reactions. Rather than following our compulsion to judge the feelings or invent a story to explain it, we simply experience *what is*. By releasing the "inner critic" one can open to pain, without stories. Meditation practice assists us to enter into the ground of *be-ing* that underlies thoughts and feelings.

Therapy addresses the need to reflect while spiritual practices help us to be more present, or to have a greater sense of presence in the world. The combination of both approaches allows for the "…unpacking of a wider felt sense, which illuminates…(the)…larger relationship to the situation in question…dissolv(ing) the emotional entanglement" (Welwood, 2002, p. 186). Behavioral problems can be viewed more as opportunities for awakening the heart and deepening our connection to life instead of trying to rid ourselves of what we believe is pathological (Welwood, 2002).

Topic Four

Freudian Defense Mechanisms

Being human means that we are all subject to the same psychological problems. Our problems arise from the unconscious according to Freud and according to him, all problems that we suffer from as adults stem from our early developmental years. He described the human psyche as a complex dynamic system, always in movement. He theories helped the world to better understand the complex nature of the human psyche. He proposed that the structures of the psyche—the *id, ego,* and *superego*—must work together harmoniously in the psyche, otherwise the person would be overcome by the conflict that was bound to occur because of the respective needs of each of these structures of the human personality. The primal needs of the *id,* coupled with the perfectionist requirements of the *superego,* create a natural conflict that our *ego* must mediate and resolve if at all possible. When the term, *ego* is used in relation to Freud's theory, we need to redefine the term from its earlier usage in the introduction to this book.

In Freud's theory, the *ego* is the mediator of the conflicts that arise between our *id* and *superego* but these decisions are also bound by the culture in which we reside. The laws and rules of the society, written and unspoken dictate the types of choices that our *ego* can comfortably make. As you all know, our *ego* may not always be strong enough to broker a solution that considers both the primal needs of the demanding *id* within the strict confines of the *superego's* ideals. Our *ego* can be weak because we are simply tired or stressed, but can be weak for other reasons as well. These other reasons come from the pressures of our culture to delay gratification, maintain behavioral standards set by society, curbing our sexual and aggressive impulses, and living up to the expectations of others all can thwart the fulfillment of primitive *id* impulses that arise within us. This constant demand on our *ego* to arbitrate among the demands of our primitive impulses, the demands of our moral conscience and idealism, and the rules of society necessitates a safety mechanism so that we are not overwhelmed. In this chapter we will explore *defense mechanisms* and how they serve to protect the ego when we are threatened on a psychological level. These tools will help us on our journey toward self-discovery and consciousness.

Freud believed that personality was the result of our ability to control our instinctual drives, meet the demands of reality, and satisfy the requirements of our moral and ethical ideals. He called these structures the *id, ego* and *superego*, respectively. The *id* is the primitive part of our personality, which seeks immediate gratification of its needs, seeking pleasure and avoiding pain.

The *superego* is the structure related to our moral *conscience* and *ego-ideal*. Our *conscience* is formed through the acts or words for which we were punished and leads to feelings of guilt if we either contemplate or actually violate these standards. The *ego-ideal* is formed through those acts or words for which we are praised and sets the image that we try to live up to or at least the image that we want others to see of us. The superego requires perfection of our personality, holding us to the highest standards possible.

These standards form the criteria by which we place pressure on our ego to be perfect even while attempting to satisfy the more primitive needs of our *id* impulses.

The *ego* is that part of our personality that is conscious and aware. The *ego* has the hardest job in the personality because it must be grounded in the reality of the world and must navigate according to the rules of nature as well as the society in which one lives. Because the *ego* is the arbiter of our instinctual drives, reality and our moral standards, it has three bosses: reality, the *id* and the *superego*. The *ego* mediates between the demands of *id* and the *superego* within the confines of the real world. This mediation creates a tension within the psyche that can result in overwhelming anxiety if the ego is not prepared for the pressure exerted by these three "bosses."

Our psyche is structured to allow for the protection of our conscious ego from being overwhelmed in the process of these psychic conflicts. Defense mechanisms protect the ego by distorting reality in some manner. When we use defense mechanisms we are not aware that we are doing so—they are unconscious devices utilized in the moment. We distort reality and thereby soften the threat to the ego (Schultz, 1990). This allows our ego the opportunity to regroup when the circumstances are not so threatening.

Freud believed that everyone uses defense mechanisms. If we did not, we would all be neurotic or psychotic. In other words, in the healthy personality defense mechanisms are a practical way to put off anxiety-provoking feelings until we are more able to deal with them on a conscious level. However, if we use defense mechanisms excessively and do not deal with the conflicts at a later point, we thwart more mature development and self-actualization.

On the road to maturity, we have had to distort our perceptions in order to blend in and conform to standards set for us, as individuals and as members of our particular gender and society. Conflicts regarding our behavior or that of others are formed not only from our instinctual drives but also by our preconceived notions of what is right, good, or acceptable. What we expect of ourselves and of others may not truly reflect our inner nature, but may instead be our conformity to more acceptable societal motifs. Consequently, when we find our more "id-like" impulses threatening to alienate us from what we have learned is acceptable we retreat to using these defense mechanisms. We cover up our true feelings somehow and postpone having to take responsibility for our thoughts, feelings, and actions.

Following are some of the defense mechanisms proposed by Freud. The list is not exhaustive but presents those distortions we may have adopted in the process of coming to terms with our sense of self. These may well have served to impede our ability to get along with others and to form more meaningful relationships as well. The knowledge and acknowledgment of the use of defense mechanisms should facilitate our ability to see how we have kept ourselves from more self-enhancing behaviors.

Repression

Repression was basic to Freud's theory of personality. *Repression* is the involuntary removal of something from consciousness. It "forces a dangerous memory, idea, or perception out of consciousness and sets up a barrier against any form of motor discharge" (Hall, 1954). We do not actively choose to forget: the forgotten memory is too threatening and painful to remember, so it is "pushed down" into our unconscious.

For example, there was a woman by the name of Eileen Franklin who as a girl claimed that she had witnessed her father rape and murder her best friend. The conflict to the ego can be seen rather clearly in that she loved her father and depended upon him for safety and security, yet what she had witnessed was too horrible for her to deal with. *Repression* allowed her to either forget this memory or perhaps lack the ability to "see" it while it was happening. It was not until she was an adult in therapy that she remembered the event 20 years later and subsequently was instrumental in the conviction of her father for the crime. She had not actively forgotten the event. It was "erased" from her conscious self (go to the following internet address to read about this case see the link at the end of this chapter).

Thus the ego was protected from the memory that would have caused much psychological discomfort and pain. Additionally, the ramifications of remembering repressed events would have disrupted the home of Eileen and her safety. Thus, with *repression*, the ego is safe and does not have to remember what could be too much for the little girl to handle.

Suppression

Similar to *repression*, *suppression* is an active forgetting of a painful idea, thought or memory. We forget or "put something out of mind because it is annoying" (Rychlak, 1981, p. 60). Whereas *repression* always occurs unconsciously, we can choose to suppress thoughts. We are thus somewhat conscious or aware that we are activating the defense mechanism. In some sense this violates the idea that all defense mechanisms are used unconsciously. At least with *suppression* there is some awareness that we are consciously attempting to forget what is bothering us because we activate the process of pushing the information into the unconscious.

As an example, I can actively decide to no longer think about the pain I feel from my father's rejection and I can "put it out of my mind." Each time the insecurities, fear, hurt, and anger arise over this past situation, I can actively start the process of suppression by shoving the awareness down, telling myself, "I don't want to think about this anymore!" When thoughts about something worrisome keep coming into consciousness, we can actively push them out of awareness. Eventually, the suppression "sticks" and we find it more difficult to remember details or feelings from that event.

Denial

Denial is another defense mechanism that resembles *repression*. This is to reject the existence of some external threat or traumatic event that has occurred (Schultz, 1990). For example, we may deny that our death is imminent even though we have been diagnosed with a fatal illness. We tell ourselves, "No way! There must be a mistake. Not me!" We refuse to acknowledge the obvious. *Denial* gives the ego time to adjust to the news. Over time, *denial* needs to give way to making conscious choices of how to face the situation but in the meantime, this defense mechanism has softened the blow to the ego.

Denial can also explain why we are sometimes blind to things that others can readily see. For example, what is happening when a woman denies that there is anything wrong between her and her spouse even when friends tell that person that they've seen her spouse with another woman? She will often defend her spouse saying that he has been working late or that that person is simply a co-worker. Although the person's friend may provide more details, the woman continues to deny that anything is wrong. She is spared the embarrassment and at the same time can continue with her life as she wants to see it. It will not be until she has had enough evidence and pain that her *denial* will melt, allowing her to "see" the facts and perhaps have enough strength to make new choices in her life or to confront her husband.

Thus, the *denial* allowed her ego to avoid the pain of confronting the infidelity and kept the superego's integrity intact. If she saw herself as a committed and loyal wife who would never leave her husband, this denial would keep her from having to alter that self-image. Thus denial protects the ego from having to face the truth and shattering her belief that "marriage is forever."

Displacement

Displacement is the shifting of an impulse towards a threatening or absent object to one that is either available or less threatening. This is the classic, "kick the dog" syndrome. We feel that we cannot express the feelings or thoughts that we are having in a situation, we hold our tongue and move on. But we don't forget. The energy invested in the suppressed emotions or thoughts are still alive and will emerge when it is safe to "let off steam." We are mad about our situation at work but feel scared and powerless to express our feelings and thoughts. So we hold it in until we get home and "kick the dog" to let off this steam. In other words, I can be ticked off at my boss, but it is too risky to tell him where to go, so at the first opportune moment and with the first unfortunate soul that does not hold so much power over me, I take it out on her/him.

Similarly, imagine that the man or woman of your dreams has just rejected you. Another man or woman that you know, who is acceptable, but not really your type, pursues you. Licking your wounded self-image, you find yourself suddenly attracted to that person even though you had never given him or her a second thought before. I think they have called this a "rebound" relationship. The energy that was invested toward the original lost love object that rejected you is now transferred to a more available one;

however, the release of libido through *displacement* is not as psychically satisfying. Much of your *libido* is still wrapped up in the former relationship and needs to be sorted before moving on and getting involved with another person.

Reaction Formation

A *reaction formation* is to act in ways that are the opposite of how you truly feel. *Reaction formation* forms when we cannot accept something within ourselves and find it so unacceptable that we assume the opposite position to our true feelings. Assuming the opposite stance protects the *ego* from the conflict between our *id* impulses and our *superego* requirements. Homophobia can be a *reaction formation* to homosexual tendencies that are latent for example. This implies that some people who protest against gay people may in fact be curious and attracted to the same sex. Because their superego is so strong, the ego needs to find a way to deal with the biological/physiological arousal to homosexuality by strongly and consciously advocating that it is wrong and bad. Think of the various congress people and public clergy in the news who were known for their position against gays but were later caught in the act themselves. Freud was brilliant.

Two more examples may make this concept clear. If we have been reared in a strict, rigid puritanical environment or have just basically incorporated rather conservative standards, we may experience conflict when we find ourselves attracted to the wild and more liberal ways of expressing ourselves. Secretly we may long to dress provocatively or to be more sexually free, but these impulses are in opposition to our superego constraints and our ego feels overwhelmed. In reaction to our urges we, we shove down the unacceptable impulses and express the opposite attitude of the original one. We become activists against "the immoral lot in society" rejecting "that kind of behavior" or "that kind of person" or "dressing like that!"

We act out the opposite of our original feelings because it protects the ego from dealing with its true position on the issue.

Another example comes from observing grade-school-aged children. Generally, children form same-sex peer groups and to associate with the opposite sex is judged as "yucky" by our peers. Our impulses however have a different agenda. We are drawn towards the "other" while our superego admonishes us to stick with our own kind. How do children handle this conflict? They have clubs that exclude the other sex, and they wear protective symbols just in case they are touched by the opposite sex, but they continue to taunt and tease. Boys pull girls' hair; girls slug boys in the arm. They like the opposite sex, but they better not show it!

Projection

This particular defense mechanism is a favorite of mine because it covers so much of what we do with our fears, worries, desires, and obsessions. *Projection* is our tendency to attribute to others those feelings, thoughts, actions or desires, which are within us but are too threatening for us to admit. Like a movie projector, we cast the image originating from within ourselves out onto others. These images characterize the unacceptable disowned aspects of our personality. We readily see these qualities in others, but deny that they are a part of our personality. We hide it within and project it out onto others when we recognize it in another person and don't realize that much is revealed about us by our projections.

This defense mechanism helps to alleviate the inner conflict experienced if we were we to own our rejected thoughts, feelings or behaviors. The old projectors in theatres used to cast images outside of the mechanism that contained those images (the film) and onto a screen far away from the source of the image. To one who is not familiar with projectors and film, it would appear that the source of the image that we see is the screen itself! This reminds me of how as a little girl I could not understand how they could miniaturize so many people and objects and get them all to appear on the television screen! But we know that this perception is based upon the magical thinking of a preoperational child.

I can say it is YOU who is biased, hateful, prejudiced, racist, bigoted, selfish and cruel, yet do I dare to turn the mirror to face myself, asking if I also possess those same qualities? It is so easy to see in something in another person, yet so difficult to see that we too possess what we cast outside of ourselves. But how can we recognize a quality in another person if we do not also have elements of those characteristics within ourselves? Do we, therefore, recognize the behaviors in others because we also "know" that quality within ourselves? *Projection* allows us to delay self-examination, absolving us of responsibility for self-analysis and change.

We may also project onto others the ideals and expectations we have about what is attractive to us. We meet someone who fits some aspect of this vision and we create an illusory vision of the person before us. We only see what we want to see in this person and cast a blind eye to anything that contradicts our belief. This lasts about three to six months when our ego boundaries finally snap back into place and we start to take all behaviors into account. We often wonder, "How could I be so blind?" Freud has an answer to that question.

Ironically, we also cast our negative expectations onto others. What we fear they may be feeling or thinking, we will accuse them of possessing. If we have been hurt in a past relationship, we expect that others will hurt us in the future. We state, "All women are like that" or "All men are like that." We carry our wounds around as if they are "who we are," but this prevents us from fully experiencing any new situation on its own merit. If we have been ridiculed and criticized in childhood, then we are sensitized to what may sound like criticism when it is aimed at us. If we had a trying relationship with our mother or father, we too often end up choosing relationships that reflect the unmet needs in that relationship. It is as if we hope to redeem the damage done in our childhood by "getting" this other person to provide us with what we missed as a child. But this generally only leads to more of the same unfulfilled expectation because the need is within us and must either be grieved or met through our own self- nurturing.

When we have unfinished business with either of our parents, the stage can be set for a reenactment of the emotional dynamics originally structured in the familial setting. We look for, expect, and desire to be "mothered" or "fathered" in our relationships. This "parenting" can take on both hopeful and horrifying forms. We can hope to attain the positive regard we craved and thrived on as children, but we may also react to others as if they were our parent. This can make for interesting dynamics. Our projected expectations and ideals may cause tunnel vision regarding the actual qualities of the person with whom we relate. This will be more fully discussed when we explore the concepts of the anima/animus archetypes of Jung's theory.

Regression

Regression is to "go backwards" and return to former behaviors that are less mature. When the *ego* is unable to mediate the demands of the *id*, reality, and the *superego*, we will often revert back to behaviors when we had less pressure on us. When responsibilities and demands overwhelm our *ego*, we are likely to lapse to behaviors that we used when we were younger and less responsibility for ourselves. Perhaps we use indirect methods to get what we want. Rather than making direct requests we "fall back" into more immature patterns of behavior, like manipulation, pouting, or throwing a tantrum. This *regression* may occur because we fear that broaching an issue may be too threatening to a relationship or situation. We are at odds with our need to eliminate the "pain" inherent in the situation, and the simultaneous need to not rock the boat. With this type of conflict we may find ourselves reverting to earlier destructive patterns (e.g., alcoholism, the silent treatment, etc.) when the internal conflict becomes too great. *Regression* is not always so extreme, however. It can take the form of simply going home for the weekend to Mom's so that she can wash your clothes, cook dinner, and pamper you a little.

Rationalization

When we rationalize, we make up plausible excuses or reasons for our behaviors. We see only a limited perspective of the situation. We all do this one and often recognize when we have done so (after the fact of course because as you remember, defense mechanisms only serve their purpose if we are *not* conscious that we are using them). For example, if I do not do as well on a test as I had hoped I would, I can say that the material was not clearly presented, or that I was "out of it" that day, it was a rotten test, or any number of excuses. The truth may be that I did not study as much as was necessary to attain a good grade on the test, but because I see myself as bright, intelligent, focused and dedicated, it may be too threatening for me to admit that I just slacked off, especially when I am in the presence of my classmates or professor. So it is easier to blame my failure on other factors for the time being. Later, when I am by myself, I may be able to see through my excuses for getting a low grade and study harder for the next exam.

As Freud described it, we all use defense mechanisms but when we use them exclusively the ego is slipping up and not taking responsibility for the situation. Therefore, if you find yourself always reaching for excuses or reasons for your behavior, it might be time to step back and analyze how you can begin to make changes in your life through your personal actions. We are then able to own our own rationalizations and grow from this realization.

Fixation

Fixation occurs, according to Freud, because our needs are either not met well enough or they are met too well. When at different stages of development, we may become fixated at that stage for these reasons. In the first case we are frustrated and continue to do things that we hope will result in having our needs met. For example, if we never felt accepted by our mother as a child, that feeling will persist into adulthood. We may never be quite certain that other women accept us, since our mother rejected us. Conversely, when our needs were met too well as a child we may become stuck and act in regressive ways that mimic how we acted and felt when we were able to get our way.

When we are afraid to take the next step toward growth and maturity because of perceived obstacles, we are psychologically *fixated*. We fear "insecurity, failure and punishment" (Hall, 1954, p.94). When the anxiety stymies us from moving ahead, we tend to *fixate* on what is familiar rather than advancing onto new vistas.

Sublimation

Freud believed that this was the healthiest defense mechanism. *Sublimation* is a form of displacement in that we substitute an original desired object with one that is attainable and socially acceptable (Hall, 1954). For example, a young teenager may sublimate his aggressive tendencies by channeling that energy into sports. A young girl enamored with a teacher may look to her peers for a boy that resembles the ideal image she has formed regarding the teacher. If a person likes to look at scantily clothed men or women, that person can become a photographer for magazines that portray these types of images.

It has even been proposed that being a dentist or doctor is a *sublimation* for sadistic tendencies! Ask your dentist or doctor if she or he agrees! At any rate, sublimation is the healthiest defense mechanism because it allows us to satisfy instinctual impulses within the boundaries of social convention.

Summary

We cannot completely avoid using defense mechanisms because they are the result of the psyche's dynamic structure. They protect our egos and allow us to get our bearings in stressful situations. The point is to recognize when we are using them so that we can rectify the situation and to become sufficiently aware to realize when we are prone to resort to a defense mechanism. As we learn to catch ourselves in the act, we evolve our consciousness away from reaction and towards response.

Topic Five

Gender

Upon initial examination, the two genders appear to be distinct. We categorize people according to physical features to distinguish to which group that person belongs. After we ascertain the person's sex, we feel comforted by the perceptual lens we have used. Pink or blue lenses, please? Not only do anatomical differences divide the sexes, but, behaviorally, we have come to understand human behavior by assigning particular characteristics and qualities as belonging in some inherent way more rightfully to one sex or the other. This dichotomization has created a reality that is colored by the filter of belief that we have developed regarding feminine and masculine behavior. We not only judge others, but self-evaluation is also perceived through that particular gender lens.

Have these distinctions evolved because of cultural attitudes and expectations, or has there been some biological logic to the differences that have evolved into what we might consider to be feminine or masculine behavior? Might nature have had some rational plan for the perpetuation of the human species by selecting behavioral strategies that would be more conducive to the survival of homo sapien existence? If so, does this imply that biology is destiny and are we therefore locked into our preprogrammed choreographed dance of gender?

What questions can we ask that will help us to unravel the complex structure of behaviors unique to each gender and reveal the variation that exists within each gender as well? Can we move beyond our genetic and evolutionary programming, using our highest cognitive faculties to help us make distinctions? Will this enable us to transcend our more animalistic nature and express the characteristics that perhaps separate us from all other species on earth? As we descend deeper into our subject of inquiry, the structural makeup of the underlying foundation that creates gender distinctions is revealed. By breaking apart the complex tapestry of gender related behaviors, our path is illuminated allowing us to more fully understand the intricate nature of this topic. When feminine and masculine strategies for survival are examined, we find more differences exist <u>within</u> each group than <u>between</u> the two groups. The more distinctions we identify, the more we realize how the behaviors assigned to each gender group actually enables us to see the interconnectedness of the two groups. Unraveling the tapestry created by the two gender worlds discloses many answers in our macro analysis of sex differences, but examination of the internal structure of each gender group is essential for our basic understanding as well.

The Biology of Belief

In the process of growing up, we began to formulate and understand what was expected of us as boys and girls, men and women. We watched our fathers and mothers in their respective roles and imagined that when we grew up, we too would be doing similar things, acting in similar ways, saying similar things. Of course, our parents also modeled for us what we did not want to be as well, but regardless of their positive or negative influence, we learned.

Before the age of about six years old, we are simply taking in the world and learning our own particular set of "truths" about the world around us. If we hear our parents speaking lovingly towards one another, we interpret this experience as being representative of what our future intimate relationship will be like. Our perspective of the world supports our beliefs about the world.

Regardless of our inherent goodness and intellect, we need others to see our true inner self so that we can nurture it. Unfortunately, there are too many of us who feel as if no one knows us. We feel unseen and almost invisible to others. If, however, parents are bitter, resentful, and emotionally broken, they are less able to give us the kind of nurturing that would enhance our natural creativity and blossoming. When we are praised, told how unbelievably talented we are and that we can achieve whatever we set our minds to, we then form beliefs that support the likelihood of those beliefs becoming realities. The converse of all this is true as well.

The importance of this early nurturing period becomes apparent when we examine the new biology. Bruce Lipton is a cellular biologist who did early some of the early stem cell research at Stanford University in Palo Alto. In his book, "The Biology of Belief," Lipton reminds us of the importance of touch and eye contact in the early days and months of development and outlines why it is so important for us to become more aware and conscious.

He demonstrates that genes are turned on or off, not through some internal mechanism, but through signals that come from the external environment. He illustrates his ideas by examining the human cell's response to environmental toxins or nutrients. In this experiment, Lipton placed cells in two Petri dishes. One dish had toxins placed in the same dish as the cells. How did the cells behave in this environment? Do you think they moved towards the toxin

117

or away from it? Instinctively, we know that the cells would naturally move away from toxins. They did exactly what most of us would do if we were placed in a similar environment. We would shift into what he refers to as a *protection mode* of action and either move away or defend ourselves. In the other Petri dish, he placed the cells with nutrients. How do you think these cells behaved? Instinctively we know that unlike the cells placed with toxins, these cells moved towards the nutrients in a *growth mode.*

All this makes good sense, but what is important is what happens to any organism in protection or growth mode. In growth mode, we move towards situations, and both our physical and mental health are enhanced. In protection mode, we are compromised in three ways: 1) growth is shut down; 2) the immune system is turned off; and, 3) we are less intelligent because the blood flow is diverted from the prefrontal cortex (the area of the brain used to think) to the hind brain, or reptilian brain (animalistic fight or flight action; habit).

When I heard this story, I envisioned the cells as representing a little child, holding up its arms to be picked up. In the case of the nutrients, I envisioned a loving, nurturing parent. As the child reaches out to the "nutrient" parent, it does so without reservation or fear. This promotes growth and happiness. However, in the case of the toxins, I pictured a negligent or abusive parent. I saw a situation when that child (the cells in the Petri dish) had at an earlier time, reached out for comfort only to be rejected through verbal abuse, or worse, by being ignored. The next time the child wanted to be held, the urge was still there, but now the child was afraid to express her needs. Instead, with arms only half stretched out, she asked in a timid voice, "Mommy?" or "Daddy?" half expecting to be yelled at or rejected again. This causes her to contract the muscles that normally are extended in a loving situation. It was formerly an open gesture but as you might imagine, it would only take a few trials of this type of negative response for her to stop asking to be picked up. Ironically, the urge may still be there, but the behavior is now stifled. This holding back of inner impulses causes what humanistic psychologists referred to as "muscular armoring." The tension builds up from holding back our impulse to reach outward and the result is often physical pain in the arms, hands, neck, shoulders, back, and chest areas.

Human beings are a collection of specialized cells that work together in harmony. Each cell is a living organism in itself and by understanding how these cells work, we can see how important the quality of nurturing and environment are to the person we have become, both psychologically and physically. Do we have any control over whether we develop diabetes, cancer, high blood pressure, schizophrenia, or depression? Equally important, do we have any control over whether we are "bright" enough to complete our education and aspire to the lifestyle career choice that we seek? Is it in our genes or is it in our opportunities and our choices to make those decisions that lead to better health, happiness, and joy? We may have the genetic predisposition to have various diseases or psychological disorders, but Lipton argues that it is the environment that controls when and whether these genes will be expressed. We also have to consider that we create our own internal "environment" with the thoughts we have and the subsequent feelings that those thoughts generate. Our thoughts and feelings have the power to create physiological and structural changes in the brain and nervous system that can lead to disease or well-being.

When we are in nurturing, supportive, growth-enhancing environments, we feel free to reach out and expand ourselves, challenging our potential to grow. We are more confident to try something new and even if we don't reach the heights to which we aspire, we are still encouraged and heartened by our efforts towards those goals. With this courage, we try again and again. In contrast to a positive environment is one in which we feel blocked, oppressed, and negativity is more abundant than encouragement. In these types of environments, we generally do what we have to do to survive, but growth and creativity are stunted. Like the cells that were put near a toxin in the Petri dish, we tend to pull back in a protective gesture to survive. It is our form of adaptation.

Evolutionary Lens on Gender

Behaviors that have survival value assure whose genes will make it into the evolutionary pool. If a particular behavior or characteristic has greater adaptive value, then the genes that encode for those qualities are passed down to the scions of the fittest. Ironically, behaviors that are adaptive within one sex group may not necessarily be adaptive in the members of the opposite sex. Those actions that allow for harmonious intragroup interaction may be disruptive when transferred to intergroup behavior. In other words, members of each separate sex group need to develop different survival strategies within their own particular gender milieu and at the same time, generate behaviors that will be complementary between the groups. This would assure that members of each group are able to pass on their genetic dowry and survive within their respective gender milieu. The best fit between the two groups ensures the greatest survival value for the collective.

Darwin's theory of natural selection, integrated with Mendel's genetic model, is applied to human behavior to explain the diversity of behaviors that exist within and between the two sex groups in their separate and collective social milieus. Through this lens, attempts to explain behavior are characterized by ascertaining their adaptive value to the survival of our species. Darwinian logic presupposes that physical and behavioral strategies that allow for the perpetuation of the species within our natural environment will prevail.

Distinct patterns of behavior have given us an evolutionary advantage on Darwin's ladder and by using the lens of natural selection, characteristic patterns of the sexes can be understood within the context of genetic proliferation. We can also see how the "natural" environment in which we live may not be the same as the environment in which these characteristics evolved; thus dysfunctional behavior may result because of the bad fit between our evolutionary inheritance and the world in which we now find ourselves battling for survival.

From an evolutionary point of view, female and male survival strategies within the sociocultural ecosystem have resulted in the variation of *within group behavior* (i.e., within male groups or female groups) and *between group behavior*. These lenses allow us to examine the different strategies and behaviors of females and males without assuming a biased stance about which behaviors are better or how they were learned. We can observe without evoking the characteristic emotions attached to such an examination. In this way we avoid perpetuating misunderstanding and division. We can depersonalize what we may have perceived as, "well, that's just the way women (or men) are." As we seek greater understanding regarding the survival strategies developed between each group, we are better equipped to understand the differences within our respective gender group as well.

From an evolutionary perspective, behaviors that have given humans an evolutionary advantage have been the most adaptable to the social habitat in which the two genders have existed. Those behaviors and characteristics that have allowed for the survival of each respective gender include the behaviors and characteristics that have enhanced each group's reproductive opportunities as well. This tells us that we have not only inherited and encoded physical characteristics through genetics, but that we inherited a specific psychic makeup as well that has provided us with greater survival value individually and collectively. Human behavioral strategies were adaptable to the social environment in which they evolved. When understood in these terms, we realize how variation within and between the sex groups developed. The behavior patterns that appear to be distinct to each gender and between the genders have created the various ways in which we relate to one another. The underlying strategies that join females and males together paradoxically, divide them as well.

Complementary Strategies

From an evolutionary perspective, the variety of gender related behaviors are seen as complementary between and within the two groups. If we go beyond the obvious we can also discover new routes that will lead us "beyond gender." Biology is not destiny but it is within those biological limitations that humans operate, but how much of our behavior is due to biology or enculturation and the learning process? On many levels, humans have a choice whether to follow the dictates that seemingly drive their behaviors.

Humans possess the capacity for insight and creative living, which can help us build a world that both honors and recognizes the commonalities we share as humans. We are not bound by our biology but can transcend our limitations and move into the transpersonal realm of being. When we understand the origin and component parts that have combined to create our unique gender experience, we can incorporate this information into our decision making of how we will "be in the world." We become less driven by unconscious forces, which may oppose our search for equality and egalitarianism. We can use our highest cognitive processes to become aware of the world we are creating and thus move beyond gender.

Peering through the various lenses provided by the discipline of psychology, we can scrutinize how we personally contribute to the continuation of this dichotomy. Our basic nature is to question all phenomena and through careful analyses, we can ascertain the basic weave underlying female and male behavior. Given our human proclivity towards reason and logic, we must also factor in the impact of socialization upon gender behavioral strategies. It is not enough to know that we are "hard-wired" to behave in specific ways, but nurture interacts with our genetic potential resulting in what appears to be distinct behaviors characteristic of each group. Evolutionary forces interact with the social environment to produce complex behavioral patterns characteristic of its members.

The subcultures that exist within the larger social environment also impact the development and perception of gender behavior. Additionally, the psychology of each individual adds even more spice to the brew, resulting in varied patterns of behaviors within and between female and male groups.

Gender Lenses

Each gender world is a microcosmic habitat filled with diverse and unique attitudes, beliefs and roles that characterize each individual within her or his group. The separate milieus of females and males create many of the differences that we believe belong to each group and by examining these separate worlds in detail we can perhaps broaden our understanding of the resulting interaction that occurs when members of the two groups encounter one another. The shaping hand of our individuality and our gender world affects our self-perception and therefore our resulting behaviors. This perceptual position also colors how we will evaluate others as well—what do we consider to be "appropriate" and characteristic of each sex? What qualities do value or devalue or think to be inherent in males and females?

Humans are thinking, reasoning creatures, and we have the power to move beyond our gender programming. With awareness of the psychosociocultural/evolutionary forces that impact our proclivities, we can advance beyond the parameters set for us and make behavioral choices based upon illuminated insight. This is a much more effective survival strategy. Knowledge illuminates and when we are players in the arena of gender this insight can be far reaching. Conscious, aware choices give us an edge in the evolutionary scheme of things and thus with lucidity we can become more proactive of the direction in which humans evolve under the rubric of gender behavior. We adapt to our individual gender group and also learn to adapt within the melting pot of the social milieu. The complementary combinations interact to determine the collective gene pool.

Our specific genderized vision determines what we will ultimately embrace or reject as part of our image of ourselves as women or men. This limited vision also affects how we relate to others—what we allow others to know about us and also, how we evaluate others. Having distinct categories from which to define what is "like me" or "not like me" enables us to follow a gender script that is "comfortable" because it is known. We model ourselves after others who are physically similar and aspire towards the models created by culture and society to reach a more comfortable "fit" within the social realm. Although this may give us a sense of belongingness, our perspective may be somewhat myopic; thus we are hindered in our experience and understanding of self and others. Through careful scrutiny and in-depth analyses regarding the etiology of gender behavior, we can develop a perspective that allows us to embrace more of what is uniquely individual. We begin to see behavior as human related instead of simply as gender related.

Beyond our more constricted beliefs about gender lies a vast territory that embraces the effects of socialization, enculturation, biology, physiology, and the inherent differences between the genders. These factors interact to create distinctiveness, yet the complexity of our task allows us to unravel the various patterns that have formed our two separate worlds. Our exploration reveals not only the differences but also the interconnectedness of the sexes. By examining the microcosm of the genderized world, we move beyond the limitations of constricted vision about the roles and the masks that we assume and emerge with a redefinition of gender that is more inclusive of our current knowledge. We begin to understand which of our beliefs, attitudes and perceptions about gender divide, rather than connect us to each other.

Topic Six

Gender and Society

Most societies are patriarchal (Myers, 1987). Traditionally, patriarchal societies adhere to the belief that the father is supreme in the family with the wife and children legally dependent upon him. In contrast to matrilineal cultures, wherein inheritance and descent are traced through the female line, patriarchal societies trace inheritance and descent through the male offspring. Contemporary usage of the term *patriarchal* also refers to a society which is "male dominated." In patriarchal cultures, males hold not only a disproportionate number of the key positions of power, but the beliefs, values, ethics, morals, behaviors and standards for success are also male-defined. This power structure and definition of superior qualities serve to reinforce established ways of thinking, acting, and being for the inhabitants of that particular society.

As social animals, we seek a sense of belongingness and adherence to these prescribed modes of behavior facilitates our attainment of the acceptance we desire. This is also pertinent to the study of gender because the definitions of feminine and masculine behaviors are defined by patriarchy. Adherence to these pre-formed gender expectations not only sets the standards by which we measure ourselves, but is the societal yardstick as well. Our success, attractiveness, femininity, or masculinity is measured against these predefined standards, which are mere caricatures of human individuality.

Historical Considerations

Patriarchal societies are characterized by a hierarchical structuring where rank and order means everything. Ranking puts a few at the top and many at the bottom. Those of higher rank get more opportunities and higher salaries. This translates into what can be called the accoutrements of power. You see this everywhere—in the workforce, the cars we drive, and the houses we live in. Unfortunately, this has translated into the idea that more is better.

Merit is claimed to be the driving factor that allows individuals to rise in the power game, yet merit is only allowed to certain groups. To be part of the "in group" is to know the rules of ascension to power and simultaneously be lucky enough to be a member of one of the more powerful groups. Patriarchy sets the standards that determine which groups will be allowed into the ranks with males ranking above females in most cases. Ethnic categories are also viewed in this manner, with some races seen as more deserving of power than others.

Regarding gender in a patriarchy, males hold a disproportionate number of the key positions of power. Congress is a good example of this unequal distribution. Generally, women still do not rise to assume the highest ranking positions in a patriarchal society, although women are making much headway in the 21st century. This has happened through a long and protracted movement that extends back to the 1848 when women first convened to begin the fight to gain the right to vote.

Today, at least in the United States, women can gain entry into any university for which they qualify and can afford. Females are also experiencing more opportunities in career choices. The problem these opportunities pose for many women, however, is that they are often single mothers with low incomes who also have childcare expenses. What happens in our society is that many women give up their ascension to power and trade it for the role of mother and wife, which pays considerably less money! This problem is compounded when these same women return to complete their education and enter the workforce because now they are "behind" others their age. If they had completed their education before motherhood responsibilities, they must update their skills so that they will be competitive in the work world. In 2008, women were still struggling to reach equality with males, earning about $.77 to the male $1.00. Even in those areas of our society where the gender barrier has been broken (e.g., the military, construction work, and road crews), females are considered to be the "weaker" sex."

This historical trend can be explained by looking at the position that women have had throughout history, especially as has been true in our society since we became a nation. Women were considered to be lower ranking citizens, had limited legal rights, and were not allowed to own property until in 1839, Mississippi became the first state to grant women the right to hold property in their own name—with their husband's permission, however.

It was not until 1920 that the 19th Amendment to the U.S. Constitution was ratified giving women the right to vote. Bear in mind that up to that time, women were required to live under the laws of the land, yet they had no voice in legislation of those laws. Both men and women were required to live under the laws of the land, but only men (certain men…) were allowed to shape the laws that ran our country. Women were believed to have other "more important" functions to tend to, such as having children and being a homemaker as evidenced by a decision by the U.S. Supreme Court. In Hoyt v. Florida, 368 U.S. 57 (1961) they upheld the "rules adopted by the state of Florida that made it far less likely for women than men to be called for jury service on the grounds that a 'woman is still regarded as the center of home and family life'" (www.legacy98.org/timeline.html). She was to be seen, but not heard when it came to politics.

The right to vote lagged even further behind when it came to color. The Civil Rights Act of 1964 helped further the cause for women and people of color. Women of ethnic minority status were under double jeopardy in this case. As women, their rights had been limited, and as minority women, their rights were even further restricted. Thus, although the laws changed to establish parity, the attitudes of the people have yet to catch up with our ideals.

You've probably heard of the notion of "marrying up." For a woman, it has been traditional that she finds a suitor who is older and better off financially than she. This practice has come to us because of the position women have had in society. Without a right to ownership in all states until 1900, a female had little means by which to better her status in life except through marriage. This power structure created an atmosphere wherein women and other minorities had to live by standards that were often unspoken in the law books, but assumed by the majority in power. If you were born into the right class, you might have the opportunity to make the most of your creativity and abilities. If not, then you still had choices, although they were limited.

Patriarchy defines the acceptable characteristics of its women and men—as children, teens, and adults. We learn, early on, that there are particular behaviors that bring us approval and others that bring us rejection or scorn. Too often, we find that it is not our individual uniqueness that brings us acceptance, but that it is our adherence to society's expectations for us as females and males that facilitates acceptance or rejection. Adherence to these pre-formed gender expectations not only sets the standards by which we measure ourselves, but is the societal yardstick as well. Our success, attractiveness, femininity, or masculinity is measured against these predefined standards, which are mere caricatures of our human individuality.

Csikszentmihalyi (1990) believed that humans seek order, yet the universe is not very accommodating to our needs. Chaos rules and we are continually confronted with challenge after challenge to adapt. "One of the major functions of every culture is to shield its members from chaos" (Csikszentmihalyi, 1990, p. 11). One way this can be achieved is by bringing order to the various roles we assume. If we are confused or unsure of the appropriate behaviors expected of us in the societal role in which we find ourselves, chaos or confusion occurs.

Take for example the changing definitions of female and male roles during courtship. Should the woman wait for the man to initiate major turning points in the relationship, should she offer to pick up the tab when they dine, should he buy her an engagement ring that costs twice his monthly salary? With the evolution and transformation of feminine and masculine roles, the blurring of gender lines confuses those who grew up during more traditional times.

Thus, the usefulness of societal defined routes helps to dispel the chaos that Csikszentmihalyi describes. Myths or stories are created by societies to serve as roadmaps for its members to follow if they are to achieve their desired goals, whether those goals are marriage, success, happiness, fulfillment, nirvana or peace. We live life believing that if we follow the "rules" set by the culture, then we will actualize that which we seek (e.g., the American Dream tells us that if you work hard, get an education, apply yourself, etc., you will be able to buy that house with the white picket fence, have two cars in the garage, a cat and dog as well as 2.5 children, and live happily ever after)

Males who are assertive, competitive, logical, unemotional, achievement-oriented and team-players are esteemed in our society. Males are encouraged to compete, achieve and "get the job done." They are to be decisive and not let emotions get in the way. In the process of growing up, the male world is personal and competitive. The more sensitive, or "soft" male is generally not able to succeed in the competitive work world because his emotionality is devalued. He is not considered a "real man." The "real" ones have learned to behave in ways that are prized in the established hierarchical order of the patriarchy. These qualities assure success in his career, but the same qualities may be lethal in his love life.

Traditional feminine role behaviors mold women for rearing a family, not climbing the ladder of achievement. Ironically, she finds that success in the professional world requires that she act more "like a man" and reject her "feminine" self (Murdock, 1990). She feels compelled to emulate male behaviors that define success. She denies her softer, feminine nature because she wants to be taken seriously by her colleagues, who define themselves by adherence to conventional male values.

When a woman has molded herself into the patriarchal definition of success, she may initially feel that she has broken into the system, but at some point, what she thought would bring her fulfillment rings empty. She may no longer recognize the woman who stares back at her in the mirror. By embracing more masculine ideas, behaviors and ideals, she has, as Jean Shinoda Bolen, author of *Goddesses in Every Woman* and *Gods in Every Man*, would describe, "dismembered herself." She may have "cut off" parts of her true nature because they did not work in the workplace. She may have over identified with the more male-like qualities she thought were necessary to succeed.

As females, we can reach back to recapture the child within who was confident about her abilities and aspirations—that younger self within the female adult body who had no doubts about her direction, who knew the sources of her joy and happiness as a young girl. Females can return psychologically to a time when no obstacle was insurmountable—generally before the age of twelve. Unfortunately, in the process of becoming adult women and men, our confidence is constrained by the molding hand of gender appropriate behavior. For both females and males, one-sidedness in our personality wrecks havoc on our personal life. The qualities deemed necessary for success may be diametrically opposed to success in personal relationships (e.g., friendships, lovers, parenting) and would therefore necessitate a balancing between the two extremes. We can "re-member" or "re-join" these submerged aspects of our self.

Our identification with societal definitions of the feminine and masculine satisfy our need to belong to the larger social order, yet when we express parts of ourselves that do not fit the traditional definition for our gender, we may feel odd. We stand out too much. We each seek to fit into the greater whole of society, yet as psychologist Otto Rank asserted, the will of each individual is to create a self that is authentic and individual (Menaker, 1982).

At the same time, however, we are driven to merge with the larger social grouping to gain a sense of symbiosis with others—a sense of belonging. We are driven to uniqueness, yet we are pulled to conformity. These paradoxical goals oppose one another—as we merge with the societal whole, we become less distinct; as we assert our individuality, we create separation. It is this tension and conflict, which is at the root of our existential struggle.

As we traverse the road of feminine and masculine development it is befitting to explore the factors that contribute to our development, assessing whether these definitions truly fit us as individuals or serve us in our quest towards completeness and maturation. Awareness of the deep psychic influences of our feminine and masculine natures will also help us to be aware of the forces involved when we act out of unconscious motivation instead of conscious choice.

Gender Styles

It has been well documented that gender differences have not only a biological basis, but an environmental one as well. The culture in which one is reared has specific sex roles that are assigned to a child from the moment of birth, and despite the perpetuation of any double standards borne from these cultural beliefs, gender identity is defined by sex roles. How we behave, how we are perceived, or how we are esteemed by others is often tied to stereotypical definitions of what is masculine and feminine, however inaccurate these representations may be.

Gutmann (1965) believed that the psychosocial ecology of females and males provides valuable insight into the ego differences, which seem to exist in the respective gender worlds. Men and women are psychologically oriented in characteristically different ways, which must be taken into account when exploring gender differences in behavior (Lipsett & Olver, 1987). Women see themselves as connected to others and their behaviors will be shaped to sustain relationships. They are seen as less competitive, more cooperative, and more concerned with social relationships than men (Gilligan, 1982). Bakan (1966) described the female style of experiencing self, others, and time as *communion*. In communion, a person focuses on the interpersonal, subjective, and immediate aspects of one's experiences (Carlson, 1971). There is also an emphasis on establishing connection to others and a female sees her self in those terms. Intimacy and connection color the interactions of females.

The male style is different and has been referred to as *agency* by Bakan (1966). This is a tendency to define one's relationship to self, others and time in individualistic, objective and distant ways. In other words, rather than being concerned with connecting and maintaining social relationships, males tend to be more personally oriented (Carlson and Levy, 1968). Males are more concerned with separation and independence rather than intimacy and connection.

Each sex creates a distinctive gender world wherein the members come to know themselves and others through uniquely ground lenses. In the developmental process, the patterns of *language* and *play* form a distinct "playground" wherein each group operates according to different rules. According to Deborah Tannen, professor of linguistics at Georgetown University in Washington DC, we become skilled in the ways of our separate gender worlds in childhood. We learn the rules of "play" for successful adaptation to our separate groups (Tannen, 1990). Although myriad factors contribute to the differences found between males and females, the rules of the playground determine how language is used and this transfers to our adult interactions and expectations.

These differences are not always apparent until we attempt to form intimate relationships with others of the opposite sex. Females use words and language to connect with others, to establish intimacy and connection. Males use language to assert their individuality, separateness and power. Females learn early in life that peer acceptance requires interactions, which are characterized by intimacy and connection to group members (Tannen, 1990). Their games and conversations reflect these female "rules" of cooperation and equality. Conversely, young males find themselves in a gender world that stresses the establishment and maintenance of status and independence. Their games are rule-bound by interactions and behaviors that create competition and a hierarchical status among the players.

As females and males move into the work world, they continue to operate from these early experiences. The traditional male role leads a man to venture out into a habitat outside of his own more familiar ecological niche—home. The male milieu continues to emphasize status and independence. He enters the work world and finds it necessary to adjust to a political structure, which is primarily impersonal and governed by rules. Fortunately, he has been "trained" for this world of hierarchy and status. His maturational environment among his childhood male peers helped him to develop the necessary skills to succeed in the competitive work market. It is practically second nature that he continues to assert independence and status in his interactions.

In contrast, the traditional female habitat (home) is more familiar and constant and reflects her hand in its shaping. For many reasons, when children enter the picture females generally become the primary caregiver, spending more time in the home to rear the little ones. Her ecological niche is filled with all the familiar surroundings of her personal world. At least until the children are grown, her involvement outside the home usually involves neighborhood groups or community projects (Gutmann, 1965). A female's ecological niche tends to blur the distinctions between self and others and thus women come to define their perceptions and self in connection to those in their social habitat (Carlson, 1971). It is a continuance of the earlier developmental patterns inherent in the young female's experience. Consequently, the ego differences between the sexes become more pronounced in a traditional setting where the woman stays home with the children and the man is the breadwinner.

Of course, contemporary society requires families to have two incomes to survival. Now both genders venture out into the more impersonal work world, but we still bring to that arena our specific genderized perspectives and patterns of behavior which impacts our adjustment. This is good to remember when we find ourselves in group settings at work. If the primary membership of a meeting is male, the male rules of hierarchy, status, and independence will prevail. Females in this type of situation will need to "speak up" or she may never find an opening in which to talk. If the group membership is primarily female, then the rules of connection, symmetry and taking-turns will predominate. I recall a man who was working with a female group in Berkeley, CA attempting to organize them into a union. He was frustrated because the group talked so much and everyone had to have a turn expressing her viewpoint. He was going mad! I reminded him that he was in an all female group and that the rules required that everyone gets a turn (Female games assured equal participation by all players. No one sat on the bench for a whole game!). When he realized this gender difference and began to recognize and honor the rules of female interaction, things went much better.

We continue to interact in the familiar patterns learned in childhood, which often translates into misunderstandings between the two sexes. "She's from Venus!" a man declares. "He's from Mars!" declares the woman. When sex or gender differences are explored, consideration of the impact of these maturational milieus will enable us to more objectively evaluate our findings. The example above is instructive to all of us as we attempt to form better communication with others. By doing so, we engender understanding and tolerance. It is not only biology that makes the two genders different. Sociocultural factors as well as biological influences impact our behavior. Both are intricately woven into the fabric of behavior.

Gender and Conformity

Our need for belongingness undoubtedly motivates us to conform and by doing so, we eliminate the "chaos" which comes with our entry into unfamiliar territory. Living with the belief that conformity will guide us to the goal we seek, we plod along with a sense of familiarity, stability, and belongingness, but may ultimately sacrifice our individuality along the way. We act in ways that are prescribed so that we accommodate the cultural template.

In closing, I would like to share a story with my readers. It comes from Greek mythology and involves a man named, *Procrustes*, who possessed two beds which "fit all as if by magic" (Richardson, 1989). One was large and the other was small. He arranged these beds at a crossroad and as a toll, travelers had lie down in one of his beds. *Procrustes* would tie his shorter guests into the large bed then hammer them like a piece of meat or stretch them until they fit the bed. Taller guests would be tied to the smaller bed and the parts of the body that did not fit would be trimmed off.

Like the Procrustean bed of Greek mythology, if a male's inner nature does not fit the societal mold he may cut off parts of his inner self or stretch himself to "fit." He may then appear to conform, but in the alteration of his individuality, he may end up feeling shallow and inauthentic. He may be a success by conventional standards, but he may not feel fulfilled. He may never realize that he has neglected a part of his true nature in order to have a sense of belonging to the "good old boy's" club. Similarly, females are likely to be rewarded for qualities that adhere to predominant gender role structures. For women, these qualities are the ability to communicate and establish connection with others. Also, beauty, nurturance, supportiveness, compliance, passivity and affiliation are valued feminine characteristics.

What have you had "cut off" or "stretched out" to fit? Is it really a part of your inherent self or was it an adaptation on your part? There is much to consider when we explore gender but the quest is a worthy one.

140

Topic Seven

Jung's Theory

For those who seek self-understanding, life seems to be a process wherein we gradually awaken to become more aware of our potential. We come to understand "who" we really are and begin to distinguish which parts of our personality are simply appendages. The process of discovery becomes a "peeling" off of the layers imposed upon us by our conditioning and environment and we begin to see the possibilities of our true nature lying embedded underneath this outer facade. It becomes an inward journey in which we uncloak the self that was always there, awaiting our discovery.

This can be a confusing quest for seldom are we uni-dimensional. We can be assertive and pragmatic in one situation yet become passive and compliant in another. Which is the true *self* and which the impostor? We struggle to understand our complexity and often become more confused in the process. We believe on some level that we "should" be consistent and predictable, but in the completeness of the self we are *not* that simple. We are complex creatures with a wide range of behaviors, perceptions, emotions, motivations, etc. Further, the constellation of these attributes is constantly shifting within the individual. There are patterns. They are not readily discernible.

Human complexity can be illustrated through the exploration into the nature of the human psyche or personality. The processes of the psyche are not static but dynamic and ever changing. My favorite personality theory was developed by a protégé of Sigmund Freud—Carl Jung's theory of personality. As you will discover, his theory explains the complexity of the psyche in a more comprehensive way than did Freud's theory. According to Jung, when we fail to acknowledge all facets of our personality and choose to live out a limited existence we become subject to psychological difficulties.

In all societies, we are encouraged, cajoled and intimidated into appropriate behaviors. Through reinforcement, reward, and punishment we are seduced into conformity to female and male ideals, which oftentimes leads us to reject those aspects of our intrinsic nature that do not fit the "womanly" or "manly" template. We view them as being aberrant and therefore something we can discard. In fact, we may categorize these traits as rightly belonging to behaviors characteristic of the opposite gender and in the process engender the loss of a valuable possession. By failing to honor those aspects of our personality that do not fit our feminine or masculine image, we deny our unique essence.

Our self-denial often manifests as an unconscious projection and we seek completion of our lost image through our relationship with another. This can lead us towards destructive patterns because our lost image can only be found within. Until we reclaim any characteristics that we have rejected about ourselves, we may well live out an unfulfilled existence waiting for another person to fill in our holes.

Jung believed that human beings are intentional, goal-oriented creatures. We are "pulled" to actualize our fullness of being. To quote Abraham Maslow, "What a man can be, he must be." This actualization is achieved through the arduous process of coming to consciousness—an awareness of the many contingencies that affect our behavior. Understanding the nature of the psyche and the workings within that structure illuminates this process. Our psyche, or personality, is the result of a complex interaction among and within the component parts. Through Jung's theory of personality we will seek to understand the complex nature of our quest for a unique identity.

Individuation

We are born with an undifferentiated psyche. Consciousness is born from the unconscious, but until distinctions are formed between these levels of the psyche, our behavior is mediated by this more primitive state. As we gradually become more aware of the world, our behavior takes on a more intentional quality, but that awareness comes slowly. Our inner world and behaviors are shaped by not only our conscious intentions, but by the forces of our unconscious that have either been submerged in the developmental process or that have not yet been raised to our conscious awareness.

These submerged parts of our personality affect our behavior and often is reflected in our *reactions*. This happens because we have not yet incorporated various aspects of our experiences or our personality. We continue to deny that we were affected, or we claim that we do not have the characteristics that we push away. Yet, until we bravely face the mirror of the unconscious and integrate these parts of our personality, we will find that our *reactions* to situations that evoke the same feelings we thought were gone demonstrate that they are still very much alive.

When we *react,* it is "from the gut"—quick, primal and emotional. When this happens, we feel as if an "alter ego" has taken control. Our reaction is usually much stronger than the situation seems to warrant. "What came over me?" we may ask ourselves, "Why does that bother me so much?" In the aftermath, we realize that the *reaction* evoked is linked to an old feeling or "button." Unresolved unconscious feelings come welling to the surface and we strike out with a force equal to the potency of the submerged contents.

To *respond* would be more appropriate but requires the intervention of our conscious evaluation—a mediation between the situation and the emotion evoked. Responses consider the current reality or circumstances rather than linking us back to circumstances in which our reactionary "buttons" were formed. Bringing consciousness to our behavior marks progression towards *individuation.*

The task of *individuation* calls upon us to discover the unconscious psychic elements that impact our behaviors and to integrate these factors into our conscious awareness. By forming distinctions between conscious and unconscious influences, we become enlightened regarding our motivations and begin to understand our reactionary behaviors. Knowing the nature of these triggers that spark reactions enables us to determine the origins of these "buttons" and permits us to respond in the present. Understanding is factored into our awareness and we become more mindful.

Individuation also requires that we become aware of those aspects of our personality that we may have discarded because they were not attractive to our conscious definition of ourselves. With this discovery, it is to our benefit to not discard all that we have found, but to accept and embrace all facets. This does not imply that we need to act out negative aspects. We simply acknowledge them and then

<u>choose</u> which characteristics are currently useful to us and which are not.

The Nature of Libido

Jung used the term *psyche* to refer to our personality. He believed that the psyche was a complex, dynamic structure that was an energy system, constantly in motion. It is fueled by psychic energy, which he called *libido*. His definition differed from Freud's more narrow interpretation of the word. Freud believed that the *libido* was primarily sexual in nature, but Jung saw *libido* as being more of a generative life force. "Libido in its natural state is appetite...(that) of hunger, thirst...sex (and)...emotions. Libido is manifested consciously as striving, desiring and willing" (Hall, C. & V. Nordby, 1973, p. 59).

Libido arises from the interplay of instincts and *archetypes* found in the *collective unconscious*. Libido is also generated from external sources through stimulation of our senses. Once libido is spawned, energy is added to the psyche. Because we continually receive stimulation from the outside world, the psyche can never truly be homeostatic. It is continually changing and can only achieve relative stability. Even small amounts of stimulation can disrupt the balance within the psyche because the new energy creates a massive redistribution of libido within the personality (Hall & Nordby, 1973). Thus, our libido, arising from these sources (e.g., instincts, archetypes, external stimuli), drives the psyche.

The body and mind are inextricably connected to our libido and therefore affect our actions and conjointly generate our behavior. Needs arise in the body. In our mind, we place a certain value on the deficiency and form a symbol through which we can satisfy our need. The more we value a need, the more psychic energy (libido) we will invest to actualize that goal. Valuation not only increases our motivation to

145

behave in ways that will help us achieve what we want, but we will be aided with the necessary perseverance to accomplish our objectives regardless of obstacles encountered.

The character of psychic energy is not haphazard but is subject to basic principles and laws. Libido is *progressive* and *regressive*. The progressive aspect of the libido satisfies the requirements of our conscious self. We channel our energy to meet the demands of the external world. The regressive nature of the libido serves to satisfy the requirements of the unconscious. We withdraw our libido from the external world and re-channel our psychic energy inward. This nature describes the ebb and flow of our personality. Sometimes we actively embark upon ventures in the physical world and at other times we find it imperative that we withdraw from the world and people to "get our bearings."

Libido is also governed by three other principles: the *principle of opposites*, which acknowledges the duality of life; the *principle of equivalence,* a concept taken from physics that explains how equal energy becomes available to both our conscious intent and its opposite; and, *the principle of entropy* that characterizes how the psyche seeks equilibrium or balance.

Principle of Opposites

To bring a full appreciation of the quality of an experience, we must be able to at least imagine its opposite. To know life, we must be able to fathom the concept of death. In fact, to feel the finality of death may be prerequisite to realizing the fullest meaning of life. Other examples of the principle of opposites describe the quality of our experiences: wet/dry; hard/soft; dark/light; abundance/scarcity. Opposites also exist in the realm of emotions, intentions, perceptions, motivations and behavior. We love and hate; can be happy or sad; we find others helpful or hindering; we want to be dependent or independent; we are sometimes passive and at other times, aggressive; there is our feminine side and our masculine side; or we can be assertive in one instance and compliant in the next.

The *principle of opposites* invites us to expand our life's options. It allows us to analyze when we are one-sided. It gives us a way to determine what we are not considering. When we feel one way about something there is also the opposite within that feeling. If I want to help others, there is another part of me that does not want to feel responsible for others.

Knowing that for each opinion, desire, or need that we have also embodies the opposite gives us a wider perspective regarding our behavior and choices. Women do not always have to be nurturing. Men do not always have to be tough. Through this dialectical process of examining the opposites that exist within our personality, we can move beyond the limitations imposed by adherence to conformity and choose more individual expressions of ourselves.

Life continually confronts us with choices and our decisions can only be as wise as the knowledge we have available to us at any given time. This may mean that through ignorance, we behave in ways that are not necessarily good for us, but because they had survival value for us as a child, we continue to act in ways that are familiar. We learned how to behave like good little girls and boys, even to the detriment of asserting our individuality. We were shaped by familial, cultural and societal expectations and may have shoved away an integral part of our personality in the name of conformity. Examining extreme opposites in life gives us a grey area. This broader range can help us to choose a blend of the two extremes, which is a position of moderation.

Principle of Equivalence

This first law of thermodynamics states that for a given quantity of energy expended or consumed in bringing about a certain condition, an equal quantity of the same or another form of energy will appear elsewhere (Hall & Nordby, 1973). No energy is lost in the psyche, which is a relatively closed system. Because of the comparatively finite nature of psychic libido available to the elements within the personality, there is invariably competition among these structures. These structures can be archetypal aspects or emotional complexes that compete for the free libido in order to become a more dominant part of the personality. As we delve deeper into Jung's theory, it will become evident that this may not necessarily be conducive to individuation.

The archetypes and complexes of the psyche, when operating from an unconscious position, covet the available libido in order to gain the "strength" necessary for a personality "take over." Depending on the relative importance of any particular facet of the psyche, *free libido* will be attached to that archetype or complex.

We expend our libido by investing energy into our interests, desires and pursuits. Generally we will only have a finite quantity of energy, time, and desire. Upon completion of a project or the abandonment of a relationship, we gain the same amount of energy that was invested in those ventures to expend elsewhere. Unless the new pursuits are of equal emotional value to us, the amount of libido transferred from the old activity to the new quest will be limited. The remaining psychic value will then be submerged into the unconscious as *free libido* to be used by other structures of the personality seeking more energy. This may not be necessarily good for us. Some structures of the psyche have an autonomy of their own and when *potentiated* can overcome the personality. It is similar to being overcome by an emotion.

An analogy may prove useful to illustrate this idea. For example, of our 24-hour day, sleep consumes approximately 8 hours each night. If we subtract that from the available 24 hours in a day, we are left with 16 hours of every day that can be allotted to other activities. We will need to decide the proportionate amount that we will invest in each activity. Of the sixteen, we generally spend eight of those hours working if we have a job. Subtracting time spent driving to and from work or school, we are left with approximately eight hours for other pursuits. Depending on our needs we can spend the remaining time doing activities of our choice: exercising, relating to others, eating, reading, writing, or meditating. If solitude ranks high on your list of needs, then you will spend less time relating to others. In fact, if you have been overwhelmed with the fast pace of life and have not found time for yourself, that aspect of your life will scream out for recognition. If the need for solitude is neglected for too long it could cause some emotional outbursts as you seek to attain the alone time that you need. Thus we allot our time to our pursuits according to their importance just as the psyche allots energy to those parts of our personality that are the most poignant.

The *principle of equivalence* also explains the nature of psychic energy to generate libido whenever we think, feel, or intend any action. When this happens, opposite intentions are conceived in the psyche and potential energy is available to either alternative (Rychlak, 1981). As long as we remain conscious that these opposites are alternatives for us to choose, there is little consequence. It is when we vigorously reject one side of the picture that libido is free to attach to any psychic structure, whether that is a complex or an archetypal pattern awaiting expression.

149

To simplify this discussion an example of what we choose to do behaviorally will be used. According to the *principle of opposites*, when we *will* or *intend* an action, the opposite intention or desire exists as well. Equal psychic energy, or libido, is available to both choices (i.e, the *principle of equivalence*). If our self-concept is that of a caring person, we will generally choose those actions that validate that self-perception. We want to be caring and for others to view us as such. In the process of accommodation, we may fail to act upon those instances when we really would rather be doing something else. We neglect a part of our personality and become what Jung would call "one-sided." The danger of this imbalanced psychic state is that we may oblige others too often and neglect our own needs. We agree to continue to nurture others and continue to neglect ourselves until one day we "explode," become ill, or "forget" our commitments.

This concept also relates to our choices regarding what we consider "gender-appropriate" behaviors. On one level we may yearn to experience and express characteristics generally ascribed to the opposite sex, but may reject that experience or expression because it makes us too uncomfortable to deviate from societal, parental or peer expectations. Thus we push down into the unconscious our rejected aspects and adhere to more traditional behaviors.

Conversely, perhaps as an act of rebellion, we may reject more traditional forms of expression for our gender and embrace their opposite. Either way, this does not rid us of the rejected aspect of our personality. It has simply been suppressed, ready to rise when the tension between our conscious and unconscious nature becomes too great. The key to individuation thus rests with our consciousness of our duality. Owning our proclivities, whether we like them or not, allows us more libido for living with conscious intent. If not, the principle of entropy will intervene to equalize the unbalanced libido in the psyche.

Principle of Entropy

The *principle of equivalence* describes the exchange of energy within the psyche, but does not explain the direction in which the libido flows. This dynamic is explained by the *principle of entropy*. This second law of thermodynamics states that, "When two bodies of different temperatures are placed in contact, heat will pass from the hotter to the colder body until the temperature of the two bodies is equalized" (Hall & Nordby, 1973, p. 68). Energy in the psyche generally flows from a stronger body to a weaker body when they are accessible to one another.

In the psyche, unequal energy between the different aspects of personality will seek to become balanced. When we are too one-sided in our position, the libido builds up tension and when the imbalance is too great, there will be a "snapping back" of psychic energy, which will manifest itself like an explosion. This is when we find that we "blow up" and act in ways that we normally would not. In other words, we may do something way out of character. Yet this expression is also a part of who we are only it is a more extreme form.

Any aspect of our personality that possesses an overwhelming amount of libido will thus rob other aspects of our personality of available energy. This unequal distribution of psychic energy acts in accordance to the basic principles of energy just described and may create tension and anxiety that will increase until the forces at play burst to equalize the imbalance.

Archetypes

The word *archetype* can be broken down into its component parts. "Arche" refers to the "beginning, origin, cause, or primal source." "Type" refers to "form, image, copy, prototype, model, order, or norm" (Jacobi, 1959, p.

48). *Archetypes* can be perceived as typical forms of human experience. They are typical in the sense that they are characteristically human ways in which we become aware, perceive, react and behave—images of life itself.

Archetypes have a mythical quality that reveals the nature of the human soul. Regardless of their origin, myths, fairy tales, and folklore share common underlying themes— archetypal situations. As contemporary human beings, we face the same images of life and situations that confronted our ancestors only we experience them in a modern context. Thus the archetypes present us with the common human predicaments or situations we inherit as possibilities. These archetypal situations are not unique to our cohort group or our individual experience—they are human-related. Like myths and their genre, these stories still have relevance in our contemporary times. They have simply taken on a modern form. Perhaps this concept will be clarified through Jung's thoughts on the *archetypes*. He said that in life

> we are confronted with the task of finding a new interpretation appropriate to each new stage of consciousness that civilization attains. We must connect the life of the past which exists within us to the life of the present which threatens to slip away from it (Cited in Jacobi, 1959, p. 46).

Thus, the experience of the past is projected forward into the present and incorporated into the collective mind of today.

Archetypes are common to all people regardless of their racial or cultural heritage and do not come from life experiences that have simply been forgotten. Archetypes are the "...unconscious content that is altered by becoming conscious and by being perceived...(taking)...its color from the individual consciousness in which it happens to appear" (Jung, 1934/1959, p. 5). In other words, the archetype appears distinctly in each individual, yet, they are all of the

152

same form. Like instincts, *archetypes* help to shape conscious content by acting as a motivational force, having a regulating quality and thus a modifying effect upon what is held in consciousness. They are a part of our life because the bridge of emotion connects these images to us.

Another way to define this concept is to see archetypes as our instinct's perception of itself—kind of a self-portrait. This self-portrait is stereotypical and not individualistic, however. Thus we are each called to bring the *archetype* into consciousness so that we can give it a personal touch. Thus, *archetypes* impact our behaviors whenever we find ourselves in situations that constellate the particular characteristics or emotions of the different *archetypes*. In other words, the jealous woman archetype (Hera, in Greek mythology) will not be evoked unless you are in a situation where you feel that you have been betrayed. Or when we avoid relationships because we are in need of finding ourselves, we cannot know if we have truly grown until we find ourselves in a relationship again. This is when we find if we can be conscious and not slip back into archetypal patterns of reaction.

Archetypes cannot be fully explained or disposed of. They represent our predisposition to perceive, apprehend and behave in characteristically human ways. Our task is to recognize these unconscious forces in our psyche in order to update their expression to more accurately fit our individuality. The best that we can hope for is to "dream the myth onwards and give it a modern dress" (Jacobi, 1959, p. 45). We can act out these patterns in an unconscious manner or take conscious control of how we will respond to these archetypal or common human situations. If we examine our behavioral predispositions, we may be able to frame our lives in such a way that we consciously formulate the content of our life images. We can define our own existence through the multiple facets of our personality, which includes all aspects of our femininity and masculinity.

153

The Seductive Quality of Archetypes

Prior to describing some of the major archetypes and how they can influence our perceptions and expectations regarding behavior, a description of how these archetypes can "seduce" us, and the necessary process to *depotentiate* its influence will be described. Archetypes possess an impelling emotional quality that when not consciously recognized, can "charge" archetypal situations. In other words, under certain circumstances a person is likely to react archetypically rather than respond to the situation as it actually presents itself. The situation will "trigger" the person's reaction by pushing her/his particular button. The response will probably be inappropriate or out of proportion to the circumstances. When we are in conflict, anxiety is generated. We are thrown into disequilibrium and until we are able to consciously sort the options and the inherent consequences of those choices, we are likely to continue to be caught in the *angst*. Angst is the middle ground between our actuality and our potentialities. It is that transitional state between the known and the unknown.

The development of Jung's theory involved his own plunge into the unconscious (Jung, 1961/1963). He found that the contents arising from the unconscious during sleep or *active imagination* required personification in order to be dealt with on a conscious level. Active imagination is to be awake but to imagine as if you are in the dream and actively work with the contents. He found that unconscious material that would stubbornly resist becoming conscious would arise in certain situations such as we sleep, during chance encounters with similar situations, or when we are traumatized. The repression weakens allowing these "bubbles in the unconscious" to rise into awareness. Unconscious memories and experiences are not easily revealed yet they still retain the power to affect our behavior, thoughts, perceptions and feelings until we can consciously confront them. We need to identify and name the symbolic images.

Archetypes have a numinous or magical quality that tends to attract or *constellate* the contents of consciousness. Constellation of the contents of consciousness refers to how separate elements tend to combine to form a pattern, like the constellations in the night sky. In this formation process an "idea" becomes perceptible to the conscious mind. Certain situations will call awake, or *constellate*, a state of consciousness that awakens attitudes or emotions that are the opposite of our current attitude. It is like a missing part of a puzzle that we may ponder and as we become conscious of the archetypal material, it is felt in the conscious state as a Eureka moment. It is as if our mind releases a relieved "Aha!" The situation is illuminated; the light is turned on, so to speak. For example, a woman may see herself as not being the possessive type. Having grown up in a family where her mother acted jealous whenever her father interacted with another woman, she swore that she would NEVER be like her mother! But, when she is feeling stressed, somewhat neglected, or insecure and then sees her partner talking to an attractive person, the pattern of reaction modeled by her mother gets constellated and the ugly accusations, jealous feelings and insecurity come out. Sound familiar?

Studying our dreams can also help *depotentiate* archetypal energy that charges our emotions. Dreams reveal messages that cannot be ignored.

> Consciousness and the unconscious...stand in dynamic relationship to the other...If we heed the signals that the unconscious sends us via the scenarios and images of our dreams, we gain significant, even vital, information about that tiny zone known as the ego. We are likely to learn...of the error that our consciousness is making and is likely to continue to make (Coursen, 1986, p. vii).

155

Thus our dreams will tell us symbolically the messages of the unconscious in an attempt to balance what is out of kilter in our personality. The compensatory nature of these messages helps us to progress further down the path of individuation. The interpretation of dream messages leads to inner growth. Our words and actions increasingly reflect our true selfhood. We begin to emulate our unique individuality and in the process move towards equilibrium or balance.

To discover the identity of our anxiety we must give the face a name for once we have identified the culprit we will be able to determine a course of action. When we call the anxiety by name, we have the power to deal with it. The unconscious content will be made conscious and in the process will be stripped of its power to overwhelm us. We will emerge from anxiety and embark upon active problem solving.

Major Archetypes

Jung (1971) claimed that there were as many archetypes as there are situations. Because archetypes represent the primitive and undeveloped form of how we will encounter new situations, these archetypal reactions are stereotypical. We are primed as humans by the collective experience of the human race and we inherit those potentialities but they are not developed. The potential that we inherit takes a personal form as we observe others and consciously imagine a more individual response to that situation. These archetypal forms of behavior become more personal as a person encounters different models of human response to that situation.

For example, the archetype of the first kiss is one of my favorite archetypes. Before a person has experienced their "first kiss," it is simply a potential situation awaiting to be encountered. How many of you who have never been kissed try to imagine what that "first kiss" will be like when it finally happens? How many of you who have already experienced that first kiss were disillusioned when you finally crossed the archetypal threshold and moved from "I have not been kissed" to "I have been kissed"? Was the actual experience exactly as you imagined it would be, or was it different? Many students have told me that they imagined it would be fireworks and rockets, music and roses, but when they actually kissed for the first time it was awkward, full of saliva, teeth crashing together, wet tongues unfamiliar in their mouth, etc. You get the picture. Our hopes and beliefs are often quite different from our actual experience.

In the following discussion, only the major archetypes identified by Jung will be given special attention. Because of their primary character, they seem to represent the more powerful psychic energetic forces that constrain our personalities. The archetypes to be discussed are the *persona, shadow, anima and animus*, and the *self*.

Persona

The *persona* is considered the conformity archetype because it constitutes the aggregate "mask" we wear so that we can present a favorable impression to society. It consists of all the different "masks" we wear in differing social and personal circumstances allowing us to function acceptably in various settings. For example, we have a "student" persona, "wife" persona, "career-person" persona, or a "boyfriend" persona. These *personae* are useful because they enable us to conform to the many situations in which we find ourselves.

There is a danger with this archetype, however, because over-identification with any persona may result in the exclusion of the person who lies behind the mask. We may surrender ourselves to the different roles we must play and become so enmeshed in our roles that we literally forget how to be authentic. If this happens we learn to hide behind our mask, suppressing the deeper and more comprehensive self—to ourselves and to others. It was said that the late actor, Peter Sellers, known mainly for his character in the Pink Panther movies, broke down crying for he had forgotten who *he* was, knowing only how to be the characters he portrayed.

Shadow

This is perhaps the most powerful and dangerous aspect of our personality. Jung defined the *shadow* as that part of our personality wherein lies everything that is unborn or not conscious in us, including our negative and positive potential. The *shadow* is animal-like and its character is more primal and dark in the sense that it represents those aspects of our personality, which we may see as either bad or evil or just plain unacceptable. We shove parts of our humanity away from our conscious depiction of our personality and allow these rejected aspects to "sink" into our *shadow* either through repression or suppression.

The *shadow* threatens us because it embodies those qualities we tend to ignore or loathe within ourselves. We reject or ignore these facets of our personality because they do not fit within the contours of a more flattering self- image. In other words, we may see ourselves as understanding, compassionate and open, yet lurking in the depths of our psyche is the *shadow* who at times wants to be selfish, narrow-minded, cruel and critical. This shadow-self waits for us in the dark, ready to emerge and claim its right to expression when the time is right.

This split in our self-perception causes a certain amount of *cognitive dissonance,* which is what happens when we find ourselves feeling one way, but acting in another opposite fashion. We then point the finger away from ourselves, identifying what we dislike as residing in others, but not as a trait we possess (called projection in Freudian terms). Can we truly recognize or understand a quality in another unless we have intimate knowledge with that characteristic ourselves?

The *shadow* exhibits itself in our projections. Perhaps in the act of casting outward, or *projection*, we are given a chance to see our own reflection. To recognize this quality in others may be a necessary first step to greater self-understanding. We can face what we have cast outwards and even say we hate it. But in the very act of recognition, we may see our own reflection.

By becoming conscious of our alter ego, we can depotentiate its power of expression and acknowledge the rejected aspects of our self. We can own our projections and reclaim the fragmented parts. We take responsibility for our feelings about those traits and act accordingly. The *shadow* hides our secrets from us.

Addressing the *shadow* can be a disquieting task. Jung believed, that should we dare to look inside at our *shadow*, it is similar to gazing into the mirror and illuminating the self. First, we will be confronted with the reflection of our own face, or our *persona*. It is the ego that we have become attached to as representing who we are. Do we dare to remove the lens of distortion created in the developmental process? Can we admit to what we may see?

Our reflection may not be congruent with our own self-concept. We risk being revealed and that image may be unattractive and difficult to accept. The reflection will not seek to flatter, but will delineate all facets of the self, complimentary and otherwise.

Facing our *shadow* is half the battle. We struggle to remain conscious to the polar opposites that exist within our personalities and that actively shape our lives. Yet, difficult as it may be to let go of our illusions, it is through the process of relinquishing control and accepting all facets to

159

our personality that we discover our true self and move forward towards actualization. This is a good time to recall what you have learned about Freud's defense mechanisms because they will likely emerge in the face of the redistribution of psychic energy that will occur during this process.

The point, however, is not to suppress the *shadow* but to tame a rampant one. The shadow seeks expression in the personality and must take some form. It is most dangerous if repressed. Thus, if we consciously acknowledge our dark side, then we can free the psychic energy normally needed for repression or suppression for more productive uses. What is needed is the conscious development of the shadow to gain a sense of realistic insight and appropriate response to external circumstances. Rejecting the *shadow* aspects of our personality would only leave us with the inability for self-truth and limited creativity. Jung believed that our creativity was the result of the shadow, and without our *shadow*, creativity would end. For those of you who are artists—musicians, dancers, painters, drawers, writers, poets—where do you get your inspiration if not from the deepest darkest recesses of the psyche? Creativity is fed by the *shadow*.

Anima/Animus

According to Jung, the archetypes of the *anima* and *animus* are personifications of the unconscious and represent our inward face that we project onto the opposite sex (Jung, 1971). The anima and animus are archetypal images borne of the collective unconscious. Through the experiences of the collective mind of humans, we have "inherited" our beliefs and expectations of males and females. These consequent ideals are the gestalt of ancestral experiences with each gender. Thus we develop inner ideals of what men and women can and should be. These ideals are developed from the collective but are also shaped by the society in which we live.

The anima and animus are not only projected images that we cast out onto males and females, but they also manifest in our personality. The anima is feminine in nature and is a part of the male psyche. Just imagine a list of what are considered to be traditional feminine qualities—weak, submissive, indecisive, dependent, emotional, nurturing, and caring. That is the nature of the anima and is generally submerged in the male personality because of cultural and societal expectations of male behaviors.

The counterpart in the female psyche is masculine in nature and is called the *animus*. Now imagine a list with traditional masculine qualities, and simply the opposite of how we generally describe the stereotypical female—strong, dominant, decisive, independent, unemotional, and concerned with separation and power. These are qualities that are generally expected of males, but represent the submerged and undeveloped aspect of the female personality. Of course, there are many variations to the range of these stereotypical characteristics that are fostered in any given family, but in our society it seems pretty clear that there is a line drawn between what we accept as masculine or feminine attributes.

The expression of these two archetypes takes on an immature form, as is true in any undeveloped archetype. The influence of archetypes needs to be made conscious if they are to evolve. Jung saw that the anima was to blame when a man was moody. That male would therefore be "out of sorts" with his true masculine nature of logic and reason. In females, Jung believed that the animus emerged when a woman expressed her opinions. Those opinions would be immature because the animus is still in its primitive form until consciousness shapes and evolves the expression of animus-like qualities.

I must digress at this point and recount Jung's attitude regarding the feminine and masculine psyche. Although he regarded the animus as corresponding to *Logos*, or reason, in the following quote he apparently found the manifestation of the animus to be more opinionated than reasonable. This can be explained by the historical context in which he developed his theories and the viewpoint of society in regards to femininity and masculinity.

> In men, Eros (connective quality)...is less developed than Logos. In women, on the other hand, Eros is an expression of their true nature, while their Logos is often only a regrettable accident. It gives rise to misunderstandings and annoying interpretations in the family circle and among friends. This is because it consists of *opinions* instead of reflection, and by opinions I mean *a priori* assumptions that lay claim to absolute truth. Such assumptions, as everyone knows, can be extremely irritating...Men can argue in a womanish way, too, when they are anima-possessed... (Jung, 1971, pp. 152-153).

As can be ascertained from his writings, his point of view regarding females was contemporary with the times in which this was documented—1951. Although his formulation of the animus in females adhered to traditional values associated with the feminine, his ideas about these two particular archetypal forces within the human psyche are worth exploring to better understand gender issues. Jung lived from 1875-1961 and was undoubtedly influenced by the gender stereotypes that were popular during his life. These sociocultural influences were factors in the shaping of Jung's thoughts. Men were logical and could be taken over by moodiness at times, but that was the "fault" of his anima. Women were primarily seen as emotional, but could venture into the region of logic and become opinionated.

Anima and animus images are also formed through our projection of the archetype onto the parent of the opposite sex. In this way, a male's image of what woman is affected not only by the collective experience of humanity, but more personally, his image of females is formed through his interactions with his mother. His future expectations of feminine behavior will therefore hold a collective image as well as a personal image. When a mother *meets the expectations of the child* then the boy forms a positive image of women in general. If his mother does not conform to traditional values of *motherhood*, then he may develop a skewed vision of women. He will be subject to seeing all women as somehow manifesting the qualities of his mother. This process is similar for a boy's relationship to his father and future males in his life.

Similarly, this same process happens in females. Her relationship to her mother will color how she expresses her femininity as well as how she relates to other females in the future. Her relationship with her father will shape her ideals or expectations of males in the future too. Conversely, her relationship to her father will impact her evaluations of how males view her. Females form their *animus* image collectively and individually—the latter from their experiences with their father. The dynamics inherent in our relationship to our parent of the opposite sex sets us up for the types of relationships we will be drawn to later as adults. Through the course of our lives, these archetypal images influence our experiences of men and women with whom we interact.

Thus, as an adult, each person's way of apprehending, experiencing and responding or reacting to males and females is a totality of these collective and personal experiences. They color the ways in which we perceive and interpret our interactions. If we are unconsciously driven by the perceptions as they are influenced by the archetype, we will undoubtedly experience men and women in ways that reflect the ideals and assumptions we have formed about each gender, limiting our ability to truly know the person. Until we dispel the image cast and see the person in reality, we may suffer the sting of the archetype's ability to influence our perceptions and behavior. We will act not so much in response to the given situation, but from a pre-formed vision. It is as if a button has been pushed. We either see only the Adonis and Venus of our dreams or the Medusa and Cyclops of our nightmares. To clarify these concepts, some examples will be used.

The anima or animus image has the archetypal quality that overpowers our more rational faculties at times. The actualization of the image is so important that we may only see those qualities that fit the image we have formed in our minds. Generally, we are attracted to those members of the opposite sex that fit our ideal image of what a man or woman *should* be. If we are swept away by the emotional charge of the romance stage of falling in love, it is the perfect time for the anima or animus to take over.

For example, if a man *falls in love* with a woman who seems to fit his image of the ideal female, he may neglect to see her characteristics that do not fit his image. He may deny that it is a significant factor to her personality or he may believe that he is exempt from the effects. A case in point would be when he has observed her repeated behavior of being cold, calculating and uncaring in her interactions with others. His image of the anima may be such that these qualities go against that form. He may say to himself, "She would never treat me that way. She loves me." Or when she begins to treat him in such a way, he may attribute the behavior to a mood rather than seeing it as part of her character. In the name of having her fit his anima image, he will distort the reality to make it all fit.

Later, probably after much disbelief and pain, he may come to the realization that he is not exempt. He is in love with an ideal he has created in his mind. He must learn to see the person in her humanity rather than as the manifestation of his projected image. This is the time when the *principle of opposites* takes over and the psychic libido activates the polar opposite of what we felt before. This is now when the *bad mother* image of women can take over.

This *bad mother* or *bad father* image is the result of unfinished business we may have with our parents. We project these desires, needs, and frustrations upon relationships with the same gender configuration. Unresolved needs with the father will manifest in adult relationships with males and the needs unmet with the mother will continue to appear in relationships with females. It is as if we unconsciously seek resolution in the face of the other, not requiring that the other be our parent, but only the appropriate gender. We will project the anima or animus image upon the unsuspecting party and anticipate that this iconic entity will fulfill our unmet needs that originated in childhood.

We can be seduced by the character of the archetype and continue to strive to complete that which was left unfinished with the parent of the opposite sex. In this attempt, we may find that although we may not like the repetition of this familial pattern, we have found it familiar. We know how to behave and respond in that type of archetypal situation. We can respond, react, behave, perceive and feel similarly to when we were children with our parents. It had survival value then, but how do these patterns of relating to others in relationships serve us in the present? Do we really want to continue this pattern or do we want to evolve to a more functional form?

Jung wrote that man's love life "reveals the psychology of this archetype in the form either of boundless fascination, overvaluation, and infatuation, or of misogyny (hatred of women) in all its gradations and variants, none of which can be explained by the real nature of the 'object' in question..." (Jung, 1959, p. 69). Jung was describing how a man will tend to either over-idealize females or deprecate them. She is either the perfect goddess or the wicked witch.

Why does this paradoxical thinking/feeling occur? The anima embodies not only the over-idealization of females, but also carries the deprecating attitudes towards females as well. The latter are especially influenced by the quality of relationship one has had with the mother. Consequently, one moment a man may be worshiping a particular female and in the next moment, see her as holding an uncanny resemblance to his overbearing, tyrant mother.

The development of the animus nature in females follows the same course. Under the influence of this archetype a female may find herself vacillating between idolizing and devaluing males. They are either gods or cold, uncommunicative, distant creatures—just like her dad.

These are just examples of the polar opposites of the anima or animus projection. Our projections are as varied as our individual experiences with our unique set of parents; our parents simply provide the ingredients for our adult expectations. Thus, consciousness of the seductive quality of the anima and animus can enable us to forestall disappointment and destructiveness in our relationships. We can take off the lens of unconsciousness imposed by the anima/animus; with full consciousness we can see the other person as she/he is in reality.

Our task therefore becomes one of separating the archetypal images from the human person. We can be blind to who a person really is and live with the belief that our expectations will be fulfilled by this mythical creature we have just met. Remember, not all mythical creatures were gods and goddesses; some were monsters. With stars in our eyes, we may try to fit the person into the form of our ideal man or woman, all the time neglecting what "is." What you see is what you get, so it is important that we remove the lenses through which we distort others. Even though we are seduced by the image of the maleness or femaleness of the other person, we would be better served if we saw the person instead of the image. To avoid relationships with others of the opposite sex is not the solution either. As

Jung stated, "The shadow can be realized only through a relation to a partner, and anima and animus only through a relation to a partner of the opposite sex, because only in such a relation do their projections become operative" (Jung, 1971, p. 161).

Self

To Jung, the *Self* is the very core of the personality and replaces the ego. It cannot emerge until we have successfully addressed the unconscious and the influences of the archetypes. Through the process of balancing the opposing tendencies within our personality, we come to terms with the true self that lies within the uncarved stone—we progress down the path of individuation. It is like a *rebirth* wherein we emerge in a new, more integrated and wise form for we have come to terms with our unacknowledged self—our dark side, the many masks we wear, and our feminine and masculine nature to name just a few. As we act more from the *Self* instead of the ego, Jung believed that intuitive powers would become stronger. We learn to trust the knowingness that is our biological wisdom. As we become more trusting of ourselves, we begin to believe in our power to create our own reality. We learn to trust our gut feelings and begin to follow our instincts instead of being ruled by the *tyranny of the shoulds*. This tendency to do those things that we feel we *should* do instead of doing what we need or want to was set forth by the neo-Freudian, Karen Horney. This is created by our compulsive need for perfection (Horney, 1966).

As the process of more conscious living becomes a way of life for the individual, synchronistic events become the norm in one's life. To Jung, *synchronicity* is defined as meaningful coincidences. They are events that seem to happen by accident or chance, but in actuality are premonitions (Rychlak, 1981). It can occur in the waking state or emerge as messages in dreams. As we draw within to know ourselves better we become more receptive to

167

intuitive messages. By becoming more open to new and different experiences and thoughts we sharpen our intuition and begin to listen to our inner messages more intently. We act in ways that honor us rather than conforming to standards that seem foreign at best.

Topic Eight

Psychological Types

As we continue on our journey towards understanding self-development, no discussion on Jung's theory would be complete without exploring his theory of psychological types. When we are aware of our orientation to the world and the ways that we perceive or apprehend the world, self-understanding is deepened.

Jung formulated his theory of psychological types from his clinical observations. He felt that knowledge of the psyche was limited at best and our attempts towards understanding are subject to the inevitable distortions of our conscious mind.

> The fact that we have only recently discovered psychology shows plainly enough that it has taken us all this time to make a clear distinction between ourselves and the contents of our minds...we must admit that what is closest to us is the very thing we know least about, although it seems to be what we know best of all (Jung, 1933, p. 76-77).

Historically, psychological type theories were based upon scientific knowledge. These theories began with what was *known* and moved towards the *unknown*. For example, in the pseudoscience of *phrenology*, proposed by Franz Gall, character type was determined by examining the degree to which bumps on the skull protruded. The skull was mapped with areas designated to denote particular qualities of character—the larger the protuberance of any particular area, the more an individual possessed of that quality.

Another example, Hans Eysenck's typological theory was based upon the Greek formulation of character as it related to the qualities of the humors, or fluids, of the body (e.g.,blood or bile). The four types described were the *phlegmatic-type* (reserved, matter-of-fact, laid-back, unemotional); *sanguine-type* (cheerful, confident, optimistic); *choleric-type* (bad-tempered, irritable); and *melancholic-type* (depressed) types. Behavior and therefore, personality traits were related to known qualities of the humors of phlegm, blood, yellow bile and black bile, respectively. Thus behavior was first observed and then explanations for those characteristics were attributed to either bumps on the skull or the humors of the body.

Jung's method deviated from the traditional methods of describing personality. Most personality theories had been formulated from the viewpoint of the observer and assumptions about personality were based upon those observations. Jung believed that this approach only described what the describer observed and did little to explain what was occurring within the individual being described.

If our behaviors are explained from the basis of what others see or observe, the description may be far removed from what is actually occurring within our psychic field. We are left at the mercy of the observer to explain our personality. Jung took an opposing route and attempted to explain personality by beginning his explanations from the perspective of the individual under scrutiny. A most appropriate saying that relates to this idea is, "If you really want to understand a person, walk a mile in his/her shoes."

Jung (1971) believed that in the study of personality, we are the most competent to judge our own psychology—we alone know what it is like to be living in our skin and what is in our conscious mind. Jung sought to fashion a theory that took this viewpoint into account. Although unconscious factors influence our behavior, Jung believed that our conscious outlook on the world determined the resulting inner state that we hold.

Consequently, Jung's typological theory describes personality by explaining what is occurring within our conscious intentions (or what we hold in our awareness) as we act. In other words, how would our personality be explained from our internal perspective? How do I orient myself to the external world? Are my actions mediated by the situation and people outside myself—the external world—or are my actions influenced more by the resulting internal stirrings triggered by those externalities?

Jung's typological scheme consists of sixteen major types. His theory describes the focus or the preferred direction of movement of the libido, or the *attitudes*. You have probably heard of these attitudes: *extraversion* and *introversion*. His scheme also described the role of our preferred perceptual and evaluative styles, referred to as *functions*. These are related to our senses and our sixth sense, thus we have *sensation* (the five senses) and *intuition* that are perceptual functions. *Thinking* and feeling are the evaluative or judging functions.

Attitudes

"Character is a fixed individual form of a human being" (Jung, 1933, p. 74). That character can take on either a passive or active orientation. Passive persons seem to reflect upon situations before acting, while active individuals appear to jump in without hesitation or forethought. Jung (1933) wrote

> there is a whole class of men who at the moment of reaction to a given situation at first draw back a little as if with an unvoiced 'no,' and only after that are able to react; and there is another class who, in the same situation, come forward with an immediate reaction, apparently confident that their behavior is obviously right. The former class would therefore be characterized by a certain negative relation to the object, and the latter by a positive one...(p. 85)

These *attitudes*, or our passive and active aspects of our libido, are termed *introversion* and *extraversion*, respectively. They describe the flow of consciousness and are distinguished by the direction of interest or the focus of the libido. Essentially, whether we are introverted or extraverted describes our *attitude* toward the object or our conscious orientation to the world. Thus our consciousness is either primarily affected by: (1) the *objective* world (things and people external to ourselves) or *extraversion*; or, (2) by our *subjective* state (what is happening within us) or *introversion*. This is the fundamental difference between the two attitudes of consciousness. Our habitual reactions are thus established by these attitudes and therefore determine not only our style of behavior, but also the nature of our subjective experience.

Extraversion and introversion are predisposed attitudes that work equally well as psychologically adaptive modes of survival. Whichever is our *dominant* attitude, it is an inherent disposition and is not normally acquired in the nurturing process. There are circumstances that can result in a falsification of our natural individual disposition, however. A caregiver could thwart a child's natural mode by being overbearing, for example. This is especially true if the caregiver and child's nature are in opposition—one being introverted, the other extraverted.

Attempting to understand the world from the point of view of a person whose natural attitude is different from yours is difficult at best. Even with the best of intentions a parent could unduly thwart the child's natural mode. The consequences for this would probably be some form of neuroses as an adult. The cure would lie in the development of the attitude consistent with that person's inherent nature.

The dominant attitude also gives rise to the character of the unconscious. For example, generally, an extravert is more affected by the objective, external world. This leaves the internal, subjective aspects of personality relatively undeveloped. These latter qualities become submerged in the extravert's unconscious taking on an archaic and infantile character ready to emerge when the psychic equilibrium is unbalanced. When this happens, the unconscious "...concentrates the libido on the subjective factor...on all those needs and demands that are stifled or repressed by the conscious attitude" (Jung, 1971, p.187).

When the psychic energy emerges in accordance to the principle of entropy, the expression of that undeveloped part of our personality is like a young child—primitive and immature. By understanding our dominant attitude, we can then come to expect the ways in which our unconscious will be expressed. Consciousness allows us to modify the rudimentary forms of our personality.

Introversion

The attitude of *introversion*, designated as an "I" in one's typology in the Myers-Briggs Type Indicator (MBTI), is an abstracting one in which libido is withdrawn from an object. Consciousness is primarily directed inward toward our subjective state and objects and people function primarily as orienting devices. They help us establish the quality of our experience.

As introverts, objects seem to possess a strong and powerful quality, which we can't consciously perceive, but imagine to be true via our unconscious perception. A certain mistrust is aroused and "(he) shrinks from making himself or his opinions felt fearing that this would increase the object's power...Anything strange and new arouses fear and mistrust as though concealing unknown perils...any change is upsetting, if not...dangerous..." and so the introvert fashions an elaborate defense system to confront the world (Jung, 1971, p. 236).

These strategies are preventative measures to keep objects or people from gaining power over us, so in this sense as introverts, our relationship to objects and people is negative. This often leads to being frequently misunderstood. In childhood, it seemed that we mistrusted and actively resisted submitting to everything unknown. Our subjective, internal stirrings far outweighed the situation in which we found ourselves.

Generally being poor communicators, it is not unusual that introverts offend others, even when not intending to do so. Introverts are simply captivated by their inner world. Often what is communicated may hold little resemblance to the actual circumstances. What becomes poignant for the introvert is the subjective experience—how that person takes it in and sees it.

The relationship of experience is only related to the object in that it has evoked something within the psyche of an introvert. The result is new psychic information which then acts as a co-determinant of one's perception of the world. Introverted consciousness is aware of external conditions, but the subjective factors always outweigh the objective situation and therefore exert a greater influence upon decisions and choices made. The externals are merely catalysts for the more important internal life of the introvert.

If you are introverted, you're probably familiar with people describing you as being aloof, unsociable, introspective, withdrawn and preoccupied. You may find it difficult to adapt to social situations and you hate crowds. Oftentimes, this leads to feelings of being lost and lonely with consequent feelings of inferiority. "What's the matter with me?" you may ask yourself.

This feeling is exacerbated by the relative minority position esteemed to introverts in a predominantly extraverted world. In our western culture, more value is given to objective or external factors rather than subjective or internal ones, thus when we are introverted we are "obliged to depreciate the subjective factor" and force ourselves to join in the extraverted overvaluation of the object and thus oppose our own specific principles (Jung, 1971).

Extraversion

Extraverts, designated as an "E" in the MBTI, direct consciousness toward the external, objective world and subordinate their inner life. Outer necessity predominates and an extravert's whole consciousness is oriented in that direction.

Libido is invested in "perceptions, thoughts and feelings about objects, people and animals, and other environmental circumstances and conditions" (Hall & Nordby, 1973, p. 97). The extravert's attitude is related to and oriented by the objective conditions rather than our subjective state. We become preoccupied with what is outside of our own body—people, things, and events in the immediate environment.

In contrast to the introvert, as extraverts, our relation to external factors and people is positive. Our libido is invested in objects and our subjective state is a secondary determinant of our behavior. Our actions are simply more highly influenced by what is going on around us. We find that we fit easily into social situations and adapt to existing conditions, making us seem more socially "normal" than the introvert.

Jung (1971) warned that the harmful consequence of an extraverted attitude was the suppression of one's subjective factor. As stated earlier, suppression of any aspect of personality results in the emergence of that facet of our psyche, but its expression would be relatively unsophisticated because it has remained undeveloped. Thus,

> the form of neurosis most likely to afflict the extravert is hysteria...(which) begins as an exaggeration of all the usual characteristics of extraversion, and then is complicated by compensatory reactions from the unconscious, forcing the individual to introvert. This constellates the inferior introversion and produces another set of symptoms, the most typical being morbid fantasy activity and the fear of being alone (Sharp, 1987, p. 40).

This fear of being alone often leads to desperate attempts to find "someone," perhaps "anyone," to do something with.

The attitudes of introversion and extraversion constitute only one aspect of Jung's typological scheme. As he sought ways to explain the diversity of personality, his theory became more complex. He needed a system that would help explain the variance found among people within the two major attitudes of consciousness. This system came to be known as the *functions* of consciousness—the filters that color our dominant attitude and through which we apprehend experience. These functions are *thinking, feeling, sensation,* and *intuition.*

Functions

Through the four functions—the *four ways of knowing*—awareness and evaluation of our world occurs. Although we use all four functions, we each favor a particular one, which then becomes the primary vehicle of consciousness through which we evaluate or perceive the world.

The preferred function is called the *primary* or *superior* function and is "...the one we automatically use because it comes most naturally and brings certain rewards" (Sharp, 1987, p. 18). The four functions seldom develop to the same degree in our psyche. The other three functions become submerged in varying degrees in the unconscious. The functions act hierarchically. Those closer to the primary function are more developed and may help to support the primary way of knowing the world. The deeper a function is submerged, the more that function resembles an undeveloped and infantile character. These are characteristics you would expect of a relatively undeveloped part of personality.

The psychic mechanism ruling the nature of the conscious and unconscious functions are also subject to the ruling principles of the libido—the principle of opposites, principle of equivalence, and the principle of entropy that were covered in an earlier chapter. *Functions* are divided into two categories: *irrational* and *rational*. *Sensation* and *intuition* make up the former category, while *thinking* and *feeling* comprise the latter.

Irrational Functions

The *irrational functions*, sensation and intuition, are perceptual modes through which we become aware of our surroundings. "...(S)ensation and intuition...are perceptive—they make us aware of what is happening but do not interpret or evaluate...They do not act selectively according to principles, but are simply receptive of what happens"

(Jung, 1971, p. 92). Sensation allows us to use our five senses to *see* what is in the external world. Intuition enables us to go beyond the five senses allowing us to see the possibilities or possible meaning behind a situation.

The term *irrational* in this context does not imply that these are illogical or nonsensical modes of knowing. Quite simply, "...they are not based upon the principles of reason and its postulates...they subordinate judgment to perception" (Jung, 1971, p. 226). Irrational functions are empirical and based exclusively upon experience—we simply register that which we perceive. The result of our perception is not categorized into an evaluation or judgment and we make no attempt to evaluate the object or situation in terms of how we think about it or feel in this situation. We simply perceive. Sensation and intuition thus form the channels through which we receive information about experience, while the evaluation or judgment of that information belongs to the province of the *rational functions*.

Rational Functions

Some people habitually do more thinking than others. They give more weight to thought processes when making decisions and use this mode to try to understand and adapt to the world. Their experiences are "subjected to consideration and reflection or at least are reconciled with some principle sanctioned by thought" (Jung, 1971, p. 89-90). In contrast, there are those who favor emotional aspects and distinctly neglect thinking. Only in extraordinary circumstances will a feeling-type utilize thought or the analytical process to make decisions and this may be prudent in the case of a person whose primary function is feeling.

"When we *think*, it is in order to judge or to reach a conclusion, and when we *feel* it is in order to attach a proper value to something" (Jung, 1971, p. 91). These functions are rational in this sense—we are discriminating, logical, and consistent according to two different criteria, but both act as methods that facilitate our ability to attach value to our experiences. Although we often consider feelings, or emotions, to be more subjective and therefore less rational, both modes of judging our world have similar conclusions: we rank things according to some criteria.

In summary, the functions can be distinguished as such: *sensation* allows us to register the incoming stimuli, helping us to establish that "something" has occurred; *thinking* enables us to derive an objective label for the event just "sensed;" *feeling* links us to our emotional evaluation; and finally, *intuition* points us to the possibilities of meaning and the future that lie within the situation.

Hierarchical Nature of Functions

Jung (1933) believed that humans could never be everything at once, never complete. Certain qualities are always developed at the expense of others and wholeness is never attained. The *superior* or *primary function* is always the preferred conscious mode of apprehending the world.

The orientation of our consciousness, or consciousness of our will, is governed by the principles of the superior function. This preferred mode of apprehending the world is the most differentiated of the functions in our psyche. Differentiation refers to a clear boundary between one thing and another. We also have a co-determining influence that is always present in consciousness exerting its influence. It is less differentiated than the primary function and is called the *auxiliary* or *secondary function.*

The nature of the secondary function (i.e., whether it is a rational or irrational function) is always different from the primary function. This is because functions of the same nature are antagonistic to one another. For example, thinking and feeling are both evaluative functions. An individual favors only one of the rational functions, which takes its place in the consciousness of that person. The other rational function becomes submerged into the unconscious and becomes the least developed of the four functions. The auxiliary function is possible and useful only inasmuch as it serves the dominant function. Thus, if the primary function is the rational mode of feeling, then the auxiliary function would be an irrational function—either sensation or intuition. The various combinations result in

> practical thinking allied with sensation, speculative thinking forging ahead with intuition, artistic intuition selecting and presenting its images with the help of feeling-values, philosophical intuition systematizing its vision into comprehensible thought by means of a powerful intellect, and so on (Jung, 1971, p. 268).

The third function in the hierarchy is called the *tertiary function* and is opposite in nature to the secondary function. In other words, in our example of INFJ, the tertiary function would be the irrational or perceptual function of sensation. The least developed of all the functions is the submerged function that is in the same category (*rational* or *irrational*) as the primary function (this would be thinking in our example). It is function that is the most resistant to integration into consciousness and is called the *inferior* or *fourth function.*

Integration of the inferior function into consciousness requires a circuitous route. A direct approach to the unconscious would pose too great a threat to the conscious position of the individual. It is therefore advisable to take an indirect approach via the auxiliary function. This protects the conscious standpoint and at the same time gives the individual a broader view of the possibilities.

At mid-life, the task of individuation beckons us to attend to the neglected aspects of our personality. The superior function must give way to the inferior function and we experience a reversal to our previous inclination. The thinking-type becomes more ruled by feelings; the sensation-type develops a keener sense of intuition; the intuitive becomes immersed in a world of sensation; and, the feeling-type becomes captured in the world of books and ideas.

I have found that Carl Jung's theory is the most comprehensive in helping me to understand the nature of the human psyche and how it works. Freud believed that human motivation comes from our sexual libido. Jung's theory of libido is broader and identifies the energy of the psyche as stemming from many different sources, including sexuality. He believed that we have libido to work, libido to create, libido for the many activities and interests in our lives. This helps us to move away from interpreting behavior as always coming from our need for sex and procreation.

By applying the principle of opposites, Jung clearly helped me to see that the world and our experience as humans is a paradox. With this in mind, when I am focused on only one aspect of a situation, his theory reminds me that the opposite tendency or belief is also a part of my psyche. For example, if I want to go visit my friend in Colusa there are factors that support that desire: I haven't seen her for awhile, we always have meaningful conversations when we visit, we enjoy each other's company. At the same time I have to consider that there are other factors in my life that I need to consider if I am to maintain a balance in my life. I have work to complete, books I'd like to read if I had some spare time, maybe even a movie or two I'd like to just "veg" out and watch.

By keeping these seeming opposing tendencies in consciousness, I am able to make a decision that is balanced. I may decide that I will visit just for an hour or two, but then go home and do some reading. If I were to only act on the first impulse, which was to go visit, I may have stayed too long and then felt overwhelmed because I didn't spend any time catching up on my work or giving myself some alone time.

Jung's theory is also instructive in that he talked about the different personality types and how we can better understand ourselves by knowing our typology. I would like for you to find out your typology according to this theory. (The link at the end of this chapter will lead you to similarminds.com where you can find out what your typology is according to Myers-Briggs. Complete the Personality Test JUNG & ENNEAGRAM that has a little over 100 questions).

After you complete the personality inventory, you will get two results. For the purpose of this discussion, only the four-letter typology reported at the top of your results will be discussed. These four letters describe the way in which you orient yourself to the world and how you take in the world. For this book, I will not be discussing your Enneagram results but you can find more information about this personality assessment tool on the internet at the same site where you took this test.

As for your typology, let us look at an example to clarify how you will interpret how you orient yourself to the world. It will describe whether you are introverted or extraverted and also indicates your preferred ways of "knowing the world," or your dominant function (i.e., sensation, intuition, thinking, or feeling).

For example, it may be INFJ (that is my typology). That would translate into a psychological type that describes you as Introverted, represented by the first letter (I); the second letter in this example represents the function of Intuition (N) and is your secondary function (I'll explain how the second and third letters may represent either your primary or secondary function depending upon the last letter of your typology).

To determine your *primary* function, refer to the last letter of your typology that will be either a *J* or a *P*. This last letter indicates whether your *primary* function is the rational function (which would be the *feeling* function for our example of INFJ) or the perceptual function (which would be *intuition* in our example of INFJ).

The two middle letters of your typology indicate your *primary* and *secondary* functions. Which of the two functions is the *primary* function will depend upon the letter at the end of the psychological type, which in the case of our example is a *J*. The *J* indicates a preference for using the *judging,* or *rational* function of *feeling (F)* rather than the *perceptual,* or *irrational* function of intuition *(N).* Therefore, for INFJ, as shown below, the *primary* function is the rational, or judging function of *feeling (F)* and the *secondary* function is the other letter, or *N, intuition.*

If you had a P at the end of your typology, as in INFP shown below, then your *primary* function would be *intuition* or *N*, the perceptual function. The *F*, of *feeling* function in this example is now the *secondary* function and supports the *primary* function of *N*, or *intuition.* As I describe below, you will find that *feeling* and *thinking* are Judging functions, while *intuition* and *sensation* are Perceptual functions.

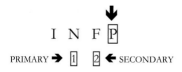

185

What Jung's typology tells us about ourselves is that our *attitude* indicates whether we either channel our libido outwards into the external, objective world in an extraverted direction *(E)*, or that we channel or energies inward or introverted *(I)* toward our subjective state. The *functions* tell us which mode of knowing the world will provide us with the most accurate answers to questions that we have. In other words, as in our example of INFJ, you will most likely find yourself very busy internally with much going on through your psyche regarding what happens within you. The external circumstances are simply triggers for your rich emotional inner self. The preference for feeling *(F)* implies that you should trust your feelings about a situation when making decisions because it is your superior function and provides you with the most accurate measure of how you are relating to the situation. Back that up with your intuition *(N)* and your decisions will likely match what your intentions and desires are.

What you will notice about your typology, however, is that there are two letters missing, or submerged, from the possible four functions (see below). This implies that you have a third, or *tertiary* function, and a fourth, or *inferior* function, that needs to be taken into account in your decision making process. The hierarchical order of your functions informs you that there is a rank order to the reliability of these functions when making decisions. The primary function will be your best bet since it is the most developed. In our example below, the *feeling* function can trusted the most. Then *intuition* supports the *feeling* function.

2 1 ⬇

I N F J

TERTIARY ➜ *(S T)* ⬅ INFERIOR

3 4

The last two functions of *sensation (S)* and *thinking (T)* for our example above generally need to be considered <u>after</u> you have evaluated your position using your *primary* and *secondary* functions that appear in your typology. This is true because your primary and secondary functions are more developed and therefore more accurate in estimating your position in a situation.

I like to think of the primary function of *feeling (F)* as being the wisest person in our "family" for the INFJ type. We can trust the decisions of the eldest and wisest of our functions. The next oldest would be the next wisest and in this case is the function of *intuition (N)*. The third or *tertiary* function would be the next person in our family we would consider when making decisions although since it is submerged we understand that it is not well developed and therefore not too reliable to help us figure out our answers yet that function still needs to be added to the total decision that we are pondering. The baby of the family is the *inferior* function, or in our case above, *thinking* function *(T)*. Although it is the least developed of all the functions for the INFJ, it still needs to be "heard" so that it doesn't later sabotage the works by throwing a fit because it was not heard in the decision making process. Does that make sense. In other words, the baby of the family wants to be able to provide input but we know that its position will have the least weight in the overall decision. Thus for an INFJ the decision-making hierarchy follows the information provided by the functions in the rank order of (1) feelings; (2) intuition; (3) sensation; and, (4) thinking.

Sometimes with a primary function of feeling, one will override the wisdom of one's emotions because in our world the thinker is preferred over the feeler. Thinking is considered more logical and rational, therefore somehow it is seen as better. The feeler may then not trust the feelings that have emerged and may resort to using the thinking function to make a decision. Feeler, be warned. You need to trust this function since it is the most developed. As a *feeler*, if you attempt to deny your *feelings* and override them with *thoughts* about the situation rather than your emotions, then you will likely resort taking the advice of the "baby" of the family! If you try to override your preferred function of *feeling* with *thinking (T)*, which is your *inferior* function and therefore the least developed in your psyche, then you'll probably be talking yourself out of your own feelings and therefore not acting on what you "know" to be the right decision for yourself.

To complete the picture for our two examples of INFJ and INFP, the type of INFP would have the submerged functions of *Thinking (T)* as the third or tertiary function, and *Sensation (S)* as the inferior function. This is illustrated below:

$$\begin{array}{cccc} & \boxed{1} & \boxed{2} & \blacktriangledown \\ \text{I} & \text{N} & \text{F} & \boxed{\text{P}} \end{array}$$

INFERIOR ➜ $(\ S \quad T\ )$ ⬅ TERTIARY

$$\boxed{4} \quad \boxed{3}$$

This implies that a decision-making hierarchy for the INFP type would be: (1) intuition; (2) feeling; (3) thinking; and, (4) sensation.

Eight Major Types

In Jung's (1971) discussion on psychological types, he focused only upon eight types—those combinations of the attitude supported by the primary function, either a rational or irrational function. In the 1920's, Katharine Cook Briggs and Isabel Briggs Myers advanced the development of Jung's typology into the sixteen types (Schultz & Schultz, 1994). The Myers-Briggs Type Indicator is the result of their work and allows for a deeper analysis of the different personality types within Jung's typological scheme. If we list all possible combinations, sixteen personality types emerge:

ESTP, ESTJ, ENTP, ENTJ, ESFP, ESFJ, ENFP, ENFJ, ISTP, ISTJ, INTP, INTJ, ISFP, ISFJ, INFP, INFJ. For the following discussion Jung's format exploring the eight types will be discussed rather than the sixteen types described by Myers and Briggs.

Extraverted-Thinking Type

The thoughts of extraverted-thinking types are guided by intellectually considered motives. Extreme extraverted-thinking is characterized by intellectual thought, which adheres to a rigid set of rules, principles and ideals. Thinking is done in terms of "shoulds" and "oughts" for others and oneself. This type of thinking involves judgment based upon external criteria which is not necessarily concrete thinking but perhaps idealism reflecting ideas from external sources extracted from tradition and education (Jung, 1971, p. 92).

In the apprehension of the world, extraverted-thinking is synthetic allowing one to take disparate hypothetical material and discover new facts or general concepts in the process. As we think, we construct as we analyze. Extraverted-thinking is found more often among males than females. When it appears in the latter, thinking tends to take on an intuitive cast.

The antagonistic and inferior function for the extraverted-thinker is feeling. Because the feeling function is inhibited in this type, the extraverted-thinker can be blatantly impersonal. This conscious detachment leads to a compensatory character in our unconscious. Because the feeling mode is undeveloped, when this mode of apprehension arises in consciousness, feelings are personal to an extreme and one becomes overly sensitive. This compensatory reaction to our conscious detachment gives rise to "secret prejudices, a readiness...to misconstrue any opposition to his formulas as personal ill-will, or a constant

189

tendency to make negative assumptions about other people..." (Jung, 1971, p. 201).

Extraverted-Feeling Type

As extraverted-feeling types, evaluation is based more upon feelings than thought. The quality or value attached to that feeling, however, is mediated by some external criteria, such as tradition, societal values, or generally accepted standards. "The object determines the quality of feeling which is harmonious with objective values" (Jung, 1971, 207). In other words, how we feel about a given situation or person is dependent upon how synchronous the situation seems in relation to our preset values. In this sense, logic always gives way to feeling. Personality adjusts to relate to the external conditions of the circumstances. For example, a female marries the "suitable" man who measures up to her reasonable expectations in such criteria as age, social status, and income. The criteria that influences our decision-making does not emanate from some hidden subjective standard. As extraverts, we would not be conscious that such a quality existed within ourselves. Our focus is always towards the external and objective.

Because introverted thinking would be the inferior function in this type, it generally appears as a negative, deprecatory voice that we usually turn against ourselves (Von Franz, 1971). This may explain why the extraverted-feeling type dislikes being alone. Especially in introverted moments, this negative inner voice tells this type, "You are nothing. Everything about you is wrong." At these times, our typical response is to distract ourselves or to seek outside stimulation, rushing to be with someone—anyone.

Extraverted-Sensation Type

Extraverted-sensation types have a keen sense of realism. Thoughts and feelings are always reduced to objective causes, to influences that seem to come from things outside the subjective realm. Having a highly developed sense for

190

objective facts, these types are described as lovers of tangible reality. There is little inclination for reflection or domination. The point of sensation is "to feel the object, to have sensations and if possible, enjoy them" (Jung, 1971, p. 218).

The more sensation rules a person's personality, the harder it is for others to be with that person. As the sensation aspect prevails, the objects and people become reduced to simply sources of stimuli. This often makes others who are trying to relate to an extraverted-sensation type, feel devalued. They are trying to have a relationship, but the focus is locked upon *sensation* as it is generated by their presence or interaction.

As the submerged and inferior function for the extraverted-sensation type, intuition arises in a manner that is colored by suspicion and mistrust. Extraverted-sensation types project these archaic intuitions onto others and believe they are detecting reasons to be suspicious and mistrustful.

Extraverted-Intuitive Type

Just as the extraverted-sensation type strives to reach the highest pitch of actuality, intuition tries to apprehend the widest range of *possibilities*. We move beyond the actualities of any given circumstance and actively seek to uncover and discover the possibilities inherent in the situation. Libido is invested in this external pursuit. The images that arise in one's psyche enhance one's perception, adding deeper insight and influencing decisions to act or abstain.

The extraverted-intuitive type can inspire courage in others or infect them with enthusiasm that is unrivaled, but there are some ramifications borne from this inherent nature. Today's inspiration may quickly fade to tomorrow's boredom for this type. Paradoxically, the dangers faced arise out of one's very nature. One is influenced by external situations and things, and can inspire others with their enthusiasm, but too often the extraverted-intuitive type abandons projects or ideas as soon as they ripen. This happens because of a belief that the possibilities are already determined and the mundane process of actualizing the idea or project holds little appeal. Because one tends to focus outside of the subjective state, extraverted-intuitives may miss living a life that can truly called their own. We chase after possibilities rather than staying put long enough to reap the fruits of our labor and instead, come away with only an empty basket.

Introverted-Thinking Type

As will be recalled, in the introvert, libido is focused inward toward subjective experience. As introverted-thinking types, evaluations do not stem from "...concrete experience back again to the object, but always (back) to the subjective content" (Jung, 1971, p. 237). This internal reckoning guides one's judgments. The external facts of any given situation are not paramount in this type of thinking except for their influence in generating internal drama. What is most important is the development and presentation of subjective ideas. We begin with our internal or subjective state and move out towards the external. Our judgments do not stop there, however, for the libido eventually always returns to our subjective analysis for the final decision.

Introverted-thinkers are by definition not so practical-minded, being more concerned with forming new views rather than accumulating new factual knowledge. Skilled at formulating questions and creating theories, this type of thinking "opens up new prospects and insights...facts are collected as evidence for a theory, never for their own sake" (Jung, 1971, p. 237). One focuses upon intensity rather than being expansive.

These types tend to lack relationship to things external to them. In relationships with others, people may feel that they matter only in a negative way to the introverted-thinker—

from indifference to aversion. Introverted-thinkers tend to get lost in a fantasy world and can lack social grace. Consequently, the introverted-thinker either tries to go unnoticed, as if they are not concerned; they may seem childishly naïve, inconsiderate, and domineering to acquaintances, often being indifferent to others' opinions. Ideas are pursued independently, which may provoke others to oppose them, especially in work settings. Paradoxically, one can be quite naive and trusting in personal matters.

As introverted-thinking types, extraverted-feeling is submerged in the unconscious. One's feelings become trapped in the inner world of thoughts and ideals. When this happens it is difficult to even identify one's feelings. This can be most unfortunate in personal relationships especially when this type may seem oblivious to what might be considered "the objective requirements of a relationship." When feelings do reach consciousness, this type is often overwhelmed, becoming uncontrollable. Von Franz (1971) described this type's expression as a "sticky attachment...like the flow of hot lava from a volcano—it only moves about five feet an hour but devastates everything in its way" (p. 73).

Introverted-Feeling Type

Jung found it difficult to describe the introverted-feeling type because "so little appears on the surface" (Sharp, 1987, p. 75). Outwardly, one's demeanor is even and inconspicuous, not caring to impress others or influence them to change in any way. On the outside, one may appear unemotional, but this is hardly the case. Introverted-feeling types are merely misunderstood, especially when an extravert attempts to understand the introverted-feeler's world. It is hidden from the extravert, whose focus is the tangible, objective world. What is hidden within the introverted-feeler is unseen and profound—a depth of spirituality, intimacy and poetry. This difference may also be a seductive quality for the extravert as well. "It gives...a mysterious power that may prove terribly fascinating to the...(extravert)...for it touches his unconscious" (Jung, 1971, p. 249).

Expression of feelings is inhibited and one appears to be self-contained. Perhaps the statement, "still waters run deep" is an apt description of this type. On the outside one appears to have no feelings or thoughts and consequently may seem cold to others, yet the inner world is rich and full of images. These images are evoked by the objective world that in turn stimulate the churning of internal images. It is this subjective experience that eventually guides decisions. We seek these images—not images based in reality, but those that are seen as a vision within.

Introverted-feeling types avoid large crowds "because...(our)...evaluative feeling function is numbed when too much comes in at once" (Sharp, 1987, p. 76). Troubles sometimes stem from the rising of one's ego (conscious factor) into the feeling aspect. We begin to "feel" what other people are thinking. We are certain that what others feel can be aptly described as meanness, scheming, contriving; plotting secret intrigues, etc. To counter these suspicions that one's elevated ego has perceived, counter-intrigues are created and one tries to uncover any suspected schemes. Of course, these internal activities lead us to exhaustion.

Introverted-Sensation Type

Introverted-sensation types don't perceive the world as it actually is. It is altered by one's subjective disposition. "What is perceived is either not found at all in the object, or is, at most, merely suggested by it (Jung, 1971, p. 253). This is similar to what an artist, such as Vincent Van Gogh, might perceive when looking out into the night sky. He saw a crescent moon, nestled among the brilliant stars, the outline of the hills in the background; yet when one views his masterpiece, "The Starry Night" it is apparent that the scene was altered by his inner-world interpretation. The introverted-sensation type senses the object, but goes beyond it. One's libido is focused upon the subjective perception elicited by the external stimuli, but not the object itself. Our intuitive nature reaches into the past and toward the future as it is inspired by what we have sensed. What is most important is not the objective perception, but the meaning that adheres to it.

Introverted-sensation types have problems with rational, judging tasks. They lack objective understanding and don't seem to do much better with self-understanding. Intuition is the inferior function of this type, and when it manifests, it is still an infant. One supposes that what others intend hold dangerous possibilities, which are seen as ambiguous, shadowy, and sordid.

Introverted-Intuitive Type

These are the mystical daydreamers. Being oriented by psychic reality—the background processes of consciousness—we have an uncanny ability to sense the possibilities of a situation. Introverted-intuitive types "...can...foresee new possibilities in more or less clear outline...it is prophetic insight" (Jung, 1971, p. 261). What fascinates this type the most is not the external object or the situation, but rather what has been released within the psyche because of the object. Intuition allows one to look behind what is happening and perceive the inner images that arise. These images in turn fascinate more intuitive activity, often stopping us in our tracks—we *must* explore the minute details of what we have just perceived. These activated new possibilities represent the possibilities of life. They represent possible views of the world and give rise to new potentials.

Unfortunately, introverted-intuitives seem to lack good judgment about themselves and others. Perhaps this is due to the internal channeling of the libido and the possibilities that are evoked. One is not affected so much by what *is*, but rather what *can be*. Little is accomplished and one becomes vague about the specifics in the real world.

Summary

To know our psychological type enables us to use our strengths. It allows us to tap into that realm of the psyche that is mysterious and often inaccessible. By understanding that our primary and secondary functions can lead us to better decision-making, we can make choices that will reflect more positive outcomes for us. Because society has preferred the extravert and the thinking function, introverts and feelers can rest at ease to know that they "know the world" more accurately through different modalities than what society encourages. The intuitives can trust their inner sense of possibilities and meanings to a greater extent since that is their primary way of bringing in information from the world. It is not encouraged in our society to use one's intuition, and in fact, we are told that intuition does not exist. There is no sense organ to detect "intuitive hunches" so it must be an anomaly—not normal. Those whose primary function is sensation can feel more certain about what their senses are telling them.

There is much to learn and much to do on the path to individuation. We can assist the process through knowledge and dedication to the discovery process. We can awaken to our highest potential and take an active part in the reality that we experience. Through learning about the complexity of the human psyche we are empowered to work with our own psyche to develop and nurture our soul. The truth lies within. We simply have to listen.

Weblinks for Topic Eight

Myers-Briggs Type Indicator: Take the 108 item Jung & Enneagram test

http://similarminds.com/personality_tests.html

Topic Nine

Transpersonal Healing

One of the more satisfying aspects of the Transpersonal approach to understanding human behavior is its emphasis on the experiential nature of investigation. This implies that we can best understand the nature of human consciousness through our direct experience of the various states of consciousness available to us. Intellectual understanding alone is not enough to give us the kind of insight that we need to help guide others. What we have not experienced directly ourselves, we know only at a conceptual level. Without a phenomenological understanding, we are simply observers.

Phenomenology is the study of the experience of the individual that requires us to "walk a mile in the other's shoes." Empathic understanding within a healing relationship with a therapist, counselor or guide is like finding a welcoming hand to hold as we travel through unknown territory. The transpersonal approach to healing therefore requires that we first embark upon our own journey to wholeness so that we can be effective guides or therapists. This doesn't mean that you have to have all the answers, but that you have had direct experience with the territory that will be encountered when a person chooses to begin this personal search for self. This direct experiential knowledge also makes us more confident that we are familiar with the journey that the other is embarked upon. Because it is familiar to us we can provide insight and guidance of what to expect along the way. This helps the person who is seeking a soulful connection to the universe to not feel alone. We are companions on a journey together and one of us has traveled this road before.

The transpersonal is interested in the ways in which we can better understand the nature of evolving our consciousness within this lifetime. It is, as the humanists would assert, living to our potential. In search of our full individuality and actualization of our unique potential, the tools that are being identified by research into non-ordinary states of consciousness are helping many people to overcome trauma and move beyond the events that have served to limit their happiness and growth. Non-ordinary states of consciousness allow us to tap into the unconscious therefore providing an opportunity for healing.

Non Ordinary States of Consciousness

What is a non-ordinary state of consciousness? Depending on the culture from which we understand consciousness, there are different answers to this question. In Western culture, ordinary consciousness is characterized by the laws of matter, space, and time according to Newton. We cannot experience something that is not present in our vicinity nor know anything that has not happened to us within our lifetime. Therefore, a non-ordinary state of consciousness is consciousness that differs from our everyday awareness. There are different methods to induce these non-ordinary states of consciousness: meditation, hypnosis, psychoactive drugs, rapid breathing, sensory deprivation, isolation tanks, sleep deprivation, prayer and lucid dreaming.

When we speak of experiences as being "non-ordinary," this implies that we know what "ordinary" or "normal" consciousness is in human beings. If a person's beliefs are limited to what we consider to be normal by western standards, then any state of consciousness that differs from this ordinary waking state would be labeled as non-ordinary or altered. Different consciousness states are thus considered to be anomalies of consciousness and therefore, not normal.

This definition is not embraced by all cultures, however. Some cultures, such as Native Americans, shamanic and other mystical traditions believe that all states of consciousness are ordinary if one pays attention. From these cultural perspectives, having an out-of-body experience or having a "vision" is seen as simply another form of consciousness available to all humans. This includes having contact with other realms of consciousness that western society considers to be paranormal, such as astral traveling or out-of-body experiences, lucid dreaming, trance states, drug induced states and other forms of "altered" states of consciousness. In these cultures and traditions, these types of consciousness states are considered as ordinary.

Even the term, "altered-states of consciousness" is ambiguous. Dr. Stanislav Grof, co-founder of transpersonal psychology who has an M.D. and was trained in Freudian psychoanalysis has stated that when we use the term *altered states* to describe the different forms of consciousness humans experience, he is reminded of what we do to our cats and dogs! He prefers the term, "holotropic states" but also uses the term, "non-ordinary" when he speaks of what many refer to as an altered state. Holotropic states are consciousness states that refer to consciousness that is "moving towards wholeness," thus he does not see all psychotic states as being a sign of mental illness. Some people will enter into a non-ordinary state of consciousness spontaneously. This can happen when a person is struggling with the conflicts that arise as we let go of old ways of thinking and being, but are unsure of the right direction to go. The psychosis is a symptom of the soul in anguish and a transpersonal practitioner who recognizes this can help lead the person through their psychosis to emerge with a renewed vision of life.

Holotropic states are healing states of consciousness that allow for the full awakening and discovery of the soulful nature of our being. It is what we refer to as our "essence." Even spontaneous psychoses fall into this category if that psychosis is an effort of consciousness to heal and "move toward wholeness."

The Realms of Consciousness

One characteristic of most psychodynamic theories is that the psyche is charted as territory formed since birth and is thus termed our biographical history. From this premise, our psychological makeup has only been influenced by the events of our lives. The time in the womb is not considered to have an influential force on our psyche, nor are evolutionary mechanisms considered to have an impact on our minds. The theory of Carl Jung is an exception to this limitation (Jung's theory is discussed in more detail in a separate chapter). Stan Grof has argued that the psychodynamic models are insufficient to provide a workable cartography of the psyche when working with the range of problems that human beings experience, especially in more severe cases of mental disturbance.

In his book, *The Holotropic Mind*, Dr. Grof outlines the three levels of human consciousness and argues that traditional psychology and psychiatry work with only one realm of human consciousness—the biographical level or postnatal experience. These are memories that are formed after birth and are limited to what has happened since that time. What has been ignored in this paradigm is the reality of how our experience in the womb and the trauma of the birth process can manifest as symptoms in our lives after birth. Otto Rank wrote of the birth trauma and how this experience forever marked the need for symbiosis and the desire for the symbolic "return to the womb," a time when all our needs were met perfectly and effortlessly. Grof describes in detail the various manifestations of symptoms that are related to our time in the womb and the stages of birth. He likens much of the mental anguish that some people experience as characteristic of the different stages of birth. This time of trauma imprints the experience on our psyche and can later produce symptoms that mimic the experience of what we encountered in the birth process.

The three stages of birth characterize what Grof calls the *Basic Perinatal Matrices* (BPM). In his LSD research and Holotropic Breathwork sessions with patients, he has charted the cartography of the psyche and how it includes three levels of the Holotropic Mind: 1) The perinatal realm of consciousness; 2) Our biographical realm of memories; and 3) The realm of the collective unconscious or the transpersonal realm.

The Perinatal Realm

There has been some argument that the trauma of birth is not "remembered" by the infant because there is insufficient myelination of the cortex at that stage of development. In the film, *Nature, Nurture and the Power of Love*, Bruce Lipton demonstrates clearly that we are learning about the environment and being conditioned even while in utero. Although we may not have conscious memories of the birth process the dilemmas of the stages of birth characterize the feelings that many of us feel in our lives: being stuck with no way out, feeling choked off or squeezed to death, and seeing the light at the end of a tunnel as we emerge.

In traditional psychology, birth is not seen as a time of psychological trauma. Grof reasons, however, that since the early experiences of being nursed and the nuances of the early nursing experience convey a sense of being loved and nurtured, then it is reasonable to assume that psychological imprinting also occurs during our experience in the womb and through the three stages of the birth process. If there is a memory of the nursing experience, there must be a memory of the birth process. Traditional psychological therapy does not access or explore this realm since it focuses only upon the experiences that have occurred postnatally.

Grof describes the Basic Perinatal Matrices (BPM) that can impact our psyche. These matrices correspond with the experience in the womb and the three stages of birth. First there is the experience in the womb from which can arise the experience of the "good womb" or "bad womb" (BPM I). This time can give rise to memories from our post natal life, such as "situations from later life in which important needs are satisfied, such as happy moments from infancy and childhood (good mothering, play with peers, harmonious periods in the family, etc.), fulfilling love, romances; trips or vacations in beautiful natural settings; exposure to artistic creations of high aesthetic value, swimming in the ocean and clear lakes" (Grof, 1985, p. 104).

Next, during the first stage of birth (or BPM II) when the contractions begin, blood supply, nourishment, oxygen and the removal of waste products are cut off during the contractions of the uterus. This is an uncomfortable time when the cervix is not yet opened. Psychological distress, later in life is analogous to this stage when we may feel constricted in our lives, being stuck with no way out, or claustrophobic. The BPM II also gives rise to memories of "situations endangering survival and body integrity (war experiences, accidents, injuries, operations, painful diseases, near drowning, episodes of suffocation, imprisonment, brainwashing, and illegal interrogations, physical abuse, etc.); severe psychological traumatization (emotional deprivation, rejection, threatening situations, oppressive family atmosphere, ridicule and humiliation, etc.) (Grof, 1985, p. 104).

In the second stage when the cervix opens, we struggle through the birth canal (BPM III). This matrix gives rise to our feelings of having had enough of oppression or abuse and we make efforts to free ourselves. This matrix can give rise to memories of struggles, fights, and adventurous activities (experiences in military service, rough airplane flights, cruises on stormy ocean, hazardous car driving, boxing); highly sensual memories (carnivals; amusement parks and nightclubs, wild parties, sexual orgies, etc.); childhood observations of adult sexual activities; experiences of seduction and rape; in females, delivering their own children (Grof, 1985, p. 104).

Lastly, we emerge from the birth canal (BPM IV) which can give rise to memories of "Fortuitous escape from dangerous situations (end of war or revolution, survival of an accident or operation); overcoming severe obstacles by active effort; episodes of strain and hard struggle resulting in a marked success; natural scenes (beginning of spring, end of an ocean storm, sunrise, etc.) (Grof, 1985, p. 104).

Allowing for the womb experience and birth process as times when the psyche is imprinted broadens the range that therapy can affect. Without considering the perinatal realm of consciousness as a source of psychological imprinting, we miss entire realms of unresolved traumas "imprinted" on our psyche. (You can listen to an interview on You Tube with Dr. Grof where he discusses his research with LSD and the encounters with these levels of the BPM. The web addresses for these interviews is found at the end of this chapter).

Phenomenologically, each of these stages represents not only a biological process but are also selective openings into the collective unconscious as described by Carl Jung. This is the third area of the Holotropic Mind that Grof describes. In the transpersonal realm of experience we venture into the land of the collective unconscious. These are the archetypal experiences of the collective human race that allow us to identify with others and all creatures, transcending space and time. This is the realm of the transpersonal where we go beyond our physical boundaries and identify with the experiences of other people, plants and animals and lose our sense of having boundaries. This is the archetypal realm of mythological heroes and heroines, creatures and situations where we experience a oneness with everything. Carl Jung spoke of this realm extensively and described how the archetypes of human experience have a profound effect upon the ways we act out these typical human conditions and situations.

Holotropic Breathwork is a natural means in which to induce a non-ordinary state of consciousness that was developed by Stan Grof and his late wife, Christina. Grof has documented hundreds of cases wherein participants in LSD research or *Holotropic Breathwork* sessions report experiences that transcend their personal lives. These reports recount experiences that range from identification with what humans face when they are imprisoned, locked in wards, living in totalitarian countries or experiences in torture chambers. This is likened to the first stage of birth, or BPM II. Transpersonal experiences of the BPM III realm reflect the struggle in the birth canal. Here, participants have experienced scenes from wars and revolutions, a feeling of having had enough of oppression and one rises up to free oneself. Being stuck in the birth canal could give rise to experiences of being in hell and surrounded by infernal landscapes. Identification with Jesus' birth/resurrection, identification with mythological figures, such as Osiris or Inanna has also been reported.

These examples illustrate how traditional approaches to understanding psychological problems and consciousness experiences limit our ability to integrate and incorporate material that has not been fully processed emotionally. By only dealing with the experiences formed during our autobiographical period, Dr. Grof and other transpersonal theorists believe that psychological understanding is thus restricted.

Holotropic Breathwork

A most interesting non-drug tool developed by Dr. Grof and his wife, Christina is what they have called *Holotropic Breathwork*. This technique was developed while he was a scholar in residence for 14 years at Esalen Institute in Big Sur, CA and represents a natural way to open consciousness and move towards wholeness. One will naturally enter into a non-ordinary state of consciousness during the process that will evoke many emotions, imagery, and memories.

> *Holotropic Breathwork* is a powerful approach to self-exploration and healing that integrates insights from modern consciousness research, anthropology, various depth psychologies, transpersonal psychology, Eastern spiritual practices, and mystical traditions of the world. The name *Holotropic* means literally "moving toward wholeness" (from the Greek *"holos"*=whole and *"trepein"*=moving in the direction of something) (www.holotropic.com/about.shtml).

In conjunction with provocative music, more rapid breathing, and internalization of the process through keeping your eyes closed within the presence of a "witness" or Sitter, one is able to achieve a non-ordinary state of consciousness. As Dr. Grof describes, through this type of breathwork, one is taken from one's body into the consciousness of other forms of life, other people, the universe, childhood, prenatal development, the birth process, and even past lives. In other words we activate universal aspects of the collective unconscious.

This internalized process is simply experienced and allowed to unfold over a 1-1/2 to 2 hour period. During this time of rapid breathing, the music facilitates the release of blockages through vibration but also enhances the visual imagery and experiences that arises.

The purpose of the "witness" or Sitter in *Holotropic Breathwork* is to be present for the Breather during the process. The Sitter helps the Breather during the process by providing nourishment or water if requested, blankets, pillows or comfort through holding. The Sitter reminds the Breather to breathe if the breathing returns to a normal pace for an extended period. Having a Sitter provides the Breather with a sense of safety during this journey. Knowing that there is someone there while we traverse this unknown territory of the psyche is comforting. He or she is our witness. The purpose of a Sitter's presence is made clear before the breathing sessions begin so that both the Sitter and Breather are confident regarding their specific role and the parameters of the process.

One other aspect of the breathwork session may include bodywork should the breathwork leave some issues unresolved. This is determined by any residual pain or discomfort that the breather is experiencing. With the breather's permission, the facilitators assist by using various bodywork techniques that help release the residual pain. This discomfort is seen as emotional pain that has been somatized, or lodged in the body. By working through the physical pain, the emotion is released and more fully processed, resulting in most cases in relief from earlier problems such as asthma, arthritic pain, depression and emotional distress. I must admit, that this part of the process was quite a spectacle to watch as I "witnessed" the working through and release of the blocked energy being processed in different participants when I attended Grof's *Holotropic Breathwork* in January 2008.

After the breathing session, the Breather is then directed to the Art Room where a mandala is created to give symbolic form to the breathwork session. The mandala is a circular ancient art form wherein the artwork is contained. This seems to bring order to disparate aspects of experience and appears to have a healing effect upon the psyche of the artist. Later in the day, all participants shared this mandala work with others in the group as a further witnessing to what unfolded during the *Holotropic Breathwork* .

My Personal Experience

My participation in the weekend workshop in San Francisco in January 2008 was nothing short of amazing. My husband, Bill, and I paired together so that we could experience *Holotropic Breathwork* together as a couple. When we had dinner with Dr. Grof in 2006 (a synchronistic meeting with Dr. Grof in a restaurant after attending one of his talks) he told us that it was a unique experience for couples because it would allow us to see one another's souls. We wondered at the time exactly what he meant by that statement. We were to find out in 2008.

Without going into the details of our breathwork sessions, I will report that being a Sitter was just as powerful as being the Breather. As the sitter I not only witnessed by husband's processing through his breathwork session, providing him with comfort and sustenance when he needed it, but was also able to witness the scene unfolding around me. There were probably over two hundred participants in the hotel conference room, each of us paired with another person, lying on sleeping bags or layers of blankets, eye shades in place and Sitters in various positions ready to assist the Breather to guide him or her to the bathroom if necessary.

The music was provocative to say the least. It was loud and evoked many emotions and images. But more amazing was the variety of experiences that breathers were having. Some screamed, many cried, some got up and assumed various positions (although we were asked to try to stay on our mats). And when necessary, Dr. Grof and the facilitators got down on the floor and helped the breather with bodywork to finish out the emotional blockages. Dr. Grof is not a young man, yet there he was, down on his hands and knees doing what he could to help each individual who needed his attention. He is a man of great status in the psychological community yet he does not hold himself aloof from others. He cares and he is there when needed.

For me, I was able to process emotional blockages related to my life that had somatized as arthritic pain in my hands. My mandala included a visual depiction of my identification of being a wild animal, like a tiger, with claws that killed and ripped other animals and beings opened. There was no horror in this experience since I could identify that that is what tigers do. Symbolically, the pain in my hands represented the inability to let go of a sense of responsibility in my life for various experiences I had had. It is a great relief to have this pain lessened. I did not ask for bodywork for this problem, however, and truly believe that if I had, the relief would have been a complete healing of the condition. But the residual pain is so much less than before that I can only attribute the release as stemming from the breathwork session. Another participant who had severe asthma reported that for the first time his lungs were open and he could freely breathe. He felt that for the first time he could play with his breath as one would play with any new toy. Much healing occurred that weekend and I look forward to attending another *Holotropic Breathwork* session when Dr. Grof facilitates another workshop in the bay area.

Weblinks (Transpersonal Healing)

Dr. Stanislav Grof and LSD Research:
(Part I)
www.youtube.com/watch?v=5ig3eU_oDS0

(Part II)

www.youtube.com/watch?v=tSRHStwOPU&feature=related

Topic Ten

Transpersonal Techniques

In the process of life, we find that we can't always express what we are feeling either because of fear or embarrassment. We think that if we suppress our urges, they will go away. When we are in psychological pain we often want to avoid the experience and learn to numb ourselves in an attempt to not feel. When we do this, however, we create numbness to life. We try not to feel pain. We push away anger. We cast aside sadness in the hopes of not feeling, but when we numb ourselves against negative feelings we compromise our ability to feel. Period. We numb all emotions in the process. We try to not feel pain, but consequently numb our ability to feel pleasure as well.

Numbing never works. Emotions have much energy attached to them. When we push feelings down, they don't go away. What we *push* down, we will literally have to *keep down* through sheer force of will. Unfortunately, this stuff always comes back to the surface, and usually when we least expect it. These suppressed emotions also seem to gain strength while hiding under our *armor*. We have our rages, depression, sadness, impatience, worry and fears. Emotions that are ignored just seem to get bigger. They become like ignored children who are trying to get our attention. The more we ignore a child, the more that child will escalate behaviors to gain our attention. It is better to express our feelings as they happen, or at least to keep the experience in consciousness so that they don't sink into the unconscious where they will create problems.

Consciousness becomes bounded through psychological processes that culminate in somatic, or bodily, changes. This process is called *armoring* which is the body's method of locking in emotions that are not expressed or that are held back (Marrone, 1996). Armoring takes on the form of tense muscles that look and feel like padding on our bodies. Physical aches and pains settle into those areas where we lock in the energy that has been suppressed and held back from expression. In transpersonal techniques to healing, these processes are addressed through active energy intervention techniques and contrast significantly from the traditional forms of talk therapy.

Some of the tools by which we can call forth blocked energy take on many forms: meditation; martial art forms such as tai chi and chi kung; yoga; acupuncture, acupressure and energy work through tapping on key acupuncture points. Within these few systems alone are many useful physical exercises that free up blocked energy, allowing vital energy to circulate through our bodies and meridians. By facilitating the free flow of our chi, greater mental and physical health can be actualized. We are less troubled by the symptoms of emotional blocking and somatization of psychological distress.

As mentioned earlier, holotropic use of drugs in research are now being studied for the first time in 40 years. Johns Hopkins, Duke University, the University of Arizona and the organization, Multidisciplinary Association for Psychedelic Studies (MAPS) are conducting studies using psychoactive substances in hopes of developing drugs that mimic the healing effects of these psychedelic drugs. Recent findings that marijuana, ketamine, and LSD can have healing effects on psychological disorders holds a promising avenue for researchers to investigate further. If you do a quick search on the internet, you will discover many articles relating to the research findings regarding the healing potential of these drugs.

Bruce Lipton and the New Biology

In a different chapter I spoke of Bruce Lipton's work on *The New Biology.* In his video, *Nature, Nurture and the Power of Love,* Dr. Bruce Lipton teaches us how our subconscious mind is the part of our mind that is programmed through the experiences we have as neonates and as young children. He convincingly shows that in the womb, we are already preparing for the environment that we will be born into at birth. As young children, we take in the world without censor and whether the environment is nurturing or not, it is the world that determines our growth and the way we will come to see the world. The mother's environment is the fetus' environment. In fact, when before the child is conceived the kind of environment that the future parents are in will cause the selection of genes that will be expressed when the mother conceives. This is powerful stuff. This means that our attitudes and perceptions that we hold prior to conception will translate into a future child that will be prepared to either survive or flourish in the environment into which he or she is born. There is a tradeoff, however. If the future parents have been in a toxic environment, the genes that will be selected for in the future child will compromise its intelligence and immune system. These are important considerations when we plan our families.

When we are in a nurturing environment, we move towards those situations. At a cellular level, we are in growth mode. In the opposite type of environment, a toxic one, we will go into protection mode. Growth can only occur in non-threatening environments because when we are in fear mode, we cannot grow—we only try to protect ourselves and our bodies respond by shutting down the viscera (major organs) so that blood can flow to the muscles to prepare us to flee or fight. When we are in a protection mode our immune system is inhibited. Simultaneously, our intelligence shuts down because we need to be able to operate from habitual reaction rather than using higher cognitive processes such as thinking so that we can protect ourselves.

He goes on to point out that we cannot change this subconscious mind through conscious effort. Affirmations would not be enough since there is an opposing belief within our psyche that must be acknowledged and balanced within the process of change. The human psyche is an energetic system that behaves in a holistic way. There are many facets to our physiology that respond to our cognitions and emotions. Because there is an intricate network of responses that occur in habit, we must use intervention techniques that address the multifaceted nature of habitual ways of behaving.

Behavioral patterns, especially those learned in childhood, may be especially difficult to change due to the classically conditioned nature of this type of programming. Lipton teaches us that our brain wave patterns as children make us especially susceptible to simple "downloading" of information. You've seen this behavior in children. What they see and hear, they will imitate without knowing whether it is right or wrong, appropriate or not. Even in the womb we are in the process of learning about the world that we will emerge into at birth. We cannot change these patterns of thinking or feeling through simply using a cognitive technique. We need to use a combined method that taps into the energy system of our bodies to break the connections that have wired together.

Energy Medicine

Energy medicine includes an effective technique that was introduced by Gary Craig. He calls this technique, *Emotional Freedom Technique*, or EFT. It is a method that has helped many people overcome such problems as Post Traumatic Stress Disorder (PTSD), anxiety, fear, phobias, depression, ADHD, chronic pain, and more. EFT is a process and I will only describe the basics of the technique and then refer you to website where he offers a free EFT manual, videos and more regarding EFT (see links at the end of this chapter).

Before I go into that technique, I want to remind you of the video, *What the Bleep Do We Know*. In that video it is demonstrated that any behavior or emotion that we experience will result in the creation of a neural network in our brain that releases neurochemicals associated with the emotion that we are experiencing. Like a chemical cocktail it acts like a drug in our brain. Each time that we repeat that emotion or behavior, that neural network is strengthened. This action is similar to what occurs in the brains of drug addicts who crave their drug of choice. The "fix" will be the only way to alleviate the craving.

Emotions essentially are an addictive process. One of the key messages of the film, *What the Bleep Do We Know*, is that all emotions are addictive. If we are going to be addicted to emotions (and we will be from what the late Candace Pert teaches us in the film), then why not choose emotions that make us feel good? I think that every person truly desires to feel happiness rather than sadness, or, peacefulness, rather than anger. Thus, we can become conscious co-creators of our reality because we can learn to consciously choose which emotions we will be addicted to! But because of the habits we have formed in the developmental process, we will have to become conscious of these reactions and intervene with a different response that weakens the neural nets that correspond with our behaviors and emotions that make our lives difficult.

If we are to follow this line of thought that runs through *What the Bleep*, then we would think that a purely cognitive process would eventually break the neural connections that make us addicted to the emotional patterns that seem to rule our lives. But, factoring in Lipton's work, we begin to see that it may take more than simply making a New Year's resolution to be happier or less anxious. We need additional tools that will help us to change the programming in our subconscious. What follows are a few of the most dynamic techniques that have emerged in the field of Energy Medicine.

EMDR

Eye Movement Desensitization and Reprocessing (EMDR) is an eclectic procedure that is having a big impact in therapeutic circles (Shapiro & Forrest, 1997). This process combines cognitive psychology, psychodynamic therapy, visualization and imagery, active imagination and eye movements to help identify and process the elements of unfinished emotional content. It is the most widely researched technique in energy medicine and is becoming more widely used to assist those with PTSD.

EMDR targets emotions that have not been fully processed. These unprocessed emotions keep a person stuck in turmoil, but through EMDR the emotions are reprocessed to completion so that the impact of the memories is lessened. Additionally, by focusing on healthier beliefs one would rather hold while engaged in the EMDR process, the new beliefs replace the old.

At the heart of one's behaviors are the beliefs that shape perception. Trauma and pain that are not fully processed emotionally become stuck and cause the discomfort, flashbacks, nightmares, and startle effect characteristic of those with PTSD. While the memories of the trauma are targeted, eye movements similar to the movement that occurs during rapid eye movement sleep, or REM, are used to help finish the emotional processing.

EMDR was developed based upon sleep research and REM deprivation studies. It has been hypothesized that one of the reasons for REM sleep is to clear the mind of extraneous information and to help complete the processing of emotional content (Shapiro & Forrest, 1997). Using imagery, cognitive techniques, body-mind awareness, and psychodynamic processing, EMDR is an eclectic approach to uncovering the stories that continue to affect our choices in life. The problems emerge because we have not been able to completely process the traumatic event or protracted trauma of dysfunctional environments. We live as if these circumstances are ever present and physiologically, we continue to react as if the trauma is stuck.

One of the results of trauma or prolonged chaos is PTSD. By seeing PTSD symptoms as a form of *spiritual emergence* that requires attention, EMDR can be a viable tool in the transpersonal approach. Pathological behavior can be interpreted as the soul's cry for attention. Exploring the transpersonal nature of the trauma, moving through it and finding the seeds of wisdom to be gleaned from that event or time in one's life, assist the individual to transcend the wounds. Reasoning guides the memories to be processed. EMDR provides an effective tool to help evolve stuck consciousness. Used in combination with other techniques that work with the chi, or energy, of the body, EMDR can be very effective. I have written an article about the use of EMDR and the Six Healing Sounds for a chi kung grand master, Mantak Chia. This article is published on his website, but is also included in this section of transpersonal intervention techniques.

The EMDR Process

EMDR is an eclectic approach that utilizes the left/right eye movement pattern, imagery, cognitive therapy, body-mind awareness, and psychodynamic techniques. We begin the process by identifying the negative cognitions or beliefs being held. We are not required to relive emotional events or re-experience trauma but simply need to identify any negative or irrational beliefs that we are holding about the situation. By making a list of these negative thoughts, we have a starting point from which to begin the EMDR process.

The negative belief or beliefs that are impacting us adversely are then rated according to the amount of discomfort they produce in us. These negative beliefs will be the target of focus when the eye movements are begun. Next, we identify a counter belief or positive belief that we would rather believe about the situation or ourselves. These positive beliefs then become the focus of the second stage of the EMDR process.

Although this section focuses upon the EMDR process, I am going to combine the Six Healing Sounds to facilitate the clearing of the stuck emotions. In EMDR, we consciously identify or detect any negative beliefs being held and then assess that belief for the level of discomfort it causes us on a scale of 1 to 10, where 1 represents a low level of discomfort and 10 the highest. These are called subjective units of discomfort (SUD). Generally people report having a high SUD in relation to the emotion or belief being processed at the beginning of the procedure.

While holding the negative belief in consciousness, using the eye movements, and applying the Six Healing Sounds with the colors associated with each organ, the processing of the negative emotion is targeted. As the clearing process continues with the eye movements, memories and feelings from the event or related events may arise that then become targets for further processing with the eye movements. One stops to discuss these memories that arise in order to bring closure to the stuck emotions associated with these memories.

As the process unfolds, clarity develops regarding the stuck emotions or memories. Remembering these associated events and feelings tap into the neural network that has kept the negative feelings alive. By stopping and revisiting these feelings from a cognitive standpoint, we are able to arrest the emotions from strengthening their connection so that we can begin to feel the positive instead. We come closer to letting the negative go and experience healing. It starts to feel as if the negative emotions are no longer something in the present, but that they are now part of the past where they rightfully belong. We are more able to let it go and put it behind us.

The EMDR process combined with the practice of the Six Healing Sounds can also give rise to a range of sensations or experiences that establish a route to further processing of emotions. There may be feelings of discomfort or changes felt in parts of the body that can then be focused upon while the person is directed to commence the eye movements again. Sometimes images may arise from past situations, or emotions of sadness, anger, frustration, worry or fear may come into consciousness that can lead to still further processing. The point is to continue with the detection and transformation until the positive emotion becomes the predominant feeling in your consciousness.

In the next step of the process, a counter or positive belief is targeted for processing. This is the belief that the person would rather have in consciousness and can be stated in a way that encompasses the associative positive emotion of the organ we are clearing out. For example, if I am clearing out my kidneys of any fear or anxiety being felt, then the counter belief would include an element of installing gentleness and stillness into my behaviors.

Although we can tell ourselves how we would rather feel, it is often hard to have confidence in the truth to that belief. Prior to processing the newly identified positive belief, we need to rate the validity of that thought using a Validity of Cognition (VOC) scale. This is a scale ranging from 1 to 7, with 1 representing "completely false" and 7 representing "completely true." One generally begins this part of the process with a low belief in the validity of that preferred cognition.

Using the eye movements to install the positive emotion or belief, focusing on the color associated with the organ while using the healing sound for that organ should result in a strengthening of the validity of that cognition. As the emotions are processed, belief in the former negative belief fades and becomes something of the past in the person's mind. The new counter and positive belief becomes more valid simultaneously. As one might suspect, as the EMDR process and the Six Healing Sounds helps to complete the emotional processing and as the positive emotions are installed, the SUD will lower while the VOC will rise.

Why EMDR Works

One of the theories that helps explain why the eye movements used in EMDR help in processing stuck emotions is based upon sleep and dream research. It is known that rapid eye movement (REM) sleep is essential for mental well-being. Sleep is characterized by five stages that progress within a 90-minute pattern. The first four stages are called non-rapid eye movement (NREM) stages because there is an absence of the rapid eye movements that characterize the fifth stage of sleep, or REM. In a typical night of sleep when we sleep for eight hours, we experience approximately five REM periods. Each REM period lasts longer than the last and we move from a 10-minute REM period at the beginning of our sleep to almost an hour of REM activity by the end of the night. REM periods are also associated with our most vivid dreams and not surprisingly, our ability to experience lucid dreams as well.

Some people report that they never dream because they have no memory of their dreams. In the sleep lab where a person can be monitored for brainwave activity, muscle tone and REM, it has been found that almost everyone dreams. Researchers are able to know when a person enters into REM sleep through various monitoring devices that are used in the sleep lab. These machines are usually the electrooculargraph (EOG) that measures eye movement; the electromyograph (EMG) that measures muscle tone; and the electroencephalograph (EEG) that measures brainwave activity. When sleepers are awakened in the sleep lab during REM periods they will generally recount that they were in fact having a dream.

In sleep deprivation studies researchers tested to determine which stages of sleep were essential to cognitive functioning and emotional balance. When a person is continually awakened during NREM stages, but is allowed to complete the approximate five REM stages during the night, the person wakes up feeling refreshed and is able to function normally. But when a person is kept from entering REM but is allowed to sleep through the NREM stages, that person is less able to function optimally the next day. This type of sleep deprivation makes it difficult to carry out simple tasks. One feels irritable and the ability to think clearly and cope with random stressors is compromised. Without a good night's sleep we just cannot function as we normally do. Simultaneously, our immune system is compromised through the lack of the "right kind" of sleep. In other words, we need REM sleep and when anything interferes with that stage, we suffer.

Emotional Freedom Technique (EFT)

Developed by Gary Craig, the Emotional Freedom Technique, or EFT, is a powerful method that is simple to learn and easy to carry out in a self-help format. You don't need a therapist to get some relief, although to work with deeper issues, a therapist is highly recommended. It involves a process that is psychodynamic (unconscious processing), cognitive (thoughts), imagery (visualization), and energetic (tapping upon acupuncture points). When combined together, the elements of EFT help to desensitize you to the connection between the stimulus and the emotional reaction that you are having.

Later, I will briefly describe Gary Craig's technique and go into more detail with a variation of his protocol. This variation was developed by one of my mentors, Dr. David Feinstein. Feinstein's technique varies slightly from Gary Craig's technique, but the effect is the same. People who are suffering from anxiety, phobias, sadness, trauma, anger, and even physical pain are helped through this simple method of tapping on specific acupuncture points. It is believed that this technique helps to deactivate the neural connections between a thought or situation that evokes a particular neurochemical response and the emotion experienced. It defuses the connection so that a former thought or memory that caused you fear, anxiety or sadness can be "deactivated" so that it no longer arouses such an extreme response to the situation.

In my teaching, I have my face-to-face classroom students use this technique prior to our exams. Because many students have exam anxiety, if they go through a couple of rounds of this tapping technique, it deactivates their fight and flight response (sympathetic nervous system arousal) and allows them to think with their prefrontal cortex—the part of our mind that we need to recall answers for exams! When we are anxious, the blood is squeezed off to the thinking part of brain (prefrontal cortex) and the blood flows to the cerebellum where we can use habitual reactionary behaviors to save ourselves from harm or to fight off impending danger, such as our fear of not remembering the answers to exam questions! Students have told me that doing a couple of rounds of this tapping (energetic intervention) accompanied by a short affirmation (this is the cognitive component), they feel more alert, calm and ready to learn or take an exam or give a speech.

How does tapping on specific acupuncture points work to defuse the connection between our thoughts or a situation that causes a particular unwanted emotional response? The acupuncture points have what are called *mechanoreceptor* sites. These cells are more sensitive to mechanical stimulation that calms the fight or flight response. The calming effect caused by the tapping combined with the upsetting thought or stimuli is a form of counter-conditioning. We reverse the original upsetting emotion that is attached to the memory or stimuli in the environment and now instead of fear, sadness, or anger, one feels calmness.

Energy Psychology

Energy Psychology uses "…techniques from acupressure, yoga, qi gong, and energy medicine that teach people simple steps for initiating changes in their inner lives" (Feinstein, 2005). Using simple tapping techniques on acupressure points while engaged in a cognitive/imagery process similar to EMDR, a person is able to desensitize to formerly disturbing situations or thoughts.

Energy Psychology in Disaster Relief was the topic of a presentation I was privileged to attend with Dr. David Feinstein as the speaker. He recounted case after case of people who had been severely traumatized in Kosovo. Out of 150 patients with "249 specific memories of torture, rape, or witnessing the massacre of a loved one, 247 of those memories were "cleared" in the sense that the memory could be activated without the body going into a stress response" (Feinstein, 2006). Those numbers are phenomenal considering the difficulty of changing our limbic system reactions to trauma! Feinstein (2006) writes,

> Trauma is known to adversely change limbic system structures (involved in various emotions such as aggression, fear, pleasure, and also in the formation of memory) that are not easily corrected through talk or self-reflection (p. 21).

It has been shown that relief is more than symptomatic using energy psychology techniques because brain physiology is changed in the process. The characteristic digitized brain EEG signature of an anxious person is changed in just 4-12 sessions to that of a normal non-anxious person. Each session lasts about 30 minutes which has great implications for the time we have to spend in therapy to get better!

These techniques access the lower personality realm, or what Lipton (2005) calls the *subconscious*. Lipton is a cellular biologist, author, and former associate professor at University of Wisconsin's School of Medicine. He also pioneered research on cloned human cells at Wisconsin and Stanford University's School of Medicine. He believes that cognitive change is not sufficient to erase the programming we received as children because much of it is stored outside of conscious awareness in the form of conditioned responses (remember Pavlov's dogs?). Self talk and affirmations fail to reach this inner realm of the subconscious, which he considers to be the central control of consciousness that overrides our conscious efforts to change.

The Technique

When you are experiencing an overwhelming emotion, that is the time to identify what it is you are dealing with. You only have to create a setup word that will be the word that represents the memory or situation that evokes the overwhelming feeling. For example, if you are anxious about walking into your class to take your exam, your set up statement would go like this:

> "Even though I have this _____, I deeply love and accept myself" or if you don't buy into the idea that you deeply love and accept yourself, use a statement such as, "Even though I have this "anxiety" or 'insecurity" I am ready to make a positive change" or "my intentions are pure."

This statement combines the negative self-evaluation that you are having with a positive cognition or recognition of an opportunity. The negative thought or situation will then become the trigger for positive choice.

The tapping sequence requires that you use your two or three fingers together to thump on the following acupuncture points on your body 7-9 times each as you say your set up statement, preferably out loud. So if you are working on anger, your statement would be something similar to, "Even though I have this anger with my mother, I deeply love and accept myself."

Craig uses the following tapping sequence:

- H – top of the head
- EB – inner edge of the eyebrow
- SE – side of the eyes
- UE – under the eyes
- UN – under the nose
- CH – center of chin
- CB – collarbone
- UA – under the arm

The following is based on Feinstein's technique as it is described in his book, *Energy Psychology Interactive: Self-*

Help Guide. It is a condensed version of the detailed technique that he describes in his book. It is the basic format, but without all the details of the process. To learn more about the details, again, I refer you to his book.

Feinstein's technique uses the following sequence, 7-9 taps per location (this is the one that I use and teach my students):

- EB – inner edge of the eyebrow (above the bridge of your nose)
- SE – side of the eyes
- UE – under the eyes
- UN – under the nose
- CH – center of chin
- CB – collarbone (both sides simultaneously)
- Thymus (middle of the breast bone)
- UA – under the arm (4 inches below the armpit)
- Middle of the thighs on the outsides of the legs
- Karate Chop (hit the outer edges of both hands together)
- Between the little finger and ring finger on the backside of your hands (called the *Triple Warmer* meridian in acupuncture

Tapping Points

medicine), use your three fingers to tap 7-9 times on this area while saying your affirmation.

Do this sequence at least 2-3 times. This is the short version that I teach in the classroom. Feinstein then adds what he calls the 9-Gamut method. While continuing to tap on the Triple Warmer area, you would do the following:

- Close your eyes
- Open your eyes
- Move your eyes to the lower left
- Move your eyes to the lower right
- Rotate your eyes in a clockwise circle (360°) or in a figure 8 pattern
- Rotate your eyes in a counterclockwise circle or figure 8 pattern
- Hum a tune for a few seconds (Feinstein uses "Happy Birthday to you")
- Count to 5
- Hum again

That's basically all you have to do, and as I mentioned I don't teach the 9 Gamut to my students. They simply do the affirmation and the tapping sequences 2-3 times and most report that they feel more alert, calmer, less anxious, headaches disappear, etc.

Practice this tapping sequence so that you will remember what to do the next time you have an overwhelming emotion. Remember to identify what you are feeling and you can just use a word (such as "Fear" or "Mom") to capture the situation or emotion that triggers the emotion combined with the affirmation of "deeply love and accept myself."

In my teaching of psychology, I have had some success stories for students who have used this technique. One student had taught her son, who has ADHD symptoms, this technique and she claimed that after he did it a few times he was calm. After he did the sequence, she stated that they were able to share one of the best hours they had had in a long time.

Another interesting case study involves a man who was in the Vietnam war working with the MediVac unit. Ron (his name has been changed to protect privacy) suffered from nightmares at least 2-3 times every week. After taking my course that introduced students to EFT and the Six Healing Sounds (see below), he creatively combined two of the energy techniques that I taught and was able to reduce the number of nightmares to about 3 per month. This is extraordinary!

His last comment for the course after having used the technique for a few months was

> The one psycho-physical thing that has changed about me is that I am now a great believer in the power of meditation. Using the E.F.T. (Emotional Freedom Technique) in combination with the 6 Cosmic Healing Sounds (from the Universal Healing Tao Center) I have been able to control over 30 years of physically debilitating nightmares, after 35 years I've been able to quit smoking, lost over 40 lbs., and in general I am much more physically fit and emotionally free of stress.

Six Healing Sounds

It is one of the chi kung practices used in the *Universal Tao* system developed by Grand Master Mantak Chia, from whom I have received personal training for a number of years. Chi Kung works with the *chi*, or energy that is believed to flow through our bodies and is available everywhere. Doing chi kung frees the flow of energy in the body and cools down the visceral organs, leading to greater physical, emotional, and spiritual health. The latter section of this chapter details the combination of the EMDR process and the Six Healing Sounds, directing you in the process of combining these two energy techniques.

Do this exercise whenever you are feeling one of the major emotions of sadness, fear, anger, impatience or worry. This technique will help you to have more conscious control over your emotions. When you feel any of the emotions arising that I've listed below, do the corresponding Healing

Sound. It should help center you and change the negative emotion into its positive counter-emotion. You can also use this technique when you feel overheated. The healing sounds actually help to cool your organs. I like to use the Six Healing Sounds and combine it with EFT to address any emotional issues I may be experiencing or as a part of my daily meditative routine to clear and transform any negative emotions that arise during my day.

This exercise is based upon a practice that I have been studying since 2004 with Grand Master Mantak Chia. He teaches his methods of chi kung in almost every country in the world and is well known in chi kung circles. He comes to the U.S. to teach in the bay area and I have been fortunate to take a number of workshops with him in San Francisco at San Francisco State University and in Santa Cruz. Specifically, I am learning Healing and Medical Chi Kung, an ancient healing art of the eastern tradition.

Chi is an energy that is believed to exist everywhere. Although it cannot be detected directly, its effects have been measured through such instruments as Kirlian photography, galvanic skin response, heart rate, blood pressure, and other physiological instrumentation (Chia, 2001). The *chi* within our bodies is the same as the electromagnetic force of the universe. Science is beginning to find answers that are supporting what chi kung masters have known for over four thousand years. The human body is an energy producing and sustaining force and can be understood by using scientific knowledge.

Chi kung is a martial arts practice that works with the energy of the universe and within our bodies. By sending vital energy into our organs and to keep the chi flowing freely through our bodies, greater physical and mental health can be achieved. Medical *chi kung,* or healing chi kung, is based on this esoteric Taoist philosophy that helps us achieve no boundary consciousness (Chia, 1986a).

231

Greater health and happiness can be achieved through various meditations and exercises that utilize the abundant energy, or *chi,* from the universe and combine it with our own inner chi, or energizing force (Chia et al., 1993; Chia, 2001). What we all want is more energy. Working with chi kung helps us increase the energy in the cells of our bodies and spirit. We become healthier and happier.

One very effective meditation that can be done just about anywhere at anytime, is the chi kung method called *The Six Healing Sounds*. The *Six Healing Sounds* were discovered by Taoist Masters thousands of years ago (Chia, 1985). These sounds were believed to be

> the correct frequencies to keep the organs in optimal condition by preventing and alleviating illness...Chinese medicine teaches that each organ is surrounded by a sac or membrane, called *fascia,* which regulates its temperature. Ideally, the membrane releases excess heat out through the skin, where it is exchanged for cool life force energy from nature. An overload of physical or emotional tension causes the membrane, or fascia, to stick to the organ so that it cannot properly release heat to the skin nor absorb cool energy from the skin. The skin becomes clogged with toxins and the organ overheats. The Six Healing Sounds speed up the heat exchange through the digestive system and the mouth (Chia, 1985, p. 67-76).

In Chinese medicine, the five major organs, or viscera, of the body are believed to store specific emotions. When we are experiencing any of the negative emotions, we are overheating the associated organ in our bodies. In like fashion, when the organs are overheated or imbalanced energetically, we will feel these negative emotions more often.

As you practice the *Six Healing Sounds*, remember to breathe deeply and release the breath slowly as you do the sounds. It is best to sit while doing this practice. Wear comfortable clothing and avoid getting chilled during the practice. There are arm movements that can also be used to help facilitate the process, but I will not be introducing those movements here. In fact, I do the Six Healing Sounds whenever possible using the imagery alone while sitting or lying down. If you are interested in incorporating the arm movements, there is a link at the end of this chapter that illustrates the process for doing the Six Healing Sounds.

Major Organ	Color Association	Negative Emotion	Positive Emotion
Lungs	White	Sadness	Courage
Kidneys	Sky Blue	Fear/Anxiety	Gentleness/Stillness
Liver	Forest Green	Anger/Cruelty	Kindness/Generosity
Heart	Red	Impatience	Love, Joy, Happiness
Spleen/Pancreas	Yellow	Worry, Pity	Compassion, Fairness

Table 1. Emotions and the major organ systems.

Table 1 above, and Table 2 that follows, charts the major organs with their associated positive and negative emotions as well as the sounds to use for this technique. When you feel any of the negative emotions, you can counter them by filling your organs with the positive emotions. For example, the lungs should be imaged as silver/white in color. While focusing on your lungs (you can place your hands over your lungs), detect any sadness or depression you may be feeling. Seek to identify the sources of your sadness or depression, then transform these negative emotions into their positive counterpart—courage and righteous feelings.

In Table 2, the Healing Sounds associated with each organ are outlined. As you do the Six Healing Sounds, take a deep breath and let the sound out slowly, but not forcefully. The first healing sound is to cool the lungs. When you are experiencing any sadness or depression, smile down to your lungs, picturing them a bright white color. Put your hands lightly touching the area where your lungs are and then do the healing sound, "sssssssssssssssssss" like the sound of a snake.

Organ	Healing Sound
Lungs	sssssssssss (teeth together)
Kidneys	choooooooo (winter wind sound)
Liver	shhhhhhhhh (quieting a baby)
Heart	hawwwwww
Spleen/Pancreas	whooooooo (guttural)
Head to Foot Zones	
Triple Warmer sound	heeeeeeeeeeeeeee

Table 2. The Six Healing Sounds

We learn to train our energy and attention to the organs that create health. We shape intention by focusing on each major organ, examining if there is any of the negative emotion present, process it by identifying, one by one, the situations in our lives that are creating the sadness, fear, anger, impatience, or worry. This is the cognitive component that brings to consciousness your reasons for these emotions. You then use the corresponding Six Healing Sound to cool that particular organ (see Table 2). Note that the sixth sound is not associated with any particular organ, but reflects one of the major meridians in acupuncture theory.

The next organ you would cleanse and cool would be the kidneys. If you are experiencing fear and anxiety, then the kidneys are believed to be weak and out of balance. The kidneys are associated with the color blue, like the sky or ocean. While lightly touching your kidneys, image them blue and proceed to identify any anxiety you might be feeling and transform that into stillness. Also, detect any fear you are experiencing and then transform it into gentleness. The healing sound for the kidneys is "chooooooooo," like a train.

Following the Kidney sound, the next organ to cool is the liver. When you are continually angry, you are hurting our liver. First, identify the source of your anger if you can and then work to transform it into kindness. Also, examine the ways in which you may have been cruel, to yourself or others, and then transform the cruelty into generosity. When you are detecting the anger or cruelty in your liver, imagine that you are consciously contacting your liver by focusing upon it (it is located on the right side under your lower ribcage) and seeing green, like the forest. You would then do the liver sound, which is "shhhhhhhhhh," as when we try to comfort a baby.

Next is the heart. The heart is imaged as red while you detect any impatience and hastiness that you have been feeling. What are the sources of these feelings? Transform them into the positive emotions of love, joy, happiness, radiance, light and spirit. Do the healing sound for the heart, which is "hawwwwww."

The next organs to image are the spleen/pancreas/stomach and the color yellow. Detect any worry or pity and then transform it into compassion and fairness after identifying the sources of your worry or pity. Do the healing sound, a guttural "whoooooooo" which comes not from your mouth, but from the throat as you do the sound. Thus the "whoooooooo" sound comes from the back of the oral cavity, closing the throat to make a guttural sound. I spend time focusing on all three organs: the stomach, spleen, and pancreas in this part of the exercise.

The last sound is an overall cool down technique called the Triple Warmer. When you do the Triple Warmer sound, imagine that heat from the upper energy centers are moving down into the cooler lower centers. Pretend as if you are pushing heat down through your torso. Exhale using the Triple Warmer sound, "heeeeeeeee" as you imagine the heat moving down through your body, releasing through your feel, and going down into the earth. As you inhale, imagine that you are drawing the coolness of the earth up through your feet, cooling your body. Master Chia recommends that we lie down when doing the Triple Warmer sound.

> The Triple Warmer refers to the three energy centers of the body. The upper level, which consists of the brain, heart, and lungs, is hot. The middle section, consisting of the liver, kidneys, stomach, pancreas, and spleen, is warm. The lower level containing the large and small intestines, the bladder, and the sexual organs, is cool. The Triple Warmer Sound balances the temperature of the three levels by bringing hot energy down to the lower center and cold energy up to the upper center, through the digestive tract. This induces a deep, relaxing sleep (Chia, 1985, p, 101).

It is important that as you do the Six Healing Sounds, that you rest for a couple of breaths in between each sound, breathing naturally. You will notice a difference in the effects of the healing sounds when you do so. Even without breathing naturally between sounds, you will still gain a positive effect from doing these six healing sounds.

In body-mind fashion, chi kung teaches us to appreciate and care for ourselves by using the chi available in the universe and combining it with our own chi to heal ourselves and others. We learn to rid ourselves of negative emotions by using imagery to compost the negative emotions, sending them into the earth, and combining them with the positive counter emotion.

Taoist methods of expanding consciousness include the idea that we have three minds: the brain, the heart, and the gut (*tan tien*). The *tan tien* (about 3 finger widths below the navel) is a much smarter brain that uses less energy and definitely less words than the brain in our head! The *tan tien* is considered our center. As Master Chia teaches, "Make three minds into one mind." When you are caught up with thinking too much, move your center of awareness down into your heart. Once you are centered there, then move down into the *tan tien*. In Aikido, if we lead with our *tan tien* as we walk, we will seem strong and rooted to the earth. We are less likely to be a *pushover* because we can firmly stand our ground. Others sense this as well.

This has been an abbreviated version of the Six Healing Sounds. Some versions use different hand movements as you do the sounds. In an effort to streamline the practice, the hand movements can be eliminated without reducing the energy balancing that occurs when you do the Six Healing Sounds. I refer you to the book, *Transform Stress Into Vitality* by Mantak Chia (1985) for more details or go to the link that is provided at the end of this chapter.

EMDR and the Six Healing Sounds

Master Chia has recently incorporated the use of Eye Movement Desensitization and Reprocessing (EMDR) when utilizing the Six Healing Sounds in the practice of the Universal Tao system. According to the literature on EMDR, it is believed that the left/right pattern of eye movements assist in completing emotional processing. Most of us are not very good at letting go of our negative emotions, but through the practice of using the Six Healing Sounds we learn to compost the less healthy emotions of sadness, depression, fear, anxiety, anger, cruelty, impatience, hastiness, worry or pity and change or transform them into their positive counterpart emotions of courage, stillness, generosity, happiness and compassion.

EMDR has helped people overcome the inability to let go of negative memories that keep them from living a full and happy life. Getting closure to unfinished emotional trauma is essential to achieving health, both psychological and physical. In psychodynamic language, we are being affected by unconscious and unfinished business. When this happens a person continues to suffer long after the event has passed and suffers from these negative emotions. When we are processing negative emotions in the practice of the Universal Tao we are essentially putting behind us emotions with which we have had a long history.

Because we are human we cannot avoid feeling negative emotions, but if we can clear our organs each time we experience something negative then we can reverse the damage this negativity has on our psyche and bodies. When we hold onto bits and pieces of hurt, anger, impatience, fear, pity or sadness the result is an accumulation of that negativity in our organ systems. We seem to stand at readiness to feel and express the negative emotion all over again.

Most of us carry stuck emotions that impact our everyday lives and we fail to realize that these heavy emotions often come from the accumulation of feelings that have not been fully processed. We tell ourselves that we are over whatever happened that originally created our negative response. Yet when similar situations arise in our lives, we are primed and ready to experience the same negative emotion again. We anticipate that the past will repeat itself and we become hypervigilant for cues that validate our fears. The residual anger, fear, impatience, or depression keeps us ready to react again. This unfinished business is cumulative and we get stuck in a pattern of reviving the emotion in similar circumstances. Sometimes out of nowhere we will feel sad again, or anxious, fearful, or impatient.

When traumatic things happen to us, either physically or emotionally, we often are not prepared to deal with the situation sufficiently to enable us to gain closure. Some things that happen in life are so significant that they need only to occur once and it is seared into our emotional memory banks. Then there are the other types of trauma that come from sustained exposure to stress such as living in a family with a parent who is abusive, depressed, alcoholic or a drug addict.

Using the Six Healing Sounds, we work on processing the negative emotions from ourselves and infuse our organs with the more positive vibrations of the strengths associated with the organs. EMDR facilitates the speed at which we are able to feel the positive emotions and be less affected by the negative. When we take our negative emotions and mix them with their more positive, more fruitful counterpart, the eye movements help to process the emotions and beliefs. It is easier to turn sadness into courage; fear into gentleness and stillness; anger into generosity and kindness; worry into compassion and fairness; and impatience into love, joy and happiness.

Summary

Energy medicine is a growing and viable resource for helping people to help themselves. By using the full range of knowledge that comes from transpersonal research, we can broaden our ability to reach those populations who have not found relief through prescription drugs or traditional therapy. It is an exciting time where we can discover and harness the potential of human consciousness towards a greater happiness and well-being. With this knowledge and these techniques we come closer to reaching our potential and finding the seat of the soul.

WEBLINKS:

Grand Master Mantak Chia and the Six Healing Sounds:

    http://www.universal-
tao.com/slide_show/cosmic_healing_sounds/index.html

Multidisciplinary Association for Psychedelic Studies:

    http://www.maps.org/

Spiritual Emergence Network

    http://www.virtualcs.com/se/resources/senciis.html

Bruce Lipton and the New Biology:

    http://www.brucelipton.com/biology-of-belief-
overview

Bruce Lipton video - Nature, Nurture & the Power of Love:

    (part I):
http://video.google.com/videoplay?docid=2303414371520
8589

    (part II):
http://video.google.com/videoplay?docid=3848079041736
317218

Topic Eleven

Why Do I Feel Guilty When I Say, "No?"

What is anxiety? Inherent in human nature is our will, or the driving force from within that is the impetus behind our assertions of individuality. As we break away from conformity to assert our individuality, we hope to form a life filled with more personal meaning. Yet we often find ourselves feeling ambivalent about change—any change. Even when the current circumstances and our present way of living are not working for us, it seems that the status quo is easier. At least it is familiar and therefore, a known value. When we embark into unknown territory, *angst* builds and we experience anxiety. We lament the past and fear the future.

Existentialist Otto Rank (Menaker, 1982) proposed that the matrix for our anxiety came from the original mother/child dyad in which we first knew perfect *symbiosis* and then, separation. Each of us experienced symbiosis (i.e., the living together of two dissimilar organisms, especially when that association is mutually beneficial) in the womb. At birth, we began the arduous process of separation—breathing, feeding, staying alive through the care of others, eventually to become self-sufficient. Thus the symbiotic attachment in the womb does not completely end with our physical birth. We are forced to continue the process for many years.

At birth we separate physically from the womb or mother and progressively strive to move from total dependence and symbiotic attachment to a state of psychological separation. This psychological separation is perhaps even more difficult to achieve than our physical separation from the womb, but it is a necessary task that marks the emergence of one's self and soul.

Letting go of the familiar is not easy. Each time we assert our *will* it is as if we step away from others. We divide ourselves from the whole (e.g., our parents, peers, friends, their approval and the societal norm) to gain autonomy and a feeling of independence. In the process, we are suspended in the angst between the known and the unknown. We are pulled to the expression of the fullness of our individuality and the assertion of our uniqueness, yet concurrently desire to remain attached to the familiar. We cling to the familiarities of the past, and yet know that our movements towards self- actualization and individuation are essential to our psychological survival. We are torn, experiencing anxiety and conflict. We want to fit in, yet we also want to live as unique individuals. The anxiety we experience also stems from our empathic nature—we do not want to hurt other people because of our need to assert that individuality when it does not coincide with what others want or expect of us.

As we became more self-reliant and learned to walk, talk, and assert our *will*, we began the process of separation. Rank believed that this separation was a natural process in which we affirmed our individuality. Unless we embark upon the painful, yet rewarding journey of individuality, we would become *neurotic*. To be neurotic is to be emotionally reactive to situations that most people are able to handle. I characterize a neurotic reaction as an emotional upset that comes on quickly and is long lasting. We react strongly to emotional situations and we take a long time to get back to what we would consider to be "even" with our emotions.

Thus, being human requires that we break away from our psychological womb and make a conscious choice to separate from our symbiotic ties. This will is expressed through our creativity, asserting our preferences, daring to be different and pushing ourselves to actualize our potential. We also realize that when things are not going well, it is up to us to make changes in our lives or our perspective so that we are not so focused on the glass as "half empty."

The Will of the Individual

Will is neither good nor evil. Our personality and environment are products of our conscious *willing*. To label our *will* as good or bad does nothing to rid us of our nature, but simply serves to judge our behaviors according to externally superimposed criteria.

Psychoanalytic theory proposes that human *will* is basically bad and must be controlled. Freud felt that our instinctual drives were primarily oriented toward pleasure and away from pain without regard to others or society. This instinctual drive, which is primarily sexual in nature, has to be controlled. We are driven to avoid pain and gain pleasure, yet we are constrained by the dictates of society (e.g., laws, rules, and norms) that impede our ability to have what we want, when we want it. We learn that we have to wait and/or work for what we desire. This is the task of the *ego* according to Freud.

In our families, cultures, and society, we are usually taught to think of others and consider their needs while we pursue the gratification of our own needs. We are taught that we are selfish if we think too much about what we need or want. From this framework, when we assert ourselves we may feel bad for our impulses. We also realize that when we assert ourselves it may push us further away from others, which can cause inner conflict.

The *will* must be expressed, however, if we are to be happy. The first assertion of our *will* comes early in life and is generally negative in expression. This is when we first recognize that a "self" exists apart from the world around us. There comes a point in the development of all children when their need to individuate is expressed with a resounding "NO!" To say "no" is a powerful thing and every child knows this. How this assertion of the child's *will* is handled will have an influence on that person's sense of autonomy as she/he grows up.

In asserting our negative *will,* we are differentiating our desires from those around us and in a sense we are creating our individual existence by the power of this negation. This negative willing is not intrinsically defiant, but simply manifests in a negative expression that conveys our assertion—the message of individuality. When the budding teenager seeks to break from the norms set by society and create a "look" that is unique and individualistic, that behavior is defined as bizarre and "bad." But is it really bad or is it just different?

Every generation has had their hallmark to fame in history. The generations to come will not differ from previous ones in this respect. These assertions of the *will* and breaking away from others, creates a tension that is experienced as anxiety. Whether the assertions come from an individual or group, separation creates consequences for expressing a singular state. We feel a sense of alienation from the larger group but simultaneously feel a sense of empowerment with our assertions of individuality.

As we grow, the developmental thrust is constantly towards differentiation, and it is essential for us to do so. Yet the paradox of striving for our freedom is that we must let go of the known and familiar and embrace the new and unknown. Something must die in order for something new to be born. It is a sort of death in exchange for the opportunities of the unknown and the unfamiliar. We are torn between what "is" and what "can be." It is the eternal push/pull of the nature of our lives.

This double-edged sword is with us in every choice we make. When we individuate, we must let go of the past and embrace all that is implied in this. According to Otto Rank's theory, others are affected by our choices, creating an ethical dilemma for us that makes us feel guilty (Menaker, 1982). We feel guilty because we may be hurting others and at the same time feel guilty if we do not remain true to ourselves and go forward. We feel guilty for action or inaction. To be or not to be—that is the question.

The Separation/Symbiotic Paradox

Choosing growth over stagnation is healthy, yet there is always uncertainty attached to any new situation. We wonder if our need and wish to master a new situation overrides our capacity to do so. We doubt ourselves and become caught in a cognitive struggle between our need to be separate and our need to maintain the symbiotic tie. As we assert our *will* to grow, we do so timidly because paradoxically we deny our dual need. We are often stymied because of our emotional attachment to the past and our fear of the unknown.

To explain this quandary, Rank, who was reared in the Freudian tradition, originally claimed that it was the actual birth experience that created our *fixation*. If you will recall, the term *fixation* describes a state in which we have either had our needs met too well or not well enough. This causes us to become preoccupied compulsively to fulfill this need. We became fixated at the moment of birth to return to the perfect state of oneness that we experienced in the womb. This extreme change from the uterine environment into the "real world" becomes the prototype for our later anxieties. While in the womb, we were safe, surrounded by the amniotic fluid, cushioned from the harsh external environment. As we emerged from the womb we were overcome with the flooding of physiological excitation that could not be overcome. This anxiety served to *fixate* us on the desire to return to the womb and its safety, warmth and familiarity. Rank called this our *primal anxiety*, which became the template for all future anxiety.

The mother and child are attached to one another in the beginning, but through growth and the passage of time *differentiation* is achieved. At first, this is a perceptual discrimination but later becomes a volitional act of "willing" that occurs in a child (and many mothers too). Although this splitting occurs, the legacy of the original *symbiotic* relationship remains in the form of shared empathy. We are thus able to put ourselves in the other's shoes because initially, we were one with the other.

Remembering that it is human nature to *individuate* (to become an individual distinct from others), it was here at the beginning of life that the problem of separation/symbiosis began. Our birth is more than a physical act and requires that we experience the birth of our own unique consciousness as we grow. Originally, Rank believed that we had to reenact a physical rebirth to achieve psychological health. He later evolved his theory to affirm that it was a *psychological birth* that one must experience—a creation of the personality.

At birth, one achieves physical separation, but a psychological division remains to be accomplished wherein we can identify with another person yet see the differences that exist as well. Whenever we assert our individuality, a conflict is set up between our self-assertion and our empathic feelings for the other, especially if our *will* opposes their *will*, wishes or needs. When applied to gender related behaviors and identity it can be seen that we may well be caught in a double bind. We seek social approval and creative individuality at the same time. The two may be diametrically opposed to one another.

One solution to this dilemma is to give up *willing* so that we can avoid the overwhelming anxiety inherent in our struggle for autonomy. At the same time we could alleviate any fear of separation from the mother so that we can maintain our symbiotic tie. Of course this would develop a masochistic life style and is hardly a creative or healthy remedy. The psychological cost of this solution would likely be neurosis. It would require an excessive suppression of our "*will* to be," to individuate, and to be emotionally spontaneous.

An alternative solution would be to become active co-creators of our own reality. Co-creation is an acknowledgement that we play an intricate role in the development of our reality. This creation implies assertion of the *will* that leads to choices—choices in the outer world and in our actions, but also choices in our perceptual outlook. Our choices in life present us with opportunities and our choices in perception help determine the color of our reality.

Hand in hand with active choosing is the weight of responsibility for our choices. Knowing that we are responsible for our lives, we move forth into the future. We cannot change the past but we can change the way that we have interpreted that past. If we allow ourselves to make the choices in our lives, we realize that we have many choices before us. We can gather as much information as possible before making a choice or decision. This gathering of information gives us a wider perspective of the alternatives in life.

A Tool for Overcoming Guilt

Feeling guilty when we say *no* comes from our birth experience according to Rank, but there are other reasons for this guilt as well. Females, especially feel guilt when they say *no* because as a gender, females are expected to be the caretakers and nurturers in our society. Our families, peers and teachers also have a hand in shaping our sense of guilt. We use guilt as a way to get others to do what we want them to do.

Guilt plagues some more than others. If you are someone who is prone to feeling guilty and therefore you never say *no,* I have developed a useful tool to help you to see things differently. It's one of my favorite tools and very inexpensive. You can make it yourself, in fact. Take a blank piece of paper and write the word "NO" on one side and "YES" on the other side. You can even make a fancier "tool" by using fancier or heavyweight paper. Paint the words on each side in fancy script if you like.

This tool's usefulness is based on the idea that we might need to change our perception of how saying *no* to others is perceived. We've probably been told that we were *selfish* when we said *no* to others. Our friends ask us for a favor and even when we are overloaded with things to do, we cannot say *no.* If we say *no,* we feel guilty. What we forget is that when we tell others *yes,* we are often saying *no* to ourselves. Telling others *no* can create guilt, but telling ourselves *no* too often creates resentment. We resent that we are over-stretched, over-committed, and under nourished. We feel neglected, but are others neglecting us, or are we neglecting ourselves because we find it difficult to tell others *no?* We need to balance our lives by creating enough space for ourselves as well as for others. We need to say *yes* to

250

ourselves as well as saying *yes* to others. By achieving more balance, we will feel less resentment and guilt. We will be taking better care of ourselves.

This is where the *Yes/No* tool comes into play. As you learn to say *no* more often without feeling guilty, you'll need to use this card less. Actually, you don't have to use it when you exercise your power to assert yourself, but it is your reminder. Hold the card in front of you with the *No* facing outward and away from your body. The *Yes* will be facing you. Now when you say *No* to others, you will see that the *Yes* is facing you. You can tell the person to whom you had to say *no* that, "I'm sorry that I have to tell you *no* at this time. Please don't take it personally, but I must say *yes* to myself first at this time. I hope that you understand." Simple, yet powerful.

Recommended Exercise:

Complete *Exercise Two – Basic Fears Exercise* after you have read this topic on feeling guilty. It should help you recognize your inner voices that hold you back through either resorting to the Desperate Child or the Tough Child.

Topic Twelve

Love or Approval

In the wisdom of the Humanistic Movement, we are motivated by an intrinsic need to *become* the fullest possible expression of our unique individuality. In other words, we have an internal mechanism that forces us to strive to discover and live our potential. We are *pulled* to the future towards *self-actualization*. Abraham Maslow, father of Humanistic psychology, strongly believed that our need to live to our fullest potential was intrinsic to being fulfilled human beings. He warned us, "You must be...the very best you are capable of becoming. If you deliberately plan to be less than you are capable of being, then I warn you that you'll be deeply unhappy for the rest of your life. You will be evading your own capacities, your own possibilities."

According to Maslow's hierarchy of needs, we are influenced by our needs. If those needs are biological or physiological, then they will exert more pressure on us than needs that are psychological, such as the needs for safety, belongingness, or esteem. He considered lower levels of his hierarchy as deficit or *Deficiency Needs* (D-Needs). These D-Needs exert a force on our behaviors to have those needs met, but he did not consider those needs to be expressions of self-actualization.

Often, the lower needs are expressions of conformity or approval seeking behaviors. We do what we need to do in order to survive and to fit in. We move up the hierarchy in our pursuit of discovering the authentic self.

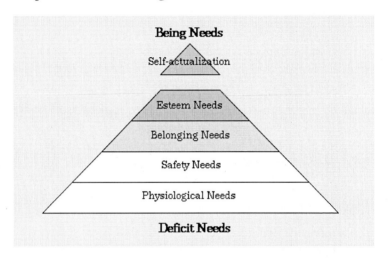

The Being Needs, or B-Needs imply that we are meta-motivated—beyond motivation. We now live with aesthetic qualities in life being more important than fitting in with others. These aesthetic qualities are seeking goodness, mercy, kindness, justice, beauty, aliveness, wholeness, simplicity and playfulness. When we are less motivated by lower instinctual needs or the need for recognition by others, we can begin to live a life of individuality. We actualize the self within.

Another famous humanistic psychologist, Carl Rogers, called this our *self-concept*, which was formed primarily through social contact and interaction with others (Schultz, 1990). One of the most powerful shaping forces to this self-concept comes from our need for *positive regard* from others. We want to feel valued not for what we do, but for who we are. When we are nurtured and our individuality is encouraged, we are able to develop a more authentic self. We discover bits of self and over time, with the right conditions we emerge as *fully-functioning* individuals.

Unfortunately, too many people are not so lucky to have been reared with tenderness, love, guidance, and acceptance. There are many variations in parenting styles and each type creates a particular challenge to children growing up in these types of families. We mustn't feel alone or different if we were reared in dysfunction because it has been estimated that approximately 97% of all people grow up in families with varying degrees of dysfunction.

When we grow up under such conditions where our sense of worth comes from what we do or don't do, then we become inauthentic and develop a *false self* so that we can fit in. "We come to see ourselves according to what others think rather than what we feel" (Schultz, 1990, p. 373). When we think of ourselves in a particular way, we are generally holding up our behaviors and characteristics to some external standard. We compare ourselves against a socially approved and formed image of what is considered to be acceptable behavior—whether it is feminine or masculine, good or bad.

Consequently, we act in ways that meet with approval so that we can get the next best thing to positive regard. We settle for *approval* and equate that with love. This can lead to the development of codependence. Codependence is not defined as being dependent upon having a significant other in a relationship as many believe. Instead, it is when our sense of self-worth and value are dependent upon meeting the needs of others! We become so focused on what others need that we have no knowledge or regard for our own needs. It is a state wherein we are unsure of our own feelings, desires, needs, and expectations. We like what others like. We try to please. We try to help others to "do the right thing" (as if we could know what is truly right for others). Codependence influences a person to ignore her inner needs, probably because she has never identified what those needs are. So, conditions-of-worth are imposed upon us by others in their attempts to shape our conformity to acceptable standards and we come to believe that our worth is dependent upon those conditions. "Little girls are supposed to be quiet! Little ladies don't act that way! Big boys are tough! Can't you take it? Suck it up, son!" Our inner nature becomes adjusted by the requirements of conformity.

In an ideal world, Rogers believed that we would not develop this *false self* if we were given *unconditional positive regard.* This is the type of acceptance from others wherein we are prized and valued for who we are without reservation (Ryckman, 1989). Even when we do something that is unacceptable, we are not ridiculed, but are given guidance and we receive positive regard acknowledging our intrinsic value. For example, when children misbehave, we need to remember to not attack the child, but to admonish the behavior. It is harmful to the children if we tell them that they are *bad.* You've heard it before, "You are a *bad* girl (or boy)!" This type of comment when heard repeatedly gets incorporated into the developing mind of a child. That child begins to believe that he or she truly is bad. Contrast that statement with one wherein the behavior is attacked, but not the child. "Honey, I love you and you are a wonderful girl (or boy), but *what you just did* is not acceptable." Then you can pose alternative behaviors that would have been better. In this way we can still express unconditional love without letting our children run wild.

Whether our childhood rearing has been beneficial to us or not requires us to ask some hard questions. How were you treated as a child? Did you feel valued or heard? Did you feel cared for or were you neglected or abused? Did your parents' expectations coincide with what you found meaningful in life? Ask yourself, "Did I feel valued and appreciated in my family? Were my feelings acknowledged? Were my parents able to give me the love that I needed? Did I *deserve* the treatment I received? Were my parents there for me emotionally? Were they overly strict and demeaning? Were they belittling to my basic feelings of worth?"

Our need for positive regard is so compelling that our self-perception may be merely a cumulative reflection cast by the mirror of others. We may feel one way, but act in ways that oppose our inner wisdom because by doing so we gain approval. We distort the inner message and believe that acceptance is more important than doing what is conducive to our growth towards being a more fully functioning human being (Rogers, 1961). Trust in our experience and assignment of meaning to that experience is therefore component processes in the development of an accurate self image.

To help us on our journey to actualization or individuation we need to heed the messages from within. Much of the process of growing up and our need for love, belongingness and acceptance cause us to distort the "gut" feelings we experience. We often times deny what we are feeling because our need for love and approval is so great that we "think away" the feeling. We rationalize the behavior of others or we internalize negative evaluations as accurate reflections of ourselves. Ultimately, we explain away any inconsistencies that we may detect on a more intuitive level. By trusting our inherent wisdom or our *biological wisdom*, we can measure our "primal response" to events and determine if we are acting or responding in self-enhancing ways. Tuning into this internal meter creates a barometer of our emotional and visceral response to experience.

"I had a dream of my Uncle Ark, standing in a bamboo grove in China…looking at me as if he had something to say…"

Topic Thirteen

Understanding Dreams

Humans are symbolic creatures. We tend to think, or imagine more in pictures or symbols rather than by using words. Erich Fromm wrote extensively on the subject in his book, *The Forgotten Language*. The saying, "A picture is worth a thousand words" is descriptive of the power of symbols to our comprehension of situations. Words limit our understanding and are subject to being misunderstood. If we paint a picture, a person is more likely to understand the deeper meaning of what we are saying.

Myths are symbolic expressions of living. At a level deeper than the conscious mind, we understand the meaning behind symbolism, metaphors, myths and fairy tales. These forms of expression speak to our unconscious, which somehow allows our conscious self to truly "know." For example, if I tell you that I am not feeling well, you get a basic idea that I am not feeling healthy, or not feeling like myself, or a number of other interpretations that may be correct or not. If I paint a picture for you, however, you will get closer to what I am trying to convey. "I feel like I'm out on the ocean in a leaking rowboat. I have no oars and no land is in sight. My hands and feet are bound and I am blindfolded. A terrible storm is brewing and the seas are beginning to rock." Get the picture?

To better explain symbolic understanding, let's look at our dreams. We dream in symbols but they are disguised. According to Jung, our dreams compensate for our conscious attitudes—they are *compensatory* to our waking life and reveal what we are *not* considering in our conscious, waking state. The meaning behind this symbolic content comes to the forefront when we sleep and is like the unconscious is tapping us on the shoulder and saying, "Excuse me. Yes, it is true that you are aware of this and that in this situation, but have you thought to look at this situation from *this* point of view? Maybe if you would pay attention to this neglected aspect of your psyche, the solution to your problems will become clearer."

Dreams are symbolic expressions of unconscious content attempting to bubble up into consciousness according to this psychoanalytic viewpoint. This awareness is not conscious when we are awake, but when we sleep it is as if the guard at the gate (our ego, according to Freud) also sleeps. Now the unconscious and possibly threatening information has a chance to rise up into our conscious mind so that we gain new information or are reminded of unfinished business.

Of course, dreams leave us with additional work. Dreams are not straightforward expressions of the unconscious. Our unconscious speaks to us in symbols, therefore, our dreams consist of images and situations that symbolize something personally meaningful to us. These images and situations in dreams are disguised, however, and require us to do more work to discover the dream's hidden meaning. We have to interpret what the symbols and situations in our dreams mean by analyzing different aspects of the dream. We look at the props that are in our dream, the people and what they are doing or not doing, what they are saying or not saying. The things and people in our dreams should not be taken literally because we must make our own unique associations to those parts of our dream in order to uncover the disguised meaning.

Since it is our dream, we alone know them meaning of that dream, but the meaning of our dream is elusive because of this symbolism. We are the writer, director, producer, actors and actresses of the dream. We have placed all the people and props in our dreams and have chosen the setting for that dream, but the meaning is disguised. We have to separately analyze each piece of the dream and every prop and person in it to discover the personal meaning these dream symbols and situations may have for us. Through perseverance, the underlying meaning presented by our unconscious can be revealed.

An example might be helpful. Perhaps you have dreamt of being in a situation where you are naked, but no one notices except for you. The meaning of this aspect of the dream can be amplified by using the technique of *association* as developed by Jung (Johnson, 1986). *Association* is a process wherein we make as many associations to the important people, objects or props, conversations or situations that were a part of the dream. The two symbolic situations I would amplify are "to be naked" and, that "no one notices."

Using the technique of association, the dreamer would take the word "naked" and associate as many meanings as possible. Put the word in a circle and then draw lines from the circle directly to each word that you associate with the dream symbol (word), object, or phrase. Additionally, the phrase "no one notices" would be a useful dream condition to amplify as well. The key to this method is to make your associations directly to the symbolic object, phrase or statement each time. For example, my associations to "naked" would be as follows: naked = vulnerable; then return to the word "naked" = open; return to the word, naked = revealed; back to naked = unadorned; naked = natural; naked = unprotected. My associations to "no one notices" are: "no one notices" = I am alone; "no one notices" = I feel unseen; "no one notices" = I have hidden emotions; "no one notices" = I am invisible; "no one notices" = I feel ignored. Once all associations have been made, select the associations that have the most significance to the situation you find yourself in at the time you had this dream. Circle them. Ask yourself how these associations reveal the hidden emotions or messages of your current situation?

From the Jungian-Senoi method (Williams, 1985) we can also analyze what others are saying or not in our dreams. If in our dream we are in danger and our family is there, but they do or say nothing, this is important to our understanding of the dream. If they do say something, what is it that they have said? Since this is our dream, we wrote the script. "Why didn't they help?" "Why didn't they say anything," or "Why did they say what they said?" Now, put yourself into the shoes of the other people in your dream and ask yourself, "How am I just like this person?" After you have made those connections you would then ask yourself, "In what ways does that part of myself that is similar to that person, treat me as I was treated by this person in my dream?"

Another method to bring meaning to dream symbols comes from the gestalt therapeutic methods of Fritz Perls (1972). I will describe what Perls referred to as the Empty Chair technique. What he meant by the Empty Chair is that we place those people in our lives with whom we are having difficulty into the chair (metaphorically or symbolically) and talk to them. We pretend that they are sitting in the empty chair and we then speak to the chair as if the person was sitting there. Your voice serves to represent both people in the interaction however—the other person and your self. So you place two chairs facing each other and you sit in one and pretend that the other person is in the other chair—the empty chair. You create a dialogue and ask your questions or state your feelings to the other person. You then get up and sit in the empty chair. You would then assume the persona of the other person and you reply to the questions or statements that you made when you were in "your" chair. Physically moving to the empty chair is helpful because it allows us to have a different perspective than if we simply reply from *our* chair. This method helps you to get at the root of your fears or feelings about the situation and helps you work out a dialogue for the "real" conversation that you might have with that person.

To duplicate this process for working with your dreams, you become the props and people who were in your dream. It is your dream where you are the director, producer, actors Remember that when you are working with your dream, these people and objects were in your dream because you put them there! To use the Empty Chair technique, you would put the person or object from your dream in the Empty Chair and then speak for them—you become their voice.

For example, take an object like a chair that happens to be in your dream. You may not think that it is very significant in the context of a dream yet you must ask yourself why you put that particular chair in your dream. What type of chair was it? Was it covered in fabric or leather? Was it new or tattered? Was it comfortable? Was it familiar? Illuminating the symbolic message of the reason for the chair being in your dream reveals its symbolic meaning. Using Perls' technique we can amplify the meaning by becoming the chair: "I am hard. People sit on me when they are tired. I endure much weight and help to support others so that they can rest. I don't mind too much if I am tipped over for I am durable and sturdy."

263

On an almost intuitive level illumination occurs when we work with symbols. With this example it could be suggested that the chair represents the part of this person's personality that feels the weight of others leaning upon her and is yet willing to allow others to continue to impose upon her to the point of being "tipped" off balance. She is tough. She can handle it, but the dreamer must then ask herself if this is really her truth. Can it be that she is feeling the need to lean on someone herself? Maybe she does not need nor want to be so tough. When the symbols are illuminated, we have an "Aha!" experience. "Aha! Now I see what is going on!" We *know* on an intuitive level what our unconscious is trying to say to us. Similar to pictures or metaphors such as, "This situation I find myself in is like a double-edged sword," association to our dream symbols enables us to relate to our dreams at a level of knowingness that is deeper than our cognitive self.

Recommended Exercise:

Complete *Exercise One - Dreamwork Exercise* after you have read this topic on Understanding Dreams. It will help you to better understand the symbolism of dreams and to help reveal the hidden contents of the unconscious.

Awakening...

Conclusion

The Awakened Self journey is never over. We traverse our path, and with each step we take, we remember who we are and who we can become. Armed with the knowledge, tools and enlightenment developed over the pages of this book, each day promises a new beginning...one in which we can awaken to recognize when we are being taken over by old paradigms that we have lived by in the past. We learn to recognize our demons and to let go of the old stories that had formerly guided our perceptions, moods, behaviors and dreams. Yet, we also know that these deeply embedded habitual reactions that were formed when we were young, may never go completely away.

The most useful thing we can do is to be awake and aware of when these old buttons surface in our psyche or behaviors. We don't need to berate ourselves when this happens, but only to acknowledge that the old ways have arisen and that we can actively choose a different response than the one that was programmed. Through this repetitive blocking of old ways of behavior, we loosen the neural nets and create new pathways for our brain to help us live our lives as we desire. When these old irritations arise again, with compassion for ourselves we acknowledge, "Ahh! Irritation again!" and we open our hearts so that we can live from our soul. No need to react any more. Breathing deeply, centering ourselves in our hearts, we mindfully take it all in and learn to respond, instead of reacting.

To be Awakened and to live from the Self is to take responsibility for our own lives without blaming our past, our parents, or society. Awakening implies that we consciously make moment-to-moment choices to live an authentic path, living from our hearts instead of our heads. Knowing that our Awakening was always what we wanted and needed, we can venture forth renewing our lives and committing to our newfound truths, changing the ways we interact with our children and grandchildren so that they too, can Awaken to their potential. It is never too late to choose a new, healthier way of living in the world. To awaken and love.

Namaste. ~

Exercises

Exercise One

Basic Fears Exercise

Many of us have a child within who is much younger than our actual chronological age. This is a result of the many unmet needs and expectations inherent in the growing process as well as from abuses or neglect we may have suffered. This exercise is designed to help you get in touch with the reactions to those basic fears that may be keeping you from achieving the wholeness you desire.

Through completion of this exercise, you will learn to recognize two inner voices that feed your perception. One is called the *Tough Child* and the other is the *Desperate Child*. As you can imagine, each voice within us serves to cover up what we are really feeling. One voice takes the position of submission, begging others to accept you or to make it better. The other voice comes from a place where we may fear that our dependence on others hinders us from moving forward. Either way, both voices are extreme positions, but in the process of identifying those voices, we can discover how we throw up defenses that seem to help us ward off anxiety. By hearing the voice of the *Desperate Child* and the *Tough Child*, you can consciously change your reactions into responses that honor your feelings and needs without becoming defensive or overly needy.

Step 1: Identifying My Fears

Try to identify at least four basic fears. These are generally statements that you tell yourself about why you cannot have what you want. For example, here is a sample list of basic fears:

1. I am not lovable.
2. There is something wrong with me.
3. I am not wanted.
4. I will be abandoned.

Step 2: The Tough Child

First you will react from the *Tough Child Within*. This is the child in you who has had to act as if she/he didn't really care—the survivor. Look at each of your statements and react to each one of them as if you are a "tough kid." Write out all the possible internal messages you may say to yourself in reaction to each of your basic fears. For example, using the above listed fears:

1. **Not lovable**: "I don't care if I am loved or not. Tough. I can handle it. I don't need them anyway! I'll show you how unlovable I am. Who needs it?!"

2. **Basically flawed**: "I will try to be perfect or an overachiever so that I cannot be criticized. Unassailability. Beyond reproach. I'll act as if I do not have this hole in my aura. In essence, I will ignore it."

3. **Not wanted**: "I will be fiercely independent. I can take care of myself. I don't need anyone to help me. I can do it myself. I don't want to be here anyway. This place stinks! There are better places than this. I don't like you anyway. If you don't want me, someone else does! You'll be sorry you didn't try harder. You'll want me someday but I won't want you."

4. **Abandoned**: "I'll leave you before you leave me. I like being alone anyway. You already left anyway, so just leave! I don't need you anyway."

Step 3: The Desperate Child

Next you will take the opposite stance and react from the Desperate Child within. This is the child who wants to please and make it all better. This voice whines, begs, pleads and says that it will do anything to gain approval. Again, write out as many thoughts as you may have to each basic fear. For example:

1. **Not lovable**: "Yes I am. I am lovable. See all the neat things I do for you. See how nice I am. I will be like you want me to be, then you will love me. I will try to figure out what you want and need, meet those needs at all costs, be the way you want me to be, then you will see how lovable I really am."

2. **Flawed**: "I feel as if I am a frog. Everyone can see the big hole in me. It is obvious. I have to hide and not let anyone close or otherwise they'll see how awful I really am. Let's focus on the imperfection in you then we won't have to look at my faults or *holes*."

3. **Not wanted**: "Why don't you want me? Why did you pretend you did in the first place? Why did you have me then? What am I doing here then? But I'm the best thing that ever happened to you. How can you not want me?"

4. **Abandoned**: "Don't leave me! Stay here right by me and don't leave me alone. I'm afraid to be alone. I'll die if you leave me. Who will take care of me? I'm, afraid of the dark! Hold me. Press me to you so we can be connected. I want to become a part of you, I want to be so essential to your life that you can't live without me. Enmeshment. A Shadowen." [Shadowen: An entity that tries to merge with another in order to be nourished and

273

feeds off of the host, becomes that host, but only in a sick way (Introduced by fantasy writer, Terry Brooks in his Shannara series).

Step 4: Insights

What insights have you had after "hearing" your two voices? What did you learn from hearing your *Tough Child* voice? Your *Desperate Child* voice? List the insights you may have had regarding this exercise. Do you understand better how your fears and your reactions to these fears may be keeping you from having what you want, whether it is more intimacy, more self confidence or a better life? What did you learn about yourself?

Exercise Two

Positive Programming Exercise

Just as a warrior prepares for battle by conditioning his body, mind and attitude, this exercise will equip you with some necessary mental and attitudinal armor for your quest. We attract to us those things that we think about. To achieve our goals, we must first get past the sentry at the gate of consciousness. That guard is our own mind. Our creative energy has to filter through our beliefs and ways of being. If we are blocking the creative process through negative, defeated attitudes, then we will be unable to actualize what we desire. In order for us to produce what we want, we have to believe that we can create and achieve those goals.

Our beliefs are formed through our experiences and they guide our actions. Like a computer, we operate according to the information that has been programmed into our minds. Even if the information is erroneous, the "computer" will process and create output based upon that data. The old tapes may be feeding you negative messages that will only serve to block your progress. As Richard Bach said in his book, *Illusions*, "Argue for your limitations and sure enough, they're yours." If you tell yourself that you will never be able to achieve something, you probably won't. When we convince ourselves, "I can do it!" somehow we find a way to make it happen. Psychologists refer to this as a *self-fulfilling prophecy*. Our belief in positive statements may have no more basis in reality than the negative statements, but they will impact our choices and actions in ways that make our statements true.

Changing the Tapes

Become aware of any negative tapes you may be playing over in your head. Every day, become more conscious of the negative statements that you may be telling yourself. You may be surprised how many times each day you may be feeding yourself negative beliefs such as, "I am so stupid!" or "I'll never get this right!" or "Bad things always happen to me!" Our perceptions help formulate the reality we experience.

In cognitive psychology, much mental dysfunction is considered a result of faulty thinking. This can range from making global conclusions based on one incident in our life, or it can consist of the damaging effects that negative self-talk can produce. Negative self-talk can be just as detrimental as if someone is constantly telling you how inadequate you are. In fact, it is the same only you do not need another person there to do it for you because you do it to yourself. These self-defeating messages are what I call our negative self-tapes. These are the hours and hours of programming that our mind and personality have undergone in the process of growing up. They generally include the demeaning and belittling messages we received such as, "You are such a bad girl (boy)! Can't you do anything right? You are so stupid! You can't do that! You'll never amount to anything."

Creating and repeating positive affirmations is a method that will help to counteract the damaging effects of these negative tapes that we all carry within us. The task is to

276

create a new library of positive messages that convey the idea that we are wonderful, worthwhile human beings and that we can achieve whatever we set out to accomplish. By creating self-affirming messages we can change the old voices for new ones.

An affirmation is a positive message that you create to declare to yourself that you can achieve what you set out to do, that you are o.k., and that life is positive. Affirmations help to "program" or "reprogram" your mind and to bolster your self-esteem. When you believe that something is possible, then you will begin to act as if it is so. Your beliefs guide your perceptions and thus affect your responses. Like a self-fulfilling prophecy we come to believe what we are told. We thus act in ways that make our beliefs a reality.

On a sheet of paper, create your chart similar to the one I've produced below, following these three steps:

Step 1

Make a list of those things that you would like to have in your life. Try to be specific: "I wish I had more confidence in myself; I wish I had my college degree; I wish I was happier; I wish I had more money. I wish that I could find love. I wish that I knew what I wanted out of life."

Step 2

Next, take each of the items in your list and below those items list all the reasons why you cannot have what you desire. Using the examples above, you might write that the reason you cannot have more confidence is because, "No one likes me." or "I'm too stupid" or, "I'm too ugly." In response to your desire to achieve your college degree, you may be telling yourself, "It will take too long," "I'm not smart enough," or there's too many people who are smarter than I am."

It is good to list more than one response for each thing that you want to have. Write as many as you can because this negative self-talk represents your core negative beliefs about yourself and life. You may be surprised at some of the messages you tell to yourself when you want something.

Step 3

Now, for each negative statement you wrote, form a positive affirmation that expresses the attainment of those qualities or achievements. Your affirmations are positive affirming statements that feel encouraging. They are also written as if they are currently true. In other words, using phrases such as "I will try to ….." implies that you won't do it. You will "try," but will you "do" it? Instead, use a phrase such as "I am…."? This programs your mind as if you are already doing what you hope to do or that you already have what you desire. Keep your affirmations in the present tense as if you are already there. An example of this process is listed below:

What I want	Why I Can't Have It	My Affirmations
1. More self-confidence	"I'm too ugly." "I'm too self conscious." "Nobody likes me." "I don't have anything important to say."	"I am self confident and assured." "I love myself." "I have many good qualities."
2. College degree	"I'm too dumb." "It takes too long." "I'll never pass my classes!" "I'm too old."	"I am achieving my educational goals." "I am excelling in my studies." "My age makes me wise."

3. Happier   "I'm too depressed."   "I am at peace with the world
              "Nothing is going right!"   and everyone in it."
                                         "I make choices that reflect
                                          my needs and desires."

4. Money   "There aren't any jobs."   "I trust myself in
            "I don't have any skills."   everything."
              "No one will hire me."   "I am a fast learner."
                                        "I am enjoying the
                                        abundance that life
                                        provides."

This is a great tool that you can use throughout your life. As you do this exercise, you'll catch yourself in your negative moments and be able to create a more positive affirmation on the spot, stopping the cycle of global catastrophic thinking.

Exercise Three

Questioning the Question

Questioning the Question is an exercise that will start the bubbles in the unconscious to churn. By asking questions we learn much about how we been programmed as children, and also how today we may be repeating these preprogrammed beliefs, actions, thoughts and feelings. We learn to query our lives so that we can live consciously.

In *The Mythic Journey*, Sam Keen stated that finding the answers to our questions was not as important as the questions we ask of ourselves. Asking questions of ourselves evokes a process that raises our awareness because we no longer live life on automatic. Each time we pose a question to ourselves about who we are, how we got that way, who contributed to this process, what those influences were, and about the beliefs we hold about ourselves and/or others, we move out of automatic conditioning and awaken our consciousness. The questioning process is endless and it is likely that you will discover that asking one question leads to several other questions. For example, if I ask myself, "What is my purpose?" it leads me to ask, "Do I have to have a purpose?" or, " How will I know when I have discovered my purpose?" This then evokes another question in me, "How will I know if it is my purpose or someone else's script for me?"

To discover the Self requires that we embark upon a journey inward to uncover and discover who we are and who we can become. Questions allow us to examine aspects of our lives that we may not have asked before. Like so many automatons we go about our lives repeating the programs we have been taught without questioning whether these programs enhance our lives or whether they fit us. Who programmed us? What did we learn? Does it work for us?

This exercise helps us explore the Existential approach in psychology where we learn that the challenges to life (or existence) stem from our mortality. The paradox of life is that we will die. More poignant is the fact that we are conscious of this fact. We are born and eventually learn that life is finite—we all die someday. So, how are we to live a life of meaning and purpose knowing that we won't always be here?

Existentialists inform us that the problems in life are focused around issues of *love, work,* and *play* and how these activities and situations fit into our lives. Can I find meaning in this life that I am living? Is my *work* meaningful? Do I believe in the causes of my chosen career? Are they in line with my larger beliefs? What part does *play* have in my life? Do I always have to be working? How much fun do I allow myself? What is love to me? When do I feel love? Who will love me? Who will I love? Can I *love* fully? Am I loveable?

Directions:

Get a piece of paper and pen or work on a computer. Ask yourself, "What questions can I ask myself that will help me on this existential journey?" Recall that existentialism

281

explains that our dilemmas in life arise from our questions about our existence. What are your questions about your existence?

You may find that there are a few categories that emerge in the process, or you can start out the process by using the areas of Love, Work, and Play to develop your questions. For example, in the category of Love, I might ask:

- What is love?
- How do I know what love is?
- Where did I learn this?
- Who makes me feel loved?
- When do I feel loved?
- Is there a difference between love and approval?

You will find that as you identify questions, you'll be tempted to answer them right then and there! Don't do it! Just keep writing down questions in your categories. These questions are jewels that will lead you to a richer life. What I love about this exercise is that as time goes by we tend to continue the process, catching ourselves in an action, thought, feeling, emotion or reaction and the asking ourselves about why we reacted that way or where did that come from? Who taught us that? This opens the door to greater self awareness and developing our own unique responses to the world around us.

I recommend that after you have exhausted development of your list, choose 3-4 of the questions from your list to work on over the next few weeks. Buy yourself a journal and start answering and exploring your chosen questions. You will discover much of who you are in this process.

Exercise Four

Core Beliefs Exercise

This exercise will help you to get to the foundation of your negative beliefs, or your core beliefs. In the exercise on Positive Programming, you began to identify some of the self-statements that you tell yourself. If you want to know more about those beliefs, try this exercise. Some of the more prevalent negative beliefs prevalent in our culture today are:

° I am powerless.
° There is scarcity in life.
° Life is a struggle.
° I am an unworthy person.
° I will fail
° I have no power.
° I do not trust myself or the process of life.

The Exercise

1. Is there a problem or situation that is troubling you that you would like to work on? Try to describe this situation as thoroughly as you can paying attention to detail.

2. How does this affect you on an emotional level? What are you feeling? Which emotion(s) is/are predominant? Elaborate on these emotions.

3. Is this situation affecting you physically? How? Are you more tired, feeling stressed, aching muscles, headaches, or experiencing an upset stomach? Describe the areas of your body that are being affected.

4. What core negative beliefs are you holding about this situation? List them as negative statements. A core negative belief fuels the uncertainty of our lives. For example, if I hold a core negative belief that "Nothing good ever happens to me," I will tend to attract and pay attention to those things in my life that verify that core negative belief.

5. Describe your worst-case scenario. What is your worst fear in this situation? Elaborate on how awful it can become. Does this worst-case scenario relate to a situation in the past? Explain. What would be the worst that could happen if this were to come true? Describe.

6. What is the best that could happen out of this situation? Describe. Try to imagine what you WANT here (as opposed to focusing on what you do NOT want).

7. Create as many affirmations as necessary to counteract the negative beliefs you are holding to be true. Be precise and form your affirmations as if they are already true. Remember, positive self-talk must replace negative, self-defeating statements. Be conscious of your self-talk.

8. Envision yourself now in a more positive way by focusing on a positive image of yourself and your future self. What are you like? What are you doing? Create a detailed future. Now is the time to let your fantasies free.

9. To live in a meaningful way, joy must be a daily part of our lives. Focus each day on what brings you joy and

choose to do that instead. What would bring joy into your life right now? List as many things as you can that make you happy. Can you include more of these in your life, maybe even one new thing each day?

10. Have you had any inner messages lately that you have not acknowledged? If so, ask yourself if you are afraid of what this inner message is saying to you. In order to dispel the power your fear has over you, you must face it head on and see it for what it is. Once you acknowledge it you can realistically assess what is required of you. By verbalizing your fear you can identify it, face it head on and meet the challenge. Describe it now and make a list of steps that you can take to move closer to your desired goal.

11. Begin to focus on what you can have in your life—not what you cannot or do not have. Manifest those realities that you desire through positive affirmations Below are some more examples of affirmations. Create some of your own. Say them to yourself silently, out loud or write them down, but be sure to give yourself positive messages daily. Construct them as if they are already happening...

° I am at peace with the world and everyone in it. (This is a helpful affirmation when you are feeling upset or find yourself obsessing over "why" something happened).

° I am enjoying an abundance of love, happiness, wealth and energy.

° I am enjoying the benefits of a fulfilling relationship that nurtures me in all ways.

° I am successfully completing my educational career goals.

° I fully trust myself to make choices that are right for me.

Exercise Five

Me, Myself, Mom and Dad: An Exercise in Jungian Archetypes

This is a great exercise to do at the conclusion of reading this book. You can, of course, do it after learning about Jung's theory, but I believe that it will be more helpful to read through at least Topic Twelve before tackling this exercise where you will try to uncover how your relationship with your parents has colored how you see other males and females. It is especially useful to help us see how we make our choices for a partner.

So, before beginning this exercise, review the Topic Seven on Jung's Theory. In this exercise you will be working with Jung's archetypes, exploring the nature of the images you hold of your parents, your dark side (shadow), the masks that you wear (persona), and your images of femininity and masculinity. By exploring these archetypes as they have manifested in our psyche, we illuminate how these internal images impact our relationships with our parents and other people in our lives. It will even reveal the nature of your relationship to yourself as a man, woman, wife, husband, mother, or father. We apply these archetypal expectations to others as well as ourselves. By working through the expectations that we hold for our mothers and fathers, we move closer to having an authentic relationship with them. We remove the blinders that may have affected our ability to appreciate our parents for the individuals that they are.

Simultaneously, working through these archetypal images, we begin to see how they have colored our ability to appreciate the individuality of others and especially, of our Self. I use the capital "S" here because it represents the awakened, actualized Self that has worked through the impediments to conscious living.

Mother

This very appropriate archetype is very powerful in both the lives of men and women. We get "hung up" in the process towards individuation because of the archetypal projections, we as children, have cast upon our mothers. Jung believed that the beginning of our problems are influenced in a limited way by the actual mother's contribution. It is true that there are corresponding effects in the child that relate to the personality traits and attitudes actually present in the mother; however, there is a stronger influence of the Mother archetype that impacts our relationship to our mother so it would be very useful for us to see how our projections may actually prevent us from knowing our "real" mother.

As children, we have an ideal image of what a mother "should be" and we project this onto our own mothers. This image is carried forth into our adult life where we will try to actualize the image in other women we know. This unresolved conflict will prevent us from relating to others in ways that take into account their personality. Our projection of the archetype of the Mother-ideal will determine our responses to that person. In other words, our expectations will get in the way.

The images that lie behind our experience with the Mother archetype represent the "entirely subjective, and very primitive needs and fears of the child, without much reference to external reality. We do not need to dissolve the archetype itself, which would be impossible, but to dissociate the projections in order to restore the contents back to the owner. We must learn to see our mother realistically and appreciate her for who she really is...not who we want her to be.

Women will find that their relationship to their actual mother affects their relationship with other women in their lives. We carry in our psyche the wounds as well as the nurturing that we received from our mothers that color our interactions with other women. If our relationship with our mother was characterized by caring, nurturing, and loving words and actions, then we go forth into the world with a confidence in women in general. They are goddesses in our eyes. If that relationship was filled with neglect, anger, unjust criticism, or abuse, our image of women will be filled with that experience. She becomes a Medusa.

Men will find that they are repeating familial patterns of behavior with other females in their lives. The power of a man's experience with his mother influences how he will relate to future females in his life. By examining the nature of his expectation and disappointments, he can begin to see each female on an individual basis. Males strive to complete the unfinished business with their mothers in their romantic relationships with women. It can never be completed there, because the issue is not with these lovers, but with the biological mother and with the man's projection of the mother-ideal. Once we recognize that much of our anguish with our parents stem from our expectations cast upon them, we can dissolve the power held over us and operate from a more realistic point of view.

° Describe the qualities of your "Ideal Mother." What is she like? What would she do or not do? How does she relate to you? Does she see you? Does she acknowledge your needs? Do you feel as if you know her as a person? Be as detailed as possible and give examples.

° What is your mother-in-reality like? Following the lead from the questions above, describe how she meets or misses the point. Be as specific as possible, listing her positive and negative qualities. Give examples.

° What qualities about your real mother disappoint you or cause you anguish? How is this related to your expectations of your mother as the *Ideal Mother*?

° What did you learn about women from your experience with your mother? Has this affected your relationship with women? How? Explain.

Father

Although Jung did not address the father as a major archetype, this exploration of feminine and masculine psychology would not be complete without addressing this other major figure in our life. His presence or absence also has a profound affect on our psyche. Similar to the effects of the Mother archetype, our expectations of how we want our father to be or our fears of how he can be will shape our relationships with other males in our lives.

The archetype's affect on a male's relationship with other males is colored by the actual relationship with one's father. If a man feels acceptance, encouragement, and guidance from his actual father, he will probably have pretty good relationships with other males. If, however, his father was emotionally distant, absent, critical, demeaning, or abusive, then when the son becomes an adult, his relationship with other men will reveal the unfinished business that he carries with his father.

A female's relationship with her father will set her standard for how she sees men in general. If she had a great relationship with her father, then she will hold other males to that high standard. If she did not feel that her father cared or was actually rejecting, abusive, or simply absent, that relationship becomes the template for the types of problems she may experience with other males when she becomes an adult.

Taking into account what has been said regarding the mother-ideal and the Mother archetype, answer the following for the Father archetype.

° Describe the qualities of your "Ideal Father." What is he like? What would he do or not do? How does he relate to you? Does he see you? Does he acknowledge your needs? Do you feel as if you know him as a person? Be as detailed as possible and give examples.

° What is your father-in-reality like? Following the lead from the questions above, describe how he meets or misses the point. Be as specific as possible, listing his positive and negative qualities. Give examples.

° What qualities about your real father disappoint you or cause you anguish? How is this related to your expectations of your father as the *Ideal Father*?

° What did you learn about men from your experiences with father? Has this affected your relationship with men? How? Explain.

Persona

Review the section on the Persona under the topic of Jung's Theory.

° How would you describe the masks that you wear?

° What are the situations?

° How do these masks help you to "fit in" in the various situations?

° Which masks seems the most "fake," or unlike the real you?

° Can you soften the mask so that more of "authentic" you can shine through? How can you accomplish this?

° Remember that we have a different persona for different social settings.

° Do you feel that any of your personas have become predominant in your life, therefore robbing you of your ability to be yourself? If so, how? Describe. How can you recapture your authentic self? Explain.

Shadow

This is our Dark Side. To discover what hides in our Shadow, we need to explore all those things that we reject or find objectionable because they are part of us but we are not conscious of it (or we at least won't admit it).

° What do you dislike in other people?

° What gets you upset?

° What attitudes do you dislike? Make an extensive list.

° How are you similar to the qualities that you just listed in the question above?

° Do you find that what you dislike in others are actually qualities that you dislike in yourself?

° Describe a scenario or two when your dark side emerges or has emerged. What are these situations and what do you believe precipitates them? What are your thoughts when this happens? Identify and discuss. Does it relate to the qualities that you listed of what you dislike? Explain.

° Any insights?

Anima/Animus

To understand what we look for in a mate, we need to explore any differences that may exist between your ideals and the actuality of your relationships. By bringing these ideals, expectations, or fears into the light on consciousness we are able to awaken and become aware of our hidden archetypal influences in our relationships.

° Describe the ideal mate. What characteristics must she/he possess?

° How would this person treat you?

° What roles will they assume in your relationship (e.g., breadwinner, homemaker, economic decision-maker, parent, etc.).

° Describe the overall relationship.

° What are your relationships like in reality?

° What kind of women or men do you actually attract?

° Do you recognize any patterns that are similar to your parent's relationship to each other?

° Or do these relationships resemble your relationship with one of your parents?

Exercise Six

Dreamwork Exercise

The following is a dreamwork exercise that you can reproduce and use for the dreams that you want to illuminate. It uses only one of the techniques described earlier so you might want to use multiple methods to really get to the core of your dream. You might also want to use one technique for one dream and another technique for a different dream. Find the method that works best for you.

It is not unusual for dreams to begin bursting through to consciousness as you travel through this journey towards self-awakening. Because you are making conscious efforts to look at different aspects of your personality, your dreams will assist you to process what emerges if you will take the time to work with your dreams.

At this point it would be a valuable asset to begin a journal in which you write down your innermost thoughts, dreams and feelings on a regular basis. It is like a promise to yourself to meet with YOU and talk things out. Research indicates that those who journalize tend to be happier and mentally healthier. Journalizing will enable you to have a log of the progression of your feelings and an account of the situations in your life. As the months go by you will be able to refer back to your entries to monitor your progress and development. If you find that you are still hashing over the same things again and again, that awareness should in itself bring enlightenment into your situation. Too often we think it is other people who are causing our problems, but when we see it in black and white (our written words) that we are once again mired in the same type of battle or challenge, we can own up to our participation in the problem. We begin to examine how perhaps our choices are creating the same scenario over and over again. It will provide a reference point from which we can measure our self-growth.

Dream journals do not have to be expensive investments. Anything that you can write on will do—a tablet, loose-leaf binder or whatever your imagination can come up with. Fabric covered hard-bound journals are available at a modest cost and are great for helping you keep track of your entries. Use what feels most comfortable for you. I have even used cash register paper or napkins when I have had the inspiration to write. Whatever works for you. Your entries can be varied. You might simply write about your feelings or you can express your feelings in the form of a poem or music lyrics. You can draw images of situations or your dream symbols. You can create a collage. The types of entries that you do are limited only by your imagination.

The method of dreamwork used here is taken from the Jungian-Senoi method (Williams,1985). It is *not* dream interpretation, but *dreamwork*. You will need to start recording your dreams in your journal upon awakening. You can simply write down key words or phrases to jog your memory later if you don't have time to write out the complete dream. Focus on the key elements that you can recall. If you prefer, record the dream content on a recorder that you keep by your beside. You'll need to be diligent about recording immediately otherwise you will no doubt have trouble remembering later.

Things to remember:

- Journal work allows us to express ourselves without censorship or judgment. It is a safe place in which we can open up and communicate with ourselves.

- Journal writing frees us from identification with our outer reality. It enables us to relate to life rather than be dominated by it.

- If integration of the personality is our goal, then the consciousness process has a direction in which to develop.

- We are our own authority. We are our own best teacher, for only *we know* how *we* think, only *we know* how *we feel.* Our opening requires that we learn to trust our intuitive-self.

- We must acknowledge the totality of ourselves in order to individuate. If we continue to deny or push down aspects of our personality, we only strengthen their force in our lives. We need to bring it to consciousness and integrate it into our conscious self.

- The questions that come forth to our mind produce consciousness. Consciousness leads to consciousness, which is the basis for evoking the powers of our unconscious mind.

- Reflection upon our questions must be taken one step further—we must test our reflections by action, not further reflection.

- Awareness must lead to action. When we gain new insight we must move into incorporating that wisdom into our lives. It is not enough to simply know something.

- Self-discovery means that we must be willing to open ourselves to receive the wisdom that is already within us. We must be willing to take the risk—to be ready and open to what will be revealed to us as we begin to explore our inner nature.

• When we are confronted with what may seem to be an obstacle, try to envision the positive lesson that may be determined from the situation.

As you delve deeper into your personality and work with the dream symbols, your dreams will undoubtedly become more meaningful and frequent. Some people cannot remember any dreams but still want to learn this method. You can work on a current or recurring dream from the past. For those who do not remember their dreams perhaps even a flash of emotion, scene, or intuitive sense of some thing having been dreamt will emerge. Write these insights down and try to expand on what you can remember. Sometimes by recalling a short scenario or incident you will be led to recall the crux of the dream.

Another technique for working with the unconscious and dreams is to make up a dream and work with the symbols, people, and actions in that imagined dream. This tact works because our brain really does not know the difference between internally generated thought/images and those that are enacted in our lives. The stories you might generate are like a projective test wherein you tell stories that reflect your unconscious thoughts and feelings. So if you don't remember your dreams, make one up and work on it as directed in the topic on Understanding Dreams and below.

In addition to the exercise, you may follow-up on these dreams by developing dream tasks for each dream. These tasks are an alteration of the dream state and allow you to move beyond the actual dream to directly contribute to your life. For example, you can complete a conversation with a key figure in your dream. You would role play both parts and become both the Dream Ego and the other. You can do this verbally or on paper. Dialoguing with the images, whether they are people or objects, allows the dreamer to gain deeper levels of understanding the dream's meaning. Zeroing in on the conceptual level of dream symbols helps bring to consciousness the hidden meaning in dreams.

Directions

Using paper and pen, or a computer, write down what you can recall of the dream that you want to work on. As you recount the dream, tell it as if it is happening in the present (i.e., use the first person "I"): "I am walking down a city street in what seems like a foreign country. I'm looking into shops and see an object that catches my attention, but I can't identify what it is. There is a person in the shop staring at me and I start to feel as if I know this person." Recount the dream in its entirety if you can remember it.

Provide as much detail as possible. What are you doing? Who is there? What is happening? What is being said? What is not being said by you or others? What emotions are present in the dream? What other objects or props in your dream? What is the atmosphere of the dream? Is it day or night? You get the point...

You will refer back to this narrative of your dream to glean any hidden symbols that you may want to illuminate through the dreamwork process. In fact, after you have recounted the dream, go back over what you wrote and circle the names of people in your dream, any objects, animals, or significant phrases that you wrote describing the dream for these can hold additional information about what your dream is all about. After writing down your dream, work on the following elements of your dream:

1. **The Dream Ego:** This is "you" in your dream. How does the Dream Ego act, talk, respond, react, feel, think, etc? What is her/his perception of the situation presented in the dream? What kinds of questions does the dream ego ask

of her/himself or others? What is the dream ego doing or not doing? Remember that details are important.

2. **Others**: Notice how others respond to the Dream Ego. What are they doing? What do they say or not say? What is their attitude towards the Dream Ego or situation? Try to recall anything that others may have said to the Dream Ego as well.

3. **Symbols**: What are the symbols in your dreams? Notice the "props" in your dream. In order to illuminate what they represent, engage in a dialogue with them using the Empty Chair technique. Ask, "What are you? Why are you in my dream?" "What do you want?" Become the object and speak for that symbol.

4. **Association:** Identify the most significant symbols or people in your dream. Now draw a circle for each and place the word that relates to the symbol in the middle of the circle. Associate to each word, always returning to the symbol to make a new association. After exhausting associations to each symbol, circle the associations that best represent what you feel or think refers to this dream at this time.

After circling the associations, review them together holistically to see if they provide you with a deeper meaning to this dream.

5. **Insights**: After you have completed the process, record any insights you have had regarding the meaning of the dream and how it relates to your life.

Exercise Seven

Journal Work Issues

As the concluding exercise in this journey, contemplate and discuss the following issues. You can use a journal for these issues or just separate pieces of paper. Be creative in your entries. By reflecting upon these themes, I hope that your outer reality will become more congruent with your inner world, allowing your life to become more sharply focused and harmonized. Knowing how we truly feel about our life issues, we can begin to live them.

Give each issue a page of it's own (some may require more attention than one page though). Write each title in bold capital letters, perhaps using color. Remember that artistic creations are a form of self-therapy that we can utilize at any point in our lives. If you feel moved to draw a symbol instead of writing in longhand, then by all means, go for it. As you explore these issues, remember that what you put down is not really your life, but your bias towards how you select from experience. We are the products of our experiences. Let your writing flow. Do not censor what you choose to write. Let the words be as big as your feelings if need be.

° **Death**: "Before I die, what must I accomplish in my life to feel that I have really lived?"

○ **Birth**: "Why was I born? What is my purpose?" Try to imagine that your soul was born for a higher purpose than day-to-day concerns. What do you think that purpose is? Ask your intuitive-self for guidance.

○ **Physical Body**: "What am I doing to you?"

○ **Wounded Side**: "What do I need to do to heal?" (We may have many wounds, but take them one at a time).

○ **Guidance**: This is the older, wiser voice within you. "What advice can you give me?"

○ **Dream Figures**: "Why are you in my dream?" How do these dream figures point the way to your actualization? What are they saying? What are they doing?

○ **Shadow**: This is the dark aspect of our personality according to Jung. It is the part of our self that we project upon others because we do not wish to claim it as our own. These are thoughts or feelings that we blame others to have, when they are in fact our own qualities. Ask yourself, "Who are you? What must I do to reconcile with you?"

○ **Passion**: "What am I passionate about?" "What is it to which I can give my total commitment?"

○ **Greed**: "In what ways am I needy?" "In what ways does this translate into my greed? "What agony creates my need?" In other words, "what is the root cause of my neediness or greediness?"

○ **Ego**: "Who do I think I am?" "What qualities do I accentuate so that others will see me in an acceptable way?" "Who am I anyway?"

○ **Birthday**: "What is in store for me in the coming year?"

Notes:

References

Abramson, P. R. (1980). *Personality*. New York: Holt, Rinehart & Winston.

Adler, A. (1957). *Understanding human nature*. New York: Fawcett.

Ainsworth, M., Blehar, M., Walters, E., & Wall, S. (1978). *Patterns of attachment: A psychological study of the strange situation*. Hillsdale, NJ: Erlbaum.

Allen, J. (1995). *Coping with trauma*. Washington, DC: American Psychiatric Press.

American Psychiatric Association (1968). *Diagnostic and statistical manual of mental disorders (2nd ed.)*. Washington, DC: American Psychiatric Association.

American Psychiatric Association (1980). *Diagnostic and statistical manual of mental disorders (3rd ed.)*. Washington, DC: American Psychiatric Association.

American Psychiatric Association (1987). *Diagnostic and statistical manual of mental disorders (rev. 3rd ed.)*. Washington, DC: American Psychiatric Association.

American Psychiatric Association (1994). *Diagnostic and statistical manual of mental disorders (4th ed.)*. Washington, DC: American Psychiatric Association.

Aronson, E. (1972). *The social animal*. San Francisco: Freeman.

Ash, M. (1990). *The zen of recovery*. New York: Tarcher/Putnam.

Assagioli, R. (1989). Self-realization and psychological disturbances. In S. Grof, & C. Grof (Eds.). *Spiritual emergency: When personal transformation becomes a crisis* (pp. 27-48). New York: Tarcher/Putnum.

Baumeister, R. (1991). *Meanings of life*. New York: Guilford Press.

Binswanger, L. (1962). Existential analysis and psychotherapy. In H. Ruitenbeek (Ed.) *Psychoanalysis and existential philosophy* (pp. 17-23). New York: Dutton.

Bohm, D. (1994). Thought as a system. New York: Routledge.

Bolen, J. (1984). *Goddesses in every woman: A new psychology of women.* New York: Harper & Row.

Bolen, J. (1988). *Gods in every man: A new psychology of men's lives and loves.* San Francisco: Harper & Row.

Bowlby, J. (1969). *Attachment and loss: Vol. 1. Attachment.* London: Hogarth.

Bowlby, J. (1973). *Attachment and loss: Vol. 2. Separation.* New York: Basic Books.

Bradshaw, J. (1991, August). We can go home again. *New Age, pp. 34-38, 94-102.*

Brazier, D. (1995). *Zen therapy: Transcending the sorrows of the human mind.* New York: Wiley & Sons.

Bruner, J. (1990). *Acts of meaning.* Cambridge, Mass: Harvard University Press.

Bucke, R. (1961). *Cosmic consciousness: The study in the evolution of the human mind.* New York: University Books.

Bugental, J. F. (1976). *The search for existential identity.* San Francisco: Jossey-Bass.

Campbell, J. (1983). *Historical atlas of world mythology.* San Francisco: Harper & Row.

Capra, F. (1980). Modern physics and eastern mysticism. In Walsh, V. & Vaughan, F. (Eds.). *Beyond ego: Transpersonal dimensions in psychology* (pp. 62-70). Los Angeles: Tarcher.

Capra, F. (1990). *The tao of physics.* Los Angeles: Audio Renaissance Tapes.

Carson, A., & Baker, R. (1994). Psychological correlates of codependence in women. *The International Journal of Addictions, 29*, 395-407.

Chia, M. (1985). *Taoist ways to transform stress into vitality.* Huntington, New York: Healing Tao Books.

Chia, M. (1986). *Chi self-massage: The Taoist way of rejuvenation.* New York: Healing Tao Books.

Chia, M. (2001). *Cosmic healing I: Cosmic Chi Kung.* Chiang Mai, Thailand: Universal Tao Publications.

Chia, M., & Chia, M. (1993). *Awaken healing light of the Tao.* New York: Healing Tao Books.

Chopra, D. (1989). *Quantum healing: Exploring the frontiers of mind/body medicine.* New York: Bantam.

Chopra, D. (1993). *Ageless body, timeless, mind: The quantum alternative to growing old.* New York: Harmony.

Coe, S. (1997). The magic of science and the science of magic: An essay on the process of healing. *Journal of Health and Social Behavior, 38*(1), 1-8.

Cohen, S., & Herbert, T. (1996). Health psychology, psychological factors and physical disease from the perspective of human psychoneuroimmunology, *Annual Review of Psychology, 47*, 113-120.

Cook, E. (1993). *Women, relationships & power: Implications for counseling.* Alexandria, VA: American Counseling Association.

Cork, M. (1969). *The forgotten children.* Markham, Ontario: Paperjacks.

Cortright, B. (1997). *Psychotherapy and spirit: Theory and practice in transpersonal psychotherapy.* New York: SUNY.

Coursen, H. R. (1986). *The compensatory psyche: A Jungian approach to Shakespeare.* Baltimore, MD: University Press of America.

Cousins, N. (1989). *Head first: The biology of hope and the healing power of the human spirit.* New York: Penguin.

Csikszentmihalyi, M. (1990). *Flow: The psychology of optimal experience.* New York: Harper Perennial.

Csikszentmihalyi, M. (1993). *The evolving self.* New York: Harper Collins.

Daniels, M. (1988). The myth of self-actualization. *Journal of Humanistic Psychology, 28*, 7-38.

Dass, R. (1989). Promises and pitfalls of the spiritual path. In S. Grof & C. Grof (Eds.). *Spiritual emergency: When personal transformation becomes a crisis* (pp. 45-51). New York: Tarcher/Putnam.

De Ropp, R. (1972). Self-transcendence and beyond. In J. White (Ed.). *The highest state of consciousness* (pp. 94-103). New York: Anchor.

Dispenza, J. (2005). *Rewiring your brain to a new reality*. Symposium conducted at the conference of What The Bleep Do We Know?!?! Santa Monica, CA.

Donlevy, J. (1996). Jung's contribution to adult development: The difficult and misunderstood path of individuation. *Journal of Humanistic Psychology, 36*(2), 92-108.

Dossey, L. (1997a). Beyond nature and nurture: Twins and quantum physics, *Psychology Today*, July/Aug, 44.

Dossey, L. (1997b). Prayer is good medicine. *The Saturday Evening Post, 269*(6), 52-55.

Dossey, L. (1998). *Recovering the soul: A scientific and spiritual search.* New York: Bantam.

Dupuy, P. (19). Women, relationships and Power. pp. 79-108.

Elkind, D. (1980). Carl Jung. In Freedman, A.M., Kaplan, H. I., & Sadock, B.J. (Eds.). *Comprehensive Textbook of Psychiatry/II* (2nd ed.).

Elkins, D. (1995). Psychotherapy and spirituality: Toward a theory of the soul. *Journal of Humanistic Psychology, 35*(2), 79-98.

Epstein, M. (1995). *Thoughts without a thinker: Psychotherapy from a Buddhist perspective.* New York: Basic Books.

Erikson, E. (1950). *Childhood and society.* New York: W. W. Norton.

Erikson, E. (1980). *Identity and the life cycle.* New York: W. W. Norton.

Fadiman, J. (1980). The transpersonal stance. In R. Walsh & F. Vaughan (Eds.). *Beyond ego: Transpersonal dimensions in psychology* (pp. 175-181). Los Angeles: Tarcher.

Faludi, S. (1991). *Backlash: The undeclared war against American women.* New York: Anchor.

Farrell, W. (1986). *Why men are the way they are.* New York: McGraw-Hill.

Feinstein, D. (1979). Personal mythology as a paradigm for a holistic public psychology. *American Journal of Orthopsychiatry, 49*, 198-217.

Feinstein, D. (1990a). Bringing a mythological perspective to clinical practice. *Psychotherapy, 27*(3), 389-396.

Feinstein, D. (1990b). How mythology got personal. *The Humanistic Psychologist, 18,* 162-175.

Feinstein, D. (1991). A mythological perspective on dreams in psychotherapy. *Psychotherapy in Private Practice, 9*(2), 85-105.

Feinstein, D. (1998). At play in the fields of the mind: Personal myths as fields of information. *Journal of Humanistic Psychology, 38*(3), 71-109.

Feinstein, D. (2005). *Introduction to energy psychology* [Film]. (Available from Innersource, www.innersource.net).

Feinstein, D. (2006, May). *Energy psychology in disaster relief.* Paper presented at the meeting of the 8th Annual International Energy Psychology Conference, Santa Clara, CA.

Feinstein, D., & Krippner, S. (1988). *Personal mythology: The psychology of your evolving self.* New York: Tarcher.

Feinstein, D., & Krippner, S. (1994). Reconciling transcendent experiences with the individual's evolving mythology. *The Humanistic Psychologist, 22,* 203-227.

Feinstein, D., Granger, D., & Krippner, S. (1988). Mythmaking and human development._Journal of Humanistic Psychology, 18,* 23-50.

Firman, J., & Gila, A. (1997). *The primal wound: A transpersonal view of trauma, addiction, and growth.* New York: SUNY.

Fischer, J., Spann, L., & Crawford, D. (1991). Measuring codependency. *Alcoholism Treatment Quarterly, 8,* 87-100.

Fordham, F. (1966). *An introduction to Jung's psychology.* Maryland: Penguin.

Freud, S. (1938a). *The basic writings of Sigmund Freud.* A.A. Brill (Ed. And Trans.) New York: Random House.

Freud, S. (1938b). The sexual abberations. In A. A. Brill (Ed. and Trans.). *The basic writings of Sigmund Freud* (pp.553-579). New York: Random House.

Friedman, H., & MacDonald, D. (1997). Toward a working definition of transpersonal assessment. *The Journal of Transpersonal Psychology, 29*(2), 105-122.

Friel, J., Subby, R., & Friel, L. (1984). *Co-dependence and the search for identity.* Pompano Beach, FL: Health Commuications, Inc.

Fromm, E. (1951). *The forgotten language: An introduction to the understanding of dreams, fairy tales and myths.* New York: Grove Press.

Fromm, E. (1983). The nature of well-being. In J. Welwood (Ed.) *Awakening the Heart: East/West approaches to psychotherapy and the healing relationship* (pp.59-69). Boston: Shambhala.

Ginsberg, C. (1984). Toward a somatic understanding of self: A reply to Leonard Geller. *Journal of Humanistic Psychology, 24, 66-92.*

Glasser, W. (1984). *Control theory.* New York: Harper & Row.

Goble, F. (1970). *The third force: The psychology of Abraham Maslow.* New York: Washington Square Press.

Goleman, D. (1980). Mental health in classical Buddhist psychology. In R. Walsh & F. Vaughan. (Eds.). *Beyond ego: Transpersonal dimensions in psychology* (pp. 89-92). Los Angeles: Tarcher.

Goleman, D. (1992). The Buddha on meditation and states of consciousness. In C. Tart (Ed.) *Transpersonal psychologies: Perspectives on the mind from seven great spiritual traditions* (pp. 203-230). San Francisco: Harper.

Goleman, D. (1995). *Emotional intelligence.* New York: Bantam.

Greene, B. (1999). *The elegant universe: Superstrings, hidden dimensions, and the quest for the ultimate theory.* New York: W.W. Norton.

Greenspan, M. (1983). *A new approach to women and therapy.* New York: McGraw-Hill.

Grof, S. (1980). Realms of the human unconscious: Observations from LSD research. In R. Walsh & F. Vaughan (Eds.) *Beyond ego: Transpersonal dimensions in psychology* (pp. 87-99). Los Angeles: Tarcher.

Grof, S. (1985). *Beyond the brain: birth, death and transcendence in psychotherapy.* New York: SUNY Press.

Grof, S. (1993). *The holotropic mind: The three levels of human consciousness and how they shape our lives.* San Francisco: Harper.

Grof, S., & Grof, C. (1989a) (Eds.). *Spiritual emergency: When personal Transformation becomes a crisis.* New York: Tarcher/Putnum.

Grof, S., & Grof, C. (1989b). Spiritual emergency: understanding evolutionary crisis. In S. Grof & C. Grof. (Eds). *Spiritual emergency: When personal transformation becomes a crisis* (pp. 1-26). New York: Tarcher/Putnum.

Grof, C., & Grof, S. (1989c). Assistance in spiritual emergency, In S. Grof & C. Grof. (Eds.). *Spiritual emergency: When personal transformation becomes a crisis* (pp. 191-198). New York: Tarcher/Putnum.

Hall, C. (1954). *A primer of Freudian psychology.* New York: Mentor Books.

Hall, C., & Nordby, V. (1973). *A primer of Jungian psychology.* New York: Mentor Books.

Hitchcock, J. (1991). *The web of the universe: Jung, the "new physics" and human spirituality.* New Jersey: Paulist Press.

Hora, T. (1962). Psychotherapy existence and religion. In H. Ruitenbeek (Ed.). *Psychoanalysis and existential philosophy* (pp. 70-89). New York: Dutton.

Hora, T. (1962). Existential psychiatry and group psychotherpy. In H. Ruitenbeek (Ed.). *Psychoanalysis and existential philosophy* (pp. 130-154). New York: Dutton.

Horgan, J. (June, 1994). Trends in neuroscience: Can science explain consciousness? *Scientific American, 271*(1), 88-94.

Horney, K. (1966). *Our inner conflicts.* New York: W. W. Norton & Co.

Horney, K. (1967). *Feminine psychology.* New York: W. W. Norton & Co.

Huxley, A. (1944). *The perennial philosophy*. New York: Harper & Row.

Huxley, A. (1956). *The doors of perception/heaven and hell*. New York: Harper Colophon.

Jacobi, J. (1959). *Complex, archetype, symbol in the psychology of C. G. Jung* (R. Manheim, Trans.). Princeton, NJ: Princeton University Press. (Original work published 1957).

Jampolsky, L. (1991). *Healing the addictive mind*. Berkeley, CA: Celestial Arts.

Jaynes, J. (1990). *The origin of consciousness in the breakdown of the bicameral mind*. Boston: Houghton-Mifflin.

Jimenez, M. (1997). Gender and psychiatry: Psychiatric conceptions of mental disorders in women, 1960-1994. *Affilia, 12*(2), 154-175.

Johnson, R. (1986). *Inner work*. San Francisco: Harper & Row.

Jordan, K., & L'Abate, L. (1995). Programmed writing and therapy with symbiotically enmeshed patients. *The American Journal of Psychotherapy, 49*(2). 225-236.

Joy, W. (1979). *Joy's way: A map for the transformational journey*. Los Angeles: Tarcher.

Jung, C. (1959). Archetypes of the collective unconscious. In R. F. C. Hull (Ed. & Trans.)_*The archetypes and the collective unconscious* (pp. 7-56). New York: Pantheon Books. (Original work published 1934).

Jung, C. (1963). *Memories, dreams, and reflections* (R. Winston & C. Winston, Trans.). New York: Pantheon. (Original work published 1961).

Jung, C. (1971a). Aion: Phenomenology of the self. In J. Campbell (Ed.) R.F.C. Hull (Trans). *The portable Jung* (pp. 13-162). New York: Viking.

Jung, C. (1971b). Psychological types. In J. Campbell (Ed.) R. F. C. Hull (Trans.) *The portable Jung* (pp. 178-269). New York: Viking.

Kaptchuk, T. (1983). *The web that has no weaver*. Chicago: Congden & Weed.

Kasprow, M., & Scotton, B. (1999). A review of transpersonal theory and its application to the practice of psychotherapy. *Journal of Psychotherapy & Practice Resources, 8*(1), 12-overle23.

Keen, S. (1991). *Fire in the belly: On being a man.* New York: Bantam.

Keen, S. (1994). *Hymns to an unknown god: Awakening the spirit in everyday life.* New York: Bantam Books.

Kepner, J. (1987). *Body process: A gestalt approach to working with the body in psychotherapy.* New York: Gardner Press.

Kornfield, J. (1989). Obstacles and vicissitudes in spiritual practice. In S. Grof & C. Grof, (Eds). *Spiritual emergency: When personal transformation becomes a crisis* (pp. 137-170). New York: Tarcher/Putnum.

Krippner, S. (1990). Personal mythology: An introduction to the concept. *The Humanistic Psychologist, 18*, 137-142.

Laing, R.D. (1962). Ontological insecurity. In H. Ruitenbeek (Ed.). *Psychoanalysis and existential philosophy* (pp. 41-69). New York: Dutton.

Laing, R.D. (1989). Transcendental experience in relation to religion and psychosis. In S. Grof. & C. Grof, C. (Eds.). *Spiritual emergency: When personal transformation becomes a crisis* (pp. 49-62). New York: Tarcher/Putnum.

Lane, J. (1992, April). *Buddhist teachings as a theory of therapy.* Symposium conducted at the meeting of the Western Psychological Association, Portland, OR.

Larsen, E. (1987). *Stage II relationships: Love beyond addiction.* San Francisco: Harper & Row.

Lee, P., Ornstein, R., Galin, D., Deikman, A., & Tart, C. (1976). *Symposium on consciousness.* New York: Viking.

Lerner, H. (1985). *The dance of anger.* New York: Harper & Row.

Lerner, H. (1988). *Women in therapy.* Northvale, New Jersey: Jason Aronson Inc.

Lerner, H. (1989). *The dance of intimacy.* New York: Harper & Row.

Linehan, M., Oldham, J., & Silk, K. (1995). Dx: Personality disorder...Now what? *Patient Care, 29*(11), 75.

Lipton, B. (2005). *The biology of belief: Unleashing the power of consciousness, matter, and miracles.* Santa Rosa, CA: Mountain of Love/Elite Books.

Lukoff, D., Lu, F., & Turner, R., (1998). From spiritual emergency to spiritual problem. The transpersonal role of the new DSM-IV category. *Journal of Humanistic Psychology, 38,* 21-50.

Lukoff, D. (1997). The psychologist as mythologist. *Journal of Humanistic Psychology, 37(3),* 34-58.

Marrone, R. (1996). *Body of knowledge: An introduction to body/mind psychology.* New York: SUNY.

Marrone, R. (1997). *Death, mourning and caring.* Pacific grove, CA: Brooks/Cole Publishing company.

Maslow, A. (1971). *The farther reaches of human nature.* New York: Penguin.

May, R. (1953). *Man's search for himself.* New York: Dell.

May, R. (1991). *The cry for myth.* New York: Norton & Co.

Menaker, E. (1982). *Otto Rank: A rediscovered legacy.* New York: Columbia University Press.

Messner, B. (1997). Archetypal evolution and "new birth" from codependency. *Communication Studies, 48*(1), 76-92.

Metzer, R. (1998). *The unfolding self.* Novato, CA: Origin Press.

Miller, A. (1981). *Drama of the gifted child and the search for the true self.* New York: Basic Books.

Miller, J. (1986). *Toward a new psychology of women.* Boston: Beacon.

Miller, R. (1998). Researching the spiritual dimensions of alcohol and other drug problems. *Addiction, 93*(7), 979-990.

Mishlove, J. (1993). *The roots of consciousness.* New York: Marlowe & Co.

Morrow, S., & Hauxhurst, D. (1998). Feminist therapy: Integrating political analysis in counseling and psychotherapy. *Women & Therapy, 21*(2), pp. 37-50.

Murdock, M. (1990). *The heroine's journey: Woman's quest for wholeness.* Boston: Shambhala.

Myers, D. G. (1987) *Social psychology* (2nd ed.). New York: McGraw-Hill.

Neher, A. (1996). Jung's theory of archetypes. A critique. *Journal of Humanistic Psychology, 36*(2), 61-91.

Ng, S. (1998). *Metaphors of the feminine and masculine: Creating a personal mythology.* New York: McGraw-Hill.

Ng, S. (2008). *Breaking the code of codependence: Becoming conscious through the transpersonal.* San Jose, CA: Wu Chi Creations.

Neumann, E. (1954). *The origins and history of consciousness.* New Jersey: Bollingen.

Norwood, R. (1985). *Women who love too much.* Los Angeles: Jeremy Tarcher.

Ornstein, R. (Ed.). (1973). *The nature of consciousness.* San Francisco, CA: Freeman & Co.

Ornstein, R. (1977). *The psychology of consciousness.* (2nd ed.). New York: Harcourt Brace Jovanovich.

Ornstein, R., & Sobel, D. (1987). *The healing brain.* New York: Touchstone.

Owens, C. (1992). Zen Buddhism. In C. Tart (Ed.) *Transpersonal psychologies: Perspectives on the mind from seven great spiritual traditions* (pp. 153-202). San Francisco: Harper.

Oyle, I. (1976). *Time, space and mind.* Milbrae, CA: Celestial Arts.

Pearsall, P. (1998). *The heart's code: The new findings about cellular memories and their role in the mind/body/spirit connection.* New York: Broadway Books.

Peck, M. (1978). *The road less traveled.* New York: Touchstone.

Perera, S. (1990). Descent to the dark Goddess. In C. Zweig (Ed.) *To be a woman.* Los Angeles: Tarcher.

Perls, F. (1972). *Gestalt therapy verbatim.* New York: Bantam.

Pert, C. (2005). *Molecules of emotion: the link between body and soul.* Symposium conducted at the conference What The Bleep Do We Know?!? Santa Monica, CA.

Perry, J. (1989). Spiritual emergence and renewal. In S. Grof & C. Grof (Eds.). *Spiritual emergency: When personal transformation becomes a crisis,* (pp. 63-76). New York: Tarcher/Putnam.

Petrie, J., Giordano, J., & Roberts, C. (1992). Characteristics of women who love too much. *Affilia, 7*(1), 7-20.

Prevatt, J., & Park, R. (1989). The spiritual emergence network (SEN). In S. Grof & C. Grof (Eds.). *Spiritual emergency: When personal transformation becomes a crisis,* (pp. 225-232). New York: Tarcher/Putnam.

Prezioso, F. (1987). Spirituality in the recovery process. *Journal of Substance Abuse Treatment, 4,* 233-238.

Radin, D. (2006). *Entangled minds: Extrasensory experiences in a quantum reality.* New York: Pocket Books.

Randolph, E. (1985). Children who shock and surprise.

Ricard, M., Lutz, A., & Davidson, R. (2014, November). Mind of the meditator, 311, 38-45.

Richardson, D. (1989). *Greek mythology for everyone: Legends of the gods and heroes.* New York: Avenel.

Rogers, C. (1961). *On becoming a person.* Boston: Houghton-Mifflin.

Rothberg, N. (1986). The alcoholic spouse and the dynamics of codependency. *Alcoholism-Treatment Quarterly, 2,* 73-86.

Ruitenbeek, H. (Ed.). (1962). *Psychoanalysis and existential philosophy.* New York: Dutton.

Russell, B. (1938). *Power: A new social analysis.* New York: W. W. Norton & Co.

Rychlak, J. F. (1981). *Introduction to personality and psychotherapy* (2nd ed.). Boston, MA: Houghton Mifflin.

Ryckman, R. (1989). *Theories of personality* (4th ed.). Pacific Grove, CA: Brooks/Cole.

Schaef, A. (1987). *When society becomes an addict.* San Francisco: Harper & Row.

Searle, J. (1994). *The rediscovery of the mind.* Cambridge, MA: MIT Press.

Scarf, M. (1987). *Intimate partners: Patterns in love and marriage.* New York: Random House.

Schultz, D. (1990). *Theories of personality* (4th ed.). Pacific Grove, CA: Brooks/Cole.

Shakespeare, W. (1975). Hamlet. In *The complete works of William Shakespeare*. New York: Avenel.

Shapiro, F., & Forrest, M. (1997). *EMDR: Eye movement desensitization and reprocessing*. New York: Harper Collins.

Sharp, D. (1987). *Personality types: Jung's model of typology*. Toronto, Canada: Inner City Books.

Sheridan, M., & Green, R. (1993). Family dynamics and individual characteristics of adult children of alcoholics: An empirical analysis. *Journal of Social Service Research, 17*(1-2), 73-97.

Shockley, G. (1994). Overcoming the obstacles of co-dependency: An interdisciplinary task. *Journal of Spiritual Formation, 15*(1), 103-108

Sperry, R. (1995). The riddle of consciousness and the changing scientific worldview. *Journal of Humanistic Psychology, 35*(2), 7-33.

Stenger, V. (1997/1998). Quantum spirituality. *Free Inquiry, 18*(1), 57-59.

Stevens, A. (1995). Jungian psychology, the body & the future. *Journal of Analytic Psychology, 40*, 353-364.

Svanberg, P. (1998). Attachment, resilience and prevention. *Journal of Mental Health, 7*(6), 543-578.

Szasz, T. (1978). *The myth of psychotherapy*. New York: Anchor Press.

Talbot, M. (1981). *Mysticism and the new physics*. New York: Bantam Books.

Talbot, M. (1991). *The holographic universe*. New York: Harper-Collins.

Tannen, D. (1990). *You just don't understand*. New York: Morrow.

Tart, C. (1980). The systems approach to consciousness. In Walsh, R. & Vaughan, F. (Eds.). *Beyond ego: Transpersonal dimensions in psychology* (pp. 115-118). Los Angeles: Tarcher.

Tart, C. (1986). *Waking up: Overcoming the obstacles to human potential*. New York: Viking.

Tart, C. (1992a). *Transpersonal psychologies: Perspectives on the mind from seven Great spiritual traditions.* San Francisco: Harper.

Tart, C. (1992b). Science, states of consciousness, and spiritual experiences: The need for state-specific sciences. In C. Tart (Ed.). *Transpersonal psychologies: Perspectives on the mind from seven great spiritual traditions* (pp. 9-58). San Francisco: Harper.

Tart, C. (1992c). The physical universe, the spiritual universe, and the paranormal. In C. Tart (Ed.) *Transpersonal psychologies: Perspectives on the mind from seven great spiritual traditions* (pp. 113-153). San Francisco: Harper.

Tart, C. (1992d). Some assumptions of orthodox, western psychology. In C. Tart (Ed.). *Transpersonal Psychologies: Perspectives on the mind from seven great spiritual traditions* (pp. 59-112). San Francisco: Harper.

Tart, C. (1993). The structure and dynamics of waking sleep. *The Journal of Transpersonal Psychology, 25*(2), 141-169.

Tart, C. (1994). *Living the mindful life.* Boston: Shambhala.

Tavris, C. (1982). *Anger: The misunderstood emotion.* New York: Touchstone.

Taylor, E. (1999). An intellectual renaissance of humanistic psychology? *The Journal of Humanistic Psychology, 39*(2), 7-25.

Theriault, S., & Holmberg, D. (1998). The new old-fashioned girl: Effects of gender and social desirability on reported gender-role ideology. *Sex Roles, 39,* 97-112.

Thoele, S. (1991). *The courage to be yourself.* New York: MJF Books.

Thompson, K. (Ed.). (1991). *To be a man: In search of the deep masculine.* Los Angeles: Tarcher.

Tillich, P. (1962). Existentialism and psychotherapy. In H. Ruitenbeek (Ed.). *_Psychoanalysis and existential philosophy* (pp. 3-16). New York: Dutton.

Trungpa, C. (1976). *The myth of freedom and the way of meditation.* Boston: Shambhala.

Vaillant, G. (1977). *Adaptation to life.* Boston: Little, Brown & Co.

Van Den Berg, J. (1962). Significance of human movement. In H. Ruitenbeek (Ed.). *Psychoanalysis and existential philosophy* (pp. 90-129). New York: Dutton.

Van Dusen, W. (1962). The theory and practice of existential analysis. In H. Ruitenbeek (Ed.). *Psychoanalysis and existential philosophy* (pp. 3-40). New York: Dutton.

Van Wormer, K. (1989). Codependency: Implications for women and therapy. *Women & Therapy, 8*(4), 51-63.

Vaughan, F. (1980). Transpersonal psychotherapy: Context, content and process. In R. Walsh & F. Vaughan (Eds.). *Beyond ego: Transpersonal dimensions in psychology* (pp. 182-189). Los Angeles: Tarcher .

Von Franz, M. (1971). *Lectures on Jung's typology.* Zurich: Spring Publications.

Walsh, R., & Vaughan, F. (1980). A comparison of psychotherapies. In Walsh, R. & F. Vaughan (Eds.). *Beyond ego: Transpersonal dimensions in psychology* (pp. 190-220). Los Angeles: Tarcher.

Wegscheider-Cruse, S. (1985). *Choicemaking.* Pompano Beach, FL: Health Communications, Inc.

Welwood, J. (1990). *Journey of the heart: The path of conscious love.* New York: HarperPerennial.

Welwood, J. (2000). *Toward a psychology of awakening: Buddhism, psychotherapy, and the path of personal and spiritual transformation.* Boston: Shambhala.

Wetzel, J. (1991). Universal mental health classification systems: Reclaiming women's experience. *Affilia, 6*(3), 8-31.

White, J. (Ed.) (1972). *The highest state of consciousness.* New York: Anchor.

Whitfield, C. (1987). *Healing the child within.* Deerfield Beach, FL: Health Communications.

Whitfield, C. (1993). *Boundaries and relationships: Knowing, protecting, and enjoying the self.* Deerfield Beach, FL: Health Communications.

Whitmont, E. (1991). *The symbolic quest: Basic concepts of analytical psychology.* New Jersey: Princeton.

Wilber, K. (1979a). *No boundary: Eastern and western approaches to personal growth.* Boston: Shambhala.

Wilber, K. (1979b). *The spectrum of consciousness.* Wheaton, Illinois: Quest.

Wilber, K. (1980a). Psychologia perennis: The spectrum of consciousness. In Walsh, R. & Vaughan, F. (Eds.). *Beyond ego: Transpersonal dimensions in psychology* (pp. 74-86). Los Angeles: Tarcher.

Wilber, K. (1980b). A developmental model of consciousness. In Walsh, V. & Vaughan, F. (Eds.). *Beyond ego: Transpersonal dimensions in psychology* (pp. 99-114). Los Angeles: Tarcher.

Wilber, K. (Ed.). (1982). *The holographic paradigm and other paradoxes.* Boulder, CO: New Science Library.

Wilber, K. (1999). Spirituality and developmental lines: Are there stages? *The Journal of Transpersonal Psychology, 31*(1), 1-10.

Wilber, K. (2000). *Integral psychology: Consciousness, spirit, psychology, and therapy.* Boston: Shambhala.

Wilkinson, H. (1999). Schizophrenic process, the emerging consciousness in recent history and phenomenological causality: The significance for psychotherapy of Julian Jaynes. *International Journal of Psychotherapy, 4*(1), 49-66.

Williams, S. K. (1985). *The Jungian-Senoi dreamwork manual.* Berkeley, CA: Journey Press.

Wise, A. (1997). *The high performance mind.* New York: Tarcher.

Wolf, F. (1994). *The dreaming universe: A mind-expanding journey into the realm where psyche and physics meet.* New York: Touchstone.

Woodward, L. (2000). Timing of separation and attachment to parents in adolescence: Results of a prospective study from birth to age 16. *Journal of Marriage & Family, 62,* 162-174.

Wright, R. (1994). *The moral animal: Why we are the way we are.* New York: Vintage

Yeshe, T. (1987). *Introduction to Tantra: A vision of totality.* Boston: Wisdom Publications.

Zukav, G. (1979). *The dancing Wu Li masters: An overview of the new physics.* New York: Quill/Wm. Morrow.

Zukav, G . (1989). *The seat of the soul.* New York: Simon & Schuster.